PRAISE FOR *POWERHOUSE*

D0964273

'A fascinating study into some of the world's most awe-inspiring organizations. From insightful interviews and research, MacNeice and Bowen have distilled the essential qualities that lead to high performance down into an actionable and enjoyable read for all business leaders.'
Sir Clive Woodward, England 2003 World Cup Winning Head Coach and Team GB Director of Sport, London 2012

'The stories of a dozen great organizations from around the world – and what we can learn from their decency and vision, as well as their success. Recommended reading for any business leader.'
Hamish McRae, Chief Economics Commentator, *The Independent*

'*Powerhouse* challenges our thinking about high performance by examining essential qualities in a wide range of leading institutions. The Powerhouse model – emphasizing Plan, Priorities, People, and Process – is a highly useful way to think about the alignment of key elements for any institution. Practical and sure to be of great value for managers from all fields.'
Phil Rosenzweig, Professor of Strategy and International Business, IMD, Switzerland and author of *The Halo Effect*

'It's hard to read a book when you are constantly stopping to take notes. The introduction and first chapter alone provoked my thinking about the ambitions of my own company and the strategies needed for success. I love this book. Each chapter is a true story about an organization and the practices and differentiators that led to its success. The organizations are highly diverse and while each is unique – most of us don't instruct our customers to build and use pit latrines – there are commonalities that can be practised by all of us. Read this book. You will be inspired and compelled to take action.'
Susan Scott, Founder of Fierce Inc and author of *Fierce Conversations*

'Thomas Edison once said, 'If we did the things we are capable of, we would astound ourselves'. This could be the credo of *Powerhouse*, written by Brian MacNeice and James Bowen. Using 12 remarkable case studies of world-renowned organizations, they make quite clear that 'high performance is by definition a collective endeavour'. In illustrating what differentiates these captivating organizations from the more humdrum ones, they make the reader familiar with the 'powerhouse approach to performance transformation'. Anybody interested in the DNA of what makes for sustainable high performance would do well to carefully study this book.'

Manfred F R Kets de Vries, Distinguished Clinical Professor of Leadership Development and Organizational Change, INSEAD and bestselling author of *The Hedgehog Effect: The secrets of building high performance teams*

'The best analysis of successful organizations since *Good to Great* and *Built to Last*. *Powerhouse* offers amazing insights into the world's best organizations and the 12 principles that drive organizational performance. This is a must-read for any executive who wants to create lasting success.'

Kevin Kruse, *New York Times* **bestselling author of** *Employee Engagement 2.0*

'Twelve very diverse institutions and yet a common thread on what it takes to succeed, brilliantly captured by the authors. A must-read for those who are passionate about succeeding.'

Ajit Shriram, Joint Managing Director, DCM Shriram, India

'*Powerhouse* is a compelling and provocative compendium of how some of the world's leading organizations have reached the pinnacle in their respective fields. This book is well researched and clearly written; a must-read for leaders who aspire to transform their organization into a world-class, high-performing institution that is built to last.'

Tom Massey, author of *The ABC's of Effective Leadership* **and** *Ten Commitments for Building High Performance Teams*

'Every now and again a new book comes along which really does add something new to our understanding of high-performance organizations. This is one of those books. A highly readable book offering real insight into how organizations become leaders in their respective fields.'

Jeff Grout, business consultant, coach, speaker and author

Powerhouse

Insider accounts into the world's top
high-performance organizations

Brian MacNeice and
James Bowen

KoganPage

First published in Great Britain and the United States in 2016 by Kogan Page Limited

2nd Floor, 45 Gee Street
London EC1V 3RS
United Kingdom
www.koganpage.com

MPHC Marketing
122 W 27th St, 10th Floor
New York NY 10001
USA

4737/23 Ansari Road
Daryaganj
New Delhi 110002
India

ISBN   978 0 7494 7831 5
E-ISBN   978 0 7494 7832 2

British Library Cataloguing-in-Publication Data

A CIP record for this book is available from the British Library.

Library of Congress Cataloging-in-Publication Data

Names: MacNeice, Brian, author. | Bowen, James, 1967 – author.
Title: Powerhouse : insider accounts into the world's top high-performance
    organizations / Brian MacNeice and James Bowen.
Description: London ; New York : Kogan Page, 2016. | Includes
    bibliographical references and index.
Identifiers: LCCN 2016033552 (print) | LCCN 2016040889 (ebook) | ISBN
    9780749478315 (alk. paper) | ISBN 9780749478322 (ebook)
Subjects: LCSH: Organizational effectiveness. | Corporate culture. |
    Performance. | Success in business.
Classification: LCC HD58.9 .M3425 2016 (print) | LCC HD58.9 (ebook) | DDC
    658—dc23
LC record available at https://lccn.loc.gov/2016033552.

Typeset by Graphicraft Limited, Hong Kong
Print production managed by Jellyfish
Printed and bound by CPI Group (UK) Ltd, Croydon, CR0 4YY

CONTENTS

For further information and resources, visit:
www.theperformancepowerhouse.com
www.koganpage.com/Powerhouse

ABOUT THE AUTHORS

Brian MacNeice is an expert in high performance and is a regular speaker on the topic at business conferences and seminars. Brian regularly runs high-performance workshops for organizations, leadership teams and senior executives. He has advised many blue-chip companies in a career spanning almost 20 years across a diverse range of industry sectors. Brian is Managing Director and co-founder of Kotinos Partners, which is a consultancy that focuses on helping CEOs and leadership teams to deliver sustained high performance.

James Bowen is an expert in strategy and organizational design and a performance consultant with 20 years of advisory experience. Over the course of his career James has worked with executive teams of blue-chip companies on a range of engagements with the achievement of step-change performance improvement as their common goal. James is also Managing Director and co-founder of Kotinos Partners.

ACKNOWLEDGEMENTS

Our journey in writing this book has been long and rewarding. Over the last five years we have received support and encouragement from many people – too many for us to namecheck every individual involved. We have met inspirational people and organizations, and been overwhelmed by the positivity and goodwill we have encountered. We have also been boosted by the total faith shown in our project by clients, colleagues, advisors, friends and family at every turn. To every one of you, we are eternally grateful. We simply could not have done this without your help. In spite of the risk of leaving some special people out, we do wish to explicitly acknowledge some of those most involved.

First, we owe an enormous debt of gratitude to the case study organizations we studied through this research – both those included in the book and those contributing to additional content available through our website. Each institution opened its doors to us and generously made available its people, facilities and resources. We have spoken to people from top to bottom within these institutions and have been granted unique access and insight into their worlds. They are the real stars of this book and we hope we have done justice to their stories.

Second, we would like to thank our clients – both past and present, and individually and collectively – as they inspired us to take on this project in the first place. Many of our perspectives on high performance have been formulated and tested through our work with their teams, addressing their ambitions and challenges. These engagements have shaped our thinking, and several – you know who you are! – can with complete legitimacy describe themselves as co-creators. We hope they are proud of what we have produced, and look forward to working with them to further push the boundaries of their powerhouse performance in the future.

Third, as first-time authors we have received huge support and patience from our publishers Kogan Page in London. Geraldine Collard, Anna Moss, Amanda Dackombe, Philippa Fiszzon, Jonathon Price, Anita Clark and all of their colleagues have been outstanding in guiding us through the writing process, sharpening our focus and putting shape on our novice ramblings. We hope the long hours they have invested have been rewarded with the final product. Paul Feldstein, our literary agent, has been invaluable in helping us to turn our idea into reality. From our first meeting in his office in

Bangor, he has never doubted us and his persistence has ultimately paid off. John Carvill at Eyecue supported us with design, and the Powerhouse Performance model and other illustrations within the book are the fruits of his work. He has been, as always, a pleasure to work with. Grant LeBoff has also helped more than he knows in getting us to the point where we can join him in calling ourselves published authors. Life is so much easier when you collaborate with good people who are great at their jobs.

Fourth, we would like to call out current and former work colleagues who have contributed to our thinking and personal development. Each, in his/her own way, has added to the perspectives, insights and skills that we hold today, and our practice reflects their input. In alphabetical order, we would like to thank the following individuals for their input, challenge and support over the years: John Bull, Alastair Campbell, John Coghlan, Caroline Currid, Alistair Gray, Fiona Gifford, Enrique Gómez, Deirdre Kilbride, Mason Kissell, Neal Kissell, Paul Limbrey, the MBA faculty at IMD in Switzerland and DCU in Ireland, Jim O'Brien, Alain Rolland and Shane Twomey.

Our support base extends well beyond the professional. Our friends have spent the last five years listening to stories of our trips to the far-flung locations we visited for this book. They have always shown interest in hearing more and have kept asking when the book would come out. We know that some thought the book was a thinly veiled excuse for touring the world at Kotinos expense – however, as they can see now, we meant it! Again we acknowledge their support and hope they enjoy it.

Finally, we wish to pay a special tribute to our respective families. Anything is possible when you have such a strong support base behind you. We are both lucky to have wonderful wives in Helen and Miriam, who were, and continue to be, with us every step of the way. And to our children Hugh, Patrick, Ben and Max, and Charlie, Jack and Dan, we hope you are as proud of your dads as we are of you. This book is dedicated to each of you.

James Bowen and Brian MacNeice

Introduction 01

Building lives through lending

Oslo, Norway, 10 December 2006. The Norwegian capital's City Hall is crammed with royalty, dignitaries and world leaders as Mosammat Taslima Begum steps forward. She is joined on the stage by Dr Muhammad Yunus and, as board members of Grameen Bank, they are awarded the Nobel Peace Prize. Meanwhile, back in their native Bangladesh, millions are cheering as they huddle around television sets in their villages to watch the proceedings. These people have borrowed money from Grameen Bank to finance micro-enterprises, and see both Begum and Yunus as representing them in Oslo too. As stakeholders in Grameen they feel that they are being awarded the Nobel Peace Prize, and are celebrating this as the greatest day of their lives.

Grameen Bank was founded by Dr Yunus – an economics professor from Dhaka – in 1976 as a vehicle to create a poverty-free world. Through Grameen, Dr Yunus invented large-scale micro-lending – providing villagers with small amounts of capital to establish micro-businesses and progress towards self-sufficiency. The basis for Grameen can be summarized using an extract from his acceptance speech:

> Human beings are not born to suffer the misery of hunger and poverty. To me, poor people are like bonsai trees. When you plant the best seed of the tallest tree in a flowerpot, you get a replica of the tallest tree, only inches tall. There is nothing wrong with the seed you planted, only the soil-base that is inadequate. Poor people are bonsai people. There is nothing wrong in their seeds. Simply, society never gave them the base to grow on. All it needs to get the poor people out of poverty is for us to create an enabling environment for them. Once the poor can unleash their energy and creativity, poverty will disappear very quickly.[1]

While over half of all borrowers have used their loans to rise from acute poverty, Grameen Bank is not a charity, rather it is a large, successful business. It has lent US$13 billion in small tranches to the poorest members of Bangladeshi society and since its foundation has been profitable in every year bar two (due to a major natural disaster in the country) – not least as

Figure 1.1 Mosammat Taslima Begum (left), representing Grameen Bank, and Muhammad Yunus pose with their Nobel Peace Prize medals and diplomas

SOURCE: Ken Opprann/©The Norwegian Nobel Institute

a result of maintaining a staggeringly high 97 per cent recovery rate for its loans. Its asset base is US$2.3 billion and growing and it maintains a workforce of over 22,000. Without question Grameen Bank is a great example of a high-performance institution.

Educating a nation

While the bankers of Grameen and their borrowers use their micro-loans with a view to consigning Bangladeshi poverty to museums, on the other side of the world in Finland, life could hardly be more different. There, the Finnish authorities have created the most equitable, yet high-achieving school education system in the world. With a radical and innovative model – in the eyes of many conventional education thinkers – they have produced amazing results. As measured by the Organization for Economic Co-operation and Development (OECD), Finland ranks at the top for educational attainment in mathematics, science and reading. More impressively, Finland has the smallest performance *gap* across its student base – in other words the difference in attainment between the best and worst performers in Finnish schools is smaller than anywhere else in the world. Delivery of education in the Finnish system is very different to that in other national education systems. Finnish children begin formal schooling much later than the norm, they have shorter school days and on average get less homework. There are virtually no private fee-paying schools in the system, no state inspectors, no published league tables comparing schools against each other, and teachers have significant autonomy for how the core curriculum is taught. In essence, Finland breaks practically every received wisdom for how a national educational system should be designed. However, despite – or more correctly *because* of this – Finland outperforms its peers.

A search for insights

Why, though, is this the case? How is it that Grameen Bank and the institution of Finnish education have reached and stayed at the top of their fields over many years, continually winning against their competitors and, in the process, setting new benchmarks for performance? Moreover, what is it that has made the New Zealand All Blacks the most winning national team in sports history? How have the St Louis Cardinals delivered – year-in, year-out – championship-winning performances on and off the baseball diamond? Why has the Kirov Ballet become so famous? And why are the Kirov Ballet and the Curtis Institute of Music so admired as leading institutions of the arts? Why has Southwest Airlines continued to succeed in the turbulent US airline industry, and how does Toyota maintain its leadership position in global automotives? How has the Tata group in India managed to become a model for ethical practice without compromising its performance as a business? Why is Mayo Clinic so revered in the world of science and medicine? And what makes the United States Marine Corps one of the best elite military units in the world? Finally, how does Médecins Sans Frontières maintain its position amongst the most effective humanitarian aid agencies globally?

Answering these questions, institution by institution, has defined our research over the last five years, with the insights forming the basis for this book. We have looked to understand each institution on its own merits and then, notwithstanding the diversity of the fields in which they operate, to identify elements of their institutional high-performance approaches that are common. Finally, we have sought to highlight those lessons that leaders of other organizations can learn from these institutions to put into practice themselves.

Background to our project

The project represents a major milestone in our personal journeys. Since the early 2000s, through working simultaneously in the fields of sports and business we have become increasingly interested in the idea and dynamics of high performance. We set up Kotinos Partners in 2010 as a niche advisory business with a particular focus on facilitating performance transformation. Our belief is that sustained, winning performance comes uniquely from great institutions, and that winning institutions are made, not born. Our passion is supporting leaders of institutions with the desire to be the best to realize those ambitions over time.

The name we chose for our business is itself connected to the idea of high performance, with the word *kotinos* coming from ancient Greek, and meaning a branch of the wild olive tree intertwined to form a circle. Worn as a crown, the kotinos was the visible symbol of victory for athletes in the ancient Olympic Games.

The process of getting to here has been intense, enlightening and fun. In framing our research – in particular in developing and refining our portfolio of case studies – we employed three basic criteria. First, consistent with our definition of high performance, we shortlisted institutions that have been demonstrably at the top of their fields over extended periods of time – both in reputation and when measured using the relevant, objective standards that matter. Second, we looked to assemble a portfolio of institutions that is diverse both in terms of what they do and where they are based. Finally, we prioritized institutions that would allow us to engage directly with the individuals and teams that make them what they are. In this way we could build our insights directly from primary research, based on exclusive access to leaders, staff and other stakeholders, on watching those people go about their business and on discussing at first hand the secrets to their institutions' sustained outperformance.

We have been privileged to be invited to study each of the institutions covered here. Our research brief in each case has been defined by three key questions: What is the high performance model in place at this institution? What were the key breakthroughs in putting this model in place? What actions are you taking now to sustain and extend your performance advantage over time?

We appreciate the time and access we have been given and have used them both to observe closely and listen intently. Through layering further discussion, investigation and analysis on top of our on-the-ground experiences, we have been able, in each case, to home in for ourselves on the bases for these institutions' enduring success.

Cutting to the chase – the 'what' and the 'how' of enduring high performance

Having completed our research of the individual institutions, and looking across the portfolio of our case studies, we can draw two conclusions from our work that relate to the delivery of sustained high performance more broadly. The first is that enduring high performance reflects a competitive advantage that is fundamentally *organizational* in nature. At the heart of every single institution whose advantage has endured lies an organizational model that works more effectively and efficiently than its competitors'. Our second conclusion is that there *are* generic lessons to be learned from studying high performance across multiple disciplines that have application in specific individual situations.

The first conclusion might seem obvious; however, we would suggest it is underappreciated and its consequences are important. Looking across all fields of endeavour, including business, sports, education, arts, military and others – we find many 'supernovas' – institutions that exploded on the scene based on particular insights, ideas or concepts, or as a result of short-term injections of resources, before shrinking back once their initial advantage was competed away. By contrast, the number of institutions achieving prominence and then staying consistently at the top is much smaller. We believe that those latter institutions share an explicit, long-term commitment to high performance, and have systematically invested the fruits of their success into mobilizing large populations of people – at many levels, and often in many locations, with diverse backgrounds, interests and skills – to act consistently and in concert towards an ambitious objective. Each has taken on a challenge that, while unique to its situation, at its core is about design and leadership, about high-performing individuals and teams, and about perseverance, focus and stamina.

Interestingly, we would propose from our research that enduring high performance is not – or at least not fundamentally – about money. While it is certainly true that, in resource terms, several institutions we discuss in this book could reasonably be described as rich, we would argue that none of them have particularly 'bought' high performance. We would suggest that their wealth has arisen as a consequence of their sustained high performance, as opposed to the other way around. That said, it is certainly the case that high performance is not free, and moreover, that an effective high-performance model, when combined with access to financial and other resources, often results in acceleration of an institution's performance advantage. However, it is not always – and in many cases not even often – that the wealthiest institution is the one that consistently comes out on top.

Switching to our second conclusion, we suggest that there *are* lessons for leaders from our broad-based study of institutional high performance. We would argue that high-performance institutions share common attributes – the 'what' of performance – albeit that they manifest themselves in different ways in different situations. Also, we propose that there is a way of thinking about their approaches to achieving and maintaining performance – the 'how' of performance – that again is a source of insight and guidance for leaders of any institution with ambition to be the best.

Starting with the 'what', the list below shows what we would identify as 12 common attributes of high-performance organizations – their Powerhouse Principles:

- Ambition:
  - a clear, unambiguous vision for what the institution is looking to achieve;
  - a description of *what winning means* that aims high – pushing the boundaries of the institution's capabilities and track record;
  - simultaneously reflecting and driving a dynamic, always-on strategy process – evolving to reflect changing circumstances within and around the institution.
- Purpose:
  - absolute clarity of why it wants to win;
  - tacit alignment of the interests of the institution and its stakeholders;
  - explicitly addressing the hearts as well as the minds, building motivation and connection in parallel.

- Measures:
  - holistic scorecards of the right performance metrics that link to the vision;
  - combining lagging and leading measures that indicate performance today, and also the creation of organizational capability and capacity to grow;
  - designing measures that are visible, understood and connected to the work of individuals and teams.
- Standards:
  - high standards embedded *and lived* as an institutional value;
  - connected to visible, objective, fast and consequential management of performance – both good and bad;
  - institution-wide intolerance of sustained underperformance.
- Gap:
  - narrow performance 'distance' between highest- and lowest-performing individuals and teams;
  - driving and maintaining the pressure to perform at all times;
  - enabling the recruitment, retention and motivation of the best talent through managing a tight performance gap effectively.
- Decisions:
  - established practice of taking decisions as close to the action as possible;
  - enabling institution-wide performance through more decisions, better decisions and better conversion of decisions into action;
  - embedded in the culture, and facilitated through structures and processes;
  - creating pace, agility and capacity to grow.
- Code:
  - behavioural standards for what it means to be a 'member' of the institution that reflect both its people and its vision;
  - establishing and setting expectations of trust as a key behavioural norm;
  - interpreted and made real throughout the organization and lived day to day at all levels;
  - enabling management on the basis of 'just enough process' – creating space for institutions and leaders to grow.

- Engagement:
  - strong connection across institutions, their leaders, their staff and their stakeholders;
  - enabling performance through shared understanding and commitment – to the institution, its vision and its people;
  - a mature and respectful approach to work – embracing tradeoffs and pushing to create win-wins;
  - adding energy to the system.
- Resilience:
  - institutional capacity to maintain performance despite negative shocks, calibrated explicitly to delivery of the vision;
  - ensuring a proactive end-to-end approach – from monitoring and prevention to reaction and adaptation.
- Feedback:
  - organization-wide interest in and focus on learning – drawing in particular from experience;
  - holistic systems, comprising multiple, nested processes progressing in parallel;
  - creating a feedback-rich culture that is objective, constructive and development-oriented – balancing institutional and individual needs, and reflecting and reinforcing trust.
- Teamwork:
  - recognition that high performance is, by definition, a collective endeavour;
  - creating teams that reflect *both* the natures and skills of the participants *and* the specifics of the challenge they face;
  - overinvestment (deliberately) in making teams work.
- Improvement:
  - constant, institution-wide focus on pushing the boundaries of performance;
  - raising the bar, then raising the game – embracing incremental and step-change improvement in parallel;
  - strategy as a capability rather than a one-off output, including organizational as well as business growth and development;
  - focus on 'improving the rate at which we improve'.

In examining this list, it is important to note that these attributes are ingrained throughout the institutions, rather than simply in the individuals or teams at the top. Further, in many of the organizations we have studied, these attributes feel integral – not just to what they do, or to how they perform, but to who they are. As such, in whatever form these attributes manifest themselves, many of them are intrinsically cultural.

The reality, however, is that achievement of these attributes is far from automatic. Rather than reflecting nature, we would suggest their existence very definitely reflects nurture. In our view they reflect a fundamental, explicit commitment on the parts of institutional leaders to enduring high performance that is backed up by a systematic approach to its achievement. In our case study discussions in the chapters that follow, we have attempted to highlight the particular principles that underpin the performance of each of the institutions we have studied, and to describe the approaches by which these principles are put in place. Having done this across the portfolio of our research (and layered in our experience of facilitating performance trans-formation with clients, which was progressing in parallel) we have concluded that there *is* a way of approaching performance transformation that can be adapted to work in any situation and any field of endeavour. For us, this involves working within and across four key pillars of high performance, which we have consolidated and captured in our Kotinos Powerhouse Performance© model (Figure 1.2).

Figure 1.2 Kotinos Powerhouse Performance© model

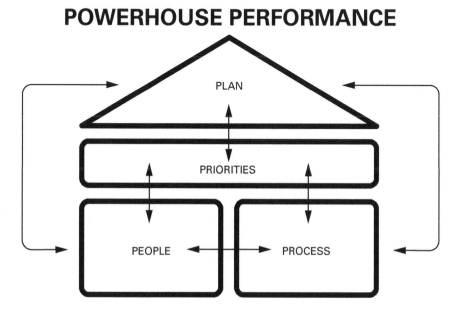

POWERHOUSE PERFORMANCE

- Pillar 1 – plan:
  - definition, articulation and communication of a medium-term vision for the institution such as to provide direction, stretch, purpose and inspiration;
  - definition – all the time – of strategies for *explicit* delivery of the vision that are grounded in outside-in (eg market, competitor, stakeholder, etc) and inside-out (eg staff, resources, financial, etc) context;
  - systematic challenging, evolution and improvement of vision and strategies on a dynamic, ongoing basis – to reflect changing circumstances and also new capabilities and capacity for performance and also changing circumstances.
- Pillar 2 – priorities:
  - institution-wide priorities for delivering the vision and strategy – defined, understood and agreed by all – that consolidate and prioritize across competing initiatives;
  - focus, explicitly designed to deliver performance *and* capability improvement;
  - take into account – at any point in time – both 'where we are' and 'where we want to go', matching work 'demand' with resource 'supply'.
- Pillar 3 – people:
  - behavioural 'codes' that define what it means to belong within the institution, driving behavioural standards for how people engage and work together and that reflect 'who we are', 'where we are' and 'where we want to go';
  - institution-wide standards, interpreted and made real for individual teams and specific situations.
- Pillar 4 – process:
  - system and model for how the institution works – 'how we do things around here?' – explicitly connected to delivery *and evolution* of the vision;
  - designed to be purposeful and outcome-oriented and avoiding drift into 'process for process sake';
  - minimizing volume of activity, while maximizing effectiveness and efficiency, working to a standard of 'just enough process';
  - influences and reflects organizational structure and definition of roles, information flows and even the set-up of physical environments, and complements the behavioural code;

- based on standard, institutional principles, but adapted for specific circumstances and situations;
- complementary to the behavioural code and, as such, maximizing effectiveness and efficiency;
- in itself a source of competitive advantage and a focus for ongoing improvement.

Taken together, the pillars of the Powerhouse Performance© model provide a basis for rapid, sustainable performance transformation. Importantly, reflecting on our research and experiences across the institutions we have studied, we suggest that for leaders of high-performance institutions, their focus should not be on any of the pillars – rather it should be on all of them, all of the time. This way, they develop the capability to relate cause and effect within and across the four pillars, and align designs to reflect the current state and achieve a specific, defined and ambitious medium-term objective. Effective leaders progress and adapt both the current and future states in parallel on a continuous basis. We observe leaders in high-performance institutions taking on and actively driving the process of converting ambitious plans into concrete actions that deliver consistent results.

There is no silver bullet to how this happens – rather, enduring high performance reflects leaders committing to, and securing institution-wide support for, a journey of broad-based organizational advantage. They assemble the pieces one by one and accelerate the pace as organizational capabilities improve. They adapt and stay the course to align with progress and unfolding events.

Making the best use of this book

Our book summarizes 12 research case studies that we have taken on over the last five years. We have already outlined the basis by which these studies were selected; however, there is no suggestion that these are the only institutions that have or do deliver sustained high performance. Neither, we should add, is there a suggestion that every element of how these institutions operate always meets the standard for high performance. They are, after all, large, complex organizations operating over long periods of time in the real world. What is uncontestable, however, is that each of these institutions is and has been a leader in its field on a sustained basis – when measured using objective, benchmark standards. What is also uncontestable, and indeed is validated by our research, is that the results achieved by these institutions have come about by design rather than by accident, and that there are core high-performance models in place at the highest levels that have resulted in the separation of the institutions we have studied from their competitors.

In writing each chapter we have attempted first to give the reader a sense of the individual institutions, the contexts within which they are delivering sustained superior performance, and the justification for their inclusion in our research. Then we have tried to describe the high-performance models in place – using our Powerhouse Performance model as an organizing framework. Finally – at the end of each chapter – we have taken the opportunities of each study to expand on the Powerhouse Principles identified earlier, with a view to providing insight to leaders for use in their own individual circumstances.

Our book is aimed at two types of readers, those interested in individual institutions and in getting under the skin of what makes them tick, and those interested in understanding high performance and the means by which it is achieved across the spectrum of our research. Readers in the former category should dip in and out of the book according to their interests, and we hope that our work helps them to gain a richer understanding of those institutions that have captured their imaginations. Readers in the second category should work their way through the book in its entirety, with a view to picking up a much richer idea for what defines high performance and how it is delivered. We hope that these readers can take away concrete ideas that they can bring to bear in driving sustained high performance in the institutions in which they are involved.

Now, allow us to open the door to the world of institutional high performance.

Note

1 Dr Muhammad Yunus speech [accessed 15 June 2016] Nobel Lecture, Oslo, 10 December 2006 [Online] http://www.nobelprize.org/nobel_prizes/peace/laureates/2006/yunus-lecture-en.html.

Grameen Bank 02

The bank of the villages

What makes Grameen Bank a performance powerhouse?

Grameen Bank is no ordinary bank. It serves the poorest people in society, those that no other bank will touch. At almost every step it has broken the conventional rules of banking. From its beginnings in 1976 as a research project led by an economics professor, Dr Muhammad Yunus, to the bank's formal establishment in 1983, and on to the present day, it has been responsible for helping some 100 million families rise out of poverty. Grameen's borrowers are asset-less and land-less, and it lends almost exclusively to women in a culture that has historically dismissed their potential for nurturing small businesses. It is not a charity but a profitable, successful business corporation. Some 40 years after Professor Yunus challenged himself to address the chronic poverty endemic throughout Bangladesh, the figures speak for themselves:[1]

- Grameen has lent some US$18.5 billion in small tranches to the poorest members of Bangladeshi society – those deemed not creditworthy by everyone else.

- The bank has 2,568 branches with over 8.8 million members located in 81,392 villages across the country, ensuring virtually complete coverage of the country's landscape.

- Of its borrowers 97 per cent are women, who are enabled to build small businesses and in so doing provide an income to support their families.

- The bank has a staggeringly high loan recovery rate of 98.48 per cent – in spite of the fact that they are lending to the poorest and most vulnerable members of Bangladeshi society.

- The bank employs in excess of 22,000 staff with total assets of over US$2,301 million.

▶

Figure 2.1 Grameen Bank Powerhouse Performance model

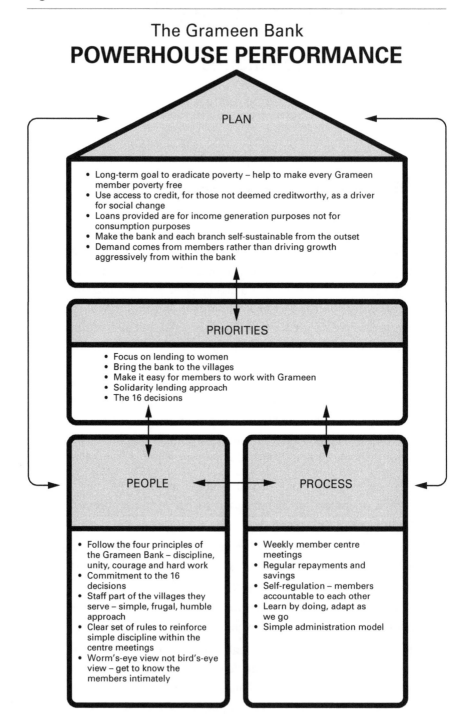

The Grameen Bank
POWERHOUSE PERFORMANCE

PLAN

- Long-term goal to eradicate poverty – help to make every Grameen member poverty free
- Use access to credit, for those not deemed creditworthy, as a driver for social change
- Loans provided are for income generation purposes not for consumption purposes
- Make the bank and each branch self-sustainable from the outset
- Demand comes from members rather than driving growth aggressively from within the bank

PRIORITIES

- Focus on lending to women
- Bring the bank to the villages
- Make it easy for members to work with Grameen
- Solidarity lending approach
- The 16 decisions

PEOPLE

- Follow the four principles of the Grameen Bank – discipline, unity, courage and hard work
- Commitment to the 16 decisions
- Staff part of the villages they serve – simple, frugal, humble approach
- Clear set of rules to reinforce simple discipline within the centre meetings
- Worm's-eye view not bird's-eye view – get to know the members intimately

PROCESS

- Weekly member centre meetings
- Regular repayments and savings
- Self-regulation – members accountable to each other
- Learn by doing, adapt as we go
- Simple administration model

- The bank has been profitable every year except 1983 (the year it was officially founded), 1991 and 1992 (in the aftermath of the catastrophic cyclone disaster in April 1991 that killed 150,000 and left millions of people without livelihoods).
- The bank reported a net profit of US$17.14 million in 2013.
- Of all Grameen Bank members 68 per cent crossed the poverty line.[2]
- Grameen Bank and Dr Muhammad Yunus were jointly awarded the Nobel Peace Prize in 2006 – Grameen Bank is the only business corporation ever to receive the prestigious accolade.

By any standards, Grameen Bank is a performance powerhouse.

Grameen Bank powerhouse

The poor professors of Jobra

The small rural village of Jobra lies close to the campus of Chittagong University in south-east Bangladesh. Muhammad Yunus drove through the village every day as he made his way from his parents' house to his post as Head of Economics at the university. As the crippling famine of 1974 swept the nation, Professor Yunus started to question why the economic principles he was teaching his students were failing the people surrounding the campus walls. 'What good were all my complex theories when people were dying of starvation on the sidewalks and porches outside my lecture hall?' It was then that he decided to immerse himself in the lives of the villagers of Jobra to see what they could teach him about poverty. As he saw it: 'I became a student again and the poorest people of Jobra my professors!'

Professor Yunus started to make regular trips to the village of Jobra. He gradually won over the confidence of the nervous villagers. As he spent more time with them he started to understand the issues they faced. He was determined to see their world from a worm's-eye rather than a bird's-eye view. 'If I wanted to understand how to help the poorest people of Jobra, I needed to get to know them at an individual level. Once you do this you see the world through a completely different set of eyes. The solutions become clearer the closer you get to the root cause of the problems.' The Jobra professors taught Dr Yunus well. He came to the realization that the cycle of poverty could only be broken by empowering the poor through access to credit.

Figure 2.2 Professor Muhammad Yunus, founder of Grameen Bank

SOURCE: Yunus Centre

US$27 that changed the lives of 100 million families

In 1976 Sufiya Begum was a 21-year-old mother of three children. She spent her days plaiting strands of bamboo cane. She used to buy the bamboo daily from local traders, work her fingers to the bone and sell finished stools back to the same traders at the end of the day. Her return for all this toil was a mere two cents! Without the means to purchase raw material herself she was unable to escape the enslavement brought on by her dependence on the traders, who charged her for bamboo at a rate that made it impossible for her to make anything more than a pittance from her toil. If she got the means to buy her own bamboo then she would be free to sell her end product in the market and command the full retail price. All she needed was 22 cents. Dr Yunus and his team of students quickly put together a list of 42 villagers who were effectively enslaved by their dependence in the same way as Sufiya Begum. He lent the group of villagers US$27. The repayment terms were simple – 'repay when you can'. The villagers used the money to buy their own raw materials and very slowly they started to reap the benefits of their hard labour. At least now, any money they made from their endeavours was going directly to them rather than back into the pockets of the traders they had been forced to deal with previously. Thus the Grameen Bank experiment was born.

To solve the problem of poverty, however, Dr Yunus knew that charity was not the answer. He knew that any long-term solution needed to be sustainable from the outset. If only he could persuade the banks to lend these people money at manageable rates. He approached the banks and asked them to provide loans to a larger group of villagers in Jobra without collateral. They scoffed at the suggestion. However, a way around the problem was found. If Dr Yunus agreed to stand as guarantor on the loans the bank would agree to lend him US$300. He could now lend money to more people in Jobra. The results slowly became clear. Not only did the money enable these people with nothing to forge a living that could sustain their families, but they also paid back the loans on time. They realized that the credit offered by Dr Yunus and his people was their only chance to break out of poverty. In fact, over time, they started to accumulate savings in excess of their outstanding loans. The pilot was an unheralded success.

Emboldened by the success of the pilot project at Jobra in the mid 1970s, Dr Yunus went back to the banks expecting them to be supportive and ready to take up the mantle. He was to be disappointed. Their response was to dismiss his results as an isolated, one-off outcome, which simply would not be replicated anywhere else. Dr Yunus became more determined to prove them wrong. He extended the pilot project to other regions where he was less well known, a long way from the walls of Chittagong University. The results were repeated. Credit was used to get people – with no hope – out of abject poverty. They paid their loans back on time and in full. They built up savings for the first time in their lives. The project was no longer an experiment. Professor Yunus took a sabbatical from the university and became a full-time banker to the poor!

'Everything they do, we do the opposite'

Muhammad Yunus was determined that Grameen Bank would not look and behave like a traditional bank. On the contrary, he wanted it to be the antithesis of a conventional bank. His philosophy was simple: 'everything a conventional bank did we started doing the opposite!'

It started with the name of the bank itself. In Sanskrit, the local language, Gram means 'rural' or 'village' and so Grameen Bank is literally the 'bank of the villages'. The conventional banks are all located where businesses operate and rich people have their offices. As a result, they are all in the cities. Grameen Bank would work exclusively in the rural villages where the poor people were. To this day you will not find a bank branch in any city or municipal area.

Conventional banks in Bangladesh serve men and generally do not lend to women. While fewer than 1 per cent of borrowers in mainstream Bangladeshi banks are female, Grameen Bank lends almost exclusively to women (97 per cent). Conventional banks ignore the poor, deeming them not to be creditworthy. Grameen Bank has proven that they are. Conventional banks operate on the basis of collateral. Grameen Bank seeks no collateral for loans. This means there is no need for lawyers and their associated costs – the basis of the relationship is one of trust. Forty years later, a loan recovery rate of 98.48 per cent says that this policy works!

Conventional banks expect their borrowers to come to them. Grameen Bank does it the other way around. The bank goes to the borrowers, wherever they live. The branch manager travels to the villages on a weekly basis to collect repayments, hear new loan applications and speak with each borrower face to face. Conventional banks are owned by powerful, corporate people seeking to maximize profit. Grameen Bank is owned by its borrowers – the poor people of Bangladesh.

Grameen is still a bank

It is easy to forget one key fact about Grameen Bank. It is not a charity. It operates as a profit-making corporate entity. Fundamentally, it makes money in the same way as any other banks. It lends money to borrowers, charging interest on the loans; and holds money on deposit, earning interest from these deposits. From the beginning, Muhammad Yunus was adamant that Grameen's operations must be financially self-sustaining and not reliant on donations to fulfil their objectives. He established the systems and procedures to ensure this would happen. Interest rates on loans are fair by local standards (20 per cent declining interest rate on the basic loans, 8 per cent on housing loans and 5 per cent on higher-education loans). Deposit schemes have grown to ensure that Grameen's amount of savings is now almost double that of outstanding borrowings across the bank. Operational procedures are very efficient. Loan administration is easy, with no under-writing of loans or involvement of lawyers. There is minimal overhead in the branches, thanks to the simple structures and modest staff costs. The growth rate of the bank and any individual branch is deliberately measured and controlled. New branch managers are not given initial investment funds to establish a branch. They must attract sufficient depositors initially to allow them to disburse loans to members. Every branch is solvent and liquid. By setting it up in this way and focusing on running the business really well, Grameen has grown its net asset base year on year to stand in excess of US$2.3 billion. This approach is the real magic of Grameen. It is a commercially astute, well-run business with a social purpose at its core. It cannot achieve the latter without ensuring it gets the former right.

The '16 Decisions'

From the outset Grameen Bank was clear that its role was to effect societal change for the people it served. However, achieving this required further innovative, radical thinking. As Dr Yunus continued to get to know his borrowers better he encouraged them to discuss their problems and concerns. These discussions proved enlightening. They led to a series of national workshops, the result of which was the adoption of the '16 Decisions', which became a critical foundation block in transforming the fortunes of Grameen families. The '16 Decisions' is essentially a charter of pledges adopted by every Grameen member. In effect, it functions as the terms and conditions of becoming a borrower within Grameen Bank. But they are very different to any other loan agreement. Included amongst the pledges contained within the 16 Decisions are 'we shall build and use pit latrines'; 'we shall drink water from tube wells'; and 'we shall keep our centre free from the curse of dowry'.[3]

Every Grameen member is educated in the 16 Decisions. They all pledge to uphold them. The weekly centre meetings held in their villages start with the reciting of the 16 Decisions. Members' green loan books, each of which documents a record of their transactions with the bank, have a copy of the 16 Decisions on the back cover. For these people the Decisions become a charter for how they will live their lives and those of their families. And it is their charter. They were the ones who devised it. They are the ones who see the positive impact it has in helping transform their futures. They are the guardians of the 16 Decisions.

Branch number 23760207

We take the 90-minute journey north from Dhaka, the capital city, to the village of Mirzanagar in the Savar Upazila (or sub-district). When we arrive we are greeted with a warm handshake by MD Sanower Hossain, the branch manager of the Mirzanagar Savar branch, who says 'Welcome to branch number 23760207'. The number signifies that this is the 2,376th branch of Grameen Bank and that it was formally established in February 2007. It is a typical branch. There are 2,365 members organized into 44 centres. The branch has six staff in total – Sanower Hossain as branch manager, four centre managers who manage approximately 600 members each, and an accountant who maintains the records of transactions from each centre meeting. The branch office is a modest rented room with no formal signage to indicate its status as a bank. There is no glass in the windows, nor security guards. It is simple by design to ensure it is not intimidating for members.

In reality it is merely a place for the six staff members to coordinate their activities in the surrounding villages, and a location for members to come at appointed times to receive loan disbursements. Most interaction with the members of this (and every other) Grameen branch happens at the centre meetings in the villages. Sanower Hossain invites me to one such meeting.

Figure 2.3 Grameen Bank borrowers' meeting centre in the village of Mirzanagar

SOURCE: Kotinos Partners

We travel approximately 20 minutes along narrow pathways to a clearing in a small, isolated village. A very basic shelter has been built there with a corrugated roof and bamboo sides. Some 40 women are already sitting under the roof of the shelter when we arrive. They welcome me into their fold and after a brief introduction the business of the meeting continues. The centre manager, who arrived before us, conducts the meeting. Each of the women brings her green Grameen book and money to make her weekly loan repayments and saving deposits. These transactions are recorded in their books and on a ledger sheet, which will be used to update the details back at the branch office in the afternoon. We ask each of the women what they

Figure 2.4 Author Brian MacNeice with MD Sanower Hossain and staff in the office of the Mirzanagar Savar branch of Grameen Bank, branch number 23760207

are using the loans for – one after the other they tell me their stories. The first woman, called Lovely, explains that her first Grameen loan allowed her to buy seeds to plant vegetables. She cultivated the crops, used them to feed her family and sold the surplus at the market. After several years she had saved enough to purchase a second-hand bus. Her family now runs a bus service in the village and on the local highways. The next woman, Fatima, explains that her borrowings enabled her family to establish a rickshaw repair business. The next woman, Nazia, runs a shop in the village. Maaryam makes decorative lights. One after another the women list the activities that are sustaining them and their families. All speak with a sense of pride and confidence when they explain their stories.

We then ask how many of the women live in a home with electricity – all except one raise their hands. We ask how many have access to clean drinking water in their homes – every hand shoots into the air. When asked how many have children attending school – again we get a full show of hands except for two older women whose children are no longer of school-going age. Finally we ask how many would have been able to raise their hands to these questions before they became Grameen members – only a couple of women now have their hands raised! It is a most powerful, yet practical demonstration of the impact that Grameen Bank has on rural Bangladeshi society.

Sustainable from the start

The following day we arrived back in Dhaka to meet with Dr Yunus. We spoke about our visit the previous day to the village and he beamed with joy as he realized we had experienced the very essence of Grameen Bank. 'You now understand why I believe that poor people are the world's greatest entrepreneurs. Every day, they must innovate in order to survive. They remain poor because they do not have the opportunities to turn their creativity into sustainable incomes. You have seen first-hand what can happen when we give them that opportunity.'

He reflects further on what he believes are some of the critical factors that are at the core of the organization he designed. 'First I wanted to make sure that what I was building was sustainable.' He continues, 'Even when I started with the pilot project in Jobra, sustainability was always a major issue. I was determined that anything we did must be capable of paying for itself.' For example, take the role of the branch manager. All of the branch managers are qualified to master's degree level. When they become branch managers they are asked to go to new villages. Branch managers must live in the villages they serve. They become part of the community. They are highly respected – few, if any, in their villages will have master's degrees – and they quickly establish themselves as key sources of advice for the villagers. They live simple lives. They dress in clean but ordinary clothes. When they go to the villages initially they don't have any money from Grameen Bank to establish a branch. They must convince a group of women to join the bank and deposit money. This allows them to start giving out loans. From there they gradually grow their branches by adding more people. Only when they have got them to a certain size will assistants be sent to help. After three years the expectation is that branches will be profitable and self-sustaining. 'Each branch is the bank – it is completely self-sufficient.'

The five-star branch

Each branch works to a five-star model. There is a colour-coded system with stars awarded for 100 per cent achievement of specific goals. A five-star branch indicates the highest level of performance possible. The five stars are:

- Green star: for any branch that maintains a 100 per cent repayment record.

- Blue star: for any branch that earns a profit.

- Violet star: for any branch that generates a surplus of deposits over the loans outstanding in the branch.

- Brown star: for any branch that ensures 100 per cent of the children of the Grameen families get a proper school education.

- Red star: for any branch that can show it has succeeded in taking 100 per cent of their borrowers' families over the poverty line.

The five-star branch concept has sparked the enthusiasm of the Grameen staff. It is proving to be a powerful and meaningful motivator for them. Each member of staff can earn 'stars' even if their branch has yet to earn any. For example, each centre manager can achieve the stars for fulfilling the same conditions for the centres they manage. This creates an internal spirit of competition, a sense of pride in achievement as stars are earned, and a sense of worth for those receiving them, knowing that the work they are doing makes a real difference to the economic and social conditions of the people they live with in their villages.

No one stands alone

Another key principle underpinning the organization's design is that of solidarity lending. Dr Yunus explains, 'in effect, no one who borrows from Grameen Bank stands alone'. The structure to achieve this is elegantly simple and highly effective. Each member belongs to a self-made group of five friends. They cannot be close family relatives but they all must be known to each other and from the same village. On average there are 10 groups in a centre.

In order to take out a loan a group member must seek the approval of the other four members of the group. Each individual member is responsible for repaying her own loan. However, they function as a group and provide support to each other in terms of encouragement, guidance and practical help when they encounter difficulties. If one member of the group defaults on her loan the others will be denied future loans. If a member of the group leaves the bank, the others are responsible for recruiting a replacement. Each group elects a Chair and that individual takes on responsibilities on behalf of the group, including presenting proposals to the centre manager should a member of the group wish to take out a new loan.

Solidarity lending works. It acts as a strong motivator to ensure that everyone within the group remains faithful to her commitments in terms of repaying loans, accumulating savings and upholding the '16 Decisions'. However, it also provides a community-oriented support system amongst the women that binds them together. The net effect across the 8.8 million borrowers is to enable each to achieve things they would not otherwise have achieved standing alone.

The four principles

The first of the 16 Decisions reads as follows: 'We shall follow and advance the four principles of Grameen Bank – discipline, unity, courage and hard work – in all walks of our lives.' These principles manifest themselves in tangible ways and are at the heart of how Grameen works. For example, the practice of making weekly loan repayments and savings deposits by members reinforces the discipline principle. This has endured from the out-set of the pilot project in Jobra. The solidarity lending approach and the self-regulation of each centre are examples of how the unity principle is implemented practically. The courage principle is emphasized by encouraging women borrowers to use their access to credit to 'invest' in their livelihoods and continually grow to enable them to provide for their families. The hard-work principle is something that comes naturally and almost does not need reinforcing. These people have worked hard all their lives, even before they had access to credit. Grameen Bank has simply ensured that the fruits of their labour have a more significant and positive impact on their lives.

Never standing still – Grameen II

Over the years Grameen Bank, like any powerhouse organization, has adapted and changed. Whilst the original raison d'être remains – to enable its members' rise out of poverty[4] – the means through which it delivers this changes. In the early years the only 'product' offered was a basic loan to provide access to credit for the first time for those previously denied. The floods of 1998 in particular prompted a major review of how the bank worked. The need to greatly increase the volume of savings deposited by members became clear, as did the need to introduce more flexible loan 'products'. The change was heralded as the emergence of Grameen II in the early 2000s and was the result of a range of ideas conceived by staff and members alike. The modern day Grameen Bank now provides a wider range of loan products, including the basic income-generating loan (the original product started in the pilot programme in Jobra in 1976); housing loans to enable members to build houses or make basic improvements to their living conditions; education loans to encourage members to provide higher-education opportunities for their children; 'struggling members' loans, which are targeted at beggars, offering interest-free credit to enable door-to-door beggars in villages to carry small merchandise such as snacks, toys or household items to offer for sale when calling door-to-door. These loans have seen large numbers of beggars become full-time salespeople.

In addition to its loan products, a range of savings products have been introduced. These include a pension fund account, which encourages members to deposit a fixed amount each week or month and which, over a 10-year period, doubles the total of their deposits. Flexi-loan repayments have been introduced for those in difficulty – for whatever reason. Essentially these allow for repayments to be spread over a longer period of time. The principle is to keep members within the bank. Loan insurance has also been introduced to ensure that, in the event of a borrower or her husband passing away, the outstanding debts are written off rather than transferring to the family at a time of great burden.

The introduction of the expanded range of products comes directly from the '16 Decisions' concept. For example, the provision of higher-education loans is a practical response to decision seven ('We shall educate our children and ensure that they can earn to pay for their education'). The product allows members to follow through on that decision. Dr Yunus summarizes the importance of this continued evolution: 'Any high-performing organization needs to be flexible enough to meet the changing needs and demands of the people it serves. Grameen Bank is no different. We must never stop developing and improving.'

'We are not job seekers, we are job creators'

As our time in Bangladesh comes to a close we sit in the office of Dr Yunus. He explains how Grameen supports young people with business ideas through the creation of social business funds. They encourage young people to come up with business ideas that the bank can invest in. In essence, Grameen becomes an angel investor with one simple difference – it does not take any profit from its investments! If a business idea is successful the owners can buy back Grameen's shares without giving the bank any profit. They pay a share transfer fee, which is a fixed amount to help cover management and advisory services.

Figure 2.5 Author Brian MacNeice with Professor Muhammad Yunus in his office at the Yunus Centre in Dhaka, Bangladesh

SOURCE: Kotinos Partners

This prompts us to discuss Dr Yunus's philosophy on the creative capability of people. It is an inspiring conversation. 'I fundamentally believe that entrepreneurship is natural to human beings. If illiterate rural women in Bangladesh can become entrepreneurs anybody can', he says. He is determined to reinforce the results demonstrated by the members of Grameen Bank in getting young people to understand that they are job creators, not job seekers. 'As long as we teach our young people to look for jobs we will have unemployment. We should educate them to see themselves as job creators.' He closes our conversation with a message he has given to many young people: 'Look to your mother as an example. Learn from her. The women of the Grameen have shown you how they harness their potential as human beings. With the support of micro-loans they have become entrepreneurs and provided for their families. They have shown you the way.'

The Museum of Poverty

Dr Yunus dreamt of a day when schoolchildren would only see poverty in a museum. He created Grameen Bank to help achieve this goal. In establishing the bank, he gave birth to the micro-lending industry. Yunus and the bank he founded are responsible for leading some 100 million families out of poverty. The Museum of Poverty does not exist yet but it is being built one family at a time.

Powerhouse Principle 1: ambition

We view ambition as a vital starting point for sustained high performance. Organizations need to have it, and need to articulate what it is. By challenging Grameen Bank to enable a future where the horrors of acute poverty were on visible display only in a museum – The Museum of Poverty – Muhammad Yunus established a powerful ambition for his institution. So what, from our experience, are the generic characteristics of a powerful ambition?

- *Ambition should be 'unreasonable' – challenging the paradigm*
  It is important to set the bar for ambition at a level that seems, at current course and speed, to be out of reach. This creates positive dissatisfaction with the status quo and challenges individuals and teams to think differently – deconstructing 'good enough' approaches and innovating to build something fundamentally better. By setting the bar as eliminating poverty forever, Dr Yunus unlocked the door to transformational thinking that in turn drove the success of Grameen Bank. In his words: 'Let us dream the wildest dream and then pursue it.' This driving force helped release 100 million families from the curse of living below the poverty line.

- *Ambition should be captivating – engaging and energizing the whole organization*
  Good ambitions appeal to the emotions as well as the intellect. They capture the imagination and provide real meaning for individuals in organizations, inspiring them to give of their very best. Exactly what it is that captivates reflects the specific circumstances of each organization and its people; however, in the case of Grameen the link is easy to see. The vision of a poverty-free world convinces well-educated individuals such as MD Sanower Hossain (Masters' qualified in a country where this is very much the exception) to become branch managers, live in the villages

▶

they serve and commit to a lifetime of serving the rural women members of the bank. Grameen staff are proud of what they do and are committed to it in ways you only see in organizations that have been energized through ambition.

- *Ambition should be connected – reflecting the organization's core purpose*
  All institutions have a core purpose. Often, this core purpose is economic in nature, for example businesses have as a primary objective the creation of value for shareholders. It is important, in setting ambition, for leaders to connect that ambition to the organization's fundamental purpose. Again, in setting the ambition that he did, Dr Yunus ticked this box at Grameen as the only path for the institution to realize its ambition lies in driving its economic viability and capacity to grow – in turn through maintaining a consistent, appropriate level of profitability. Achieving real alignment – in essence of stakeholder and shareholder value – is an important challenge for leaders to address.

- *Ambition should be 'two-sided', recognizing and reflecting an appreciation of risk*
  It is argued that unfettered ambition was at the heart of the global financial services crisis triggered in 2007. However, we would suggest that a more fundamental issue was insufficient implicit and explicit accounting for risk. President John F Kennedy in 1961 delivered one of the best practical examples of ambition setting when he challenged the US people to put a man on the moon before the end of the decade and bring him back alive. As the story of Apollo 13 bears out, this overt acknowledgement of risk, when it came to the crunch, enabled Mission Control to prioritize bringing the astronauts home over having them walk on the moon. Appreciation of risk is implicit but nonetheless present in Grameen's statement of ambition – again as the challenge of eliminating poverty is a clear one for the long term. We can see the effect of Grameen's understanding of risk, and its commitment to long-term viability, in the principles and practices it adopts to ensure minimal defaults on its loans.

- *Ambition should be non-directive – capturing the destination, without prescribing the journey*
  A core rationale for setting ambition is to provoke creativity and 'game-changing' behaviour. In instances where, in addition to the destination being defined so also is the means of arriving at that destination, we find that the scope for new ideas, paradigms and behaviours is accordingly reduced. There are always constraints on how the journey might be undertaken – whether imposed from the outside by legal or regulatory

institutions, or self-imposed from the inside. However, to the extent possible, ambitions should be framed such as to leave the widest possible scope for individuals and organizations to innovate in respect of their approach. In the case of Grameen Bank, it is obvious how the simple ambition to be at the heart of eliminating poverty creates huge scope for innovating how the institution might make its ambition happen.

- *Ambition should be managed to build momentum and confidence over time*

  At the point when institutions initially set out their ambitions, typically large subsets of their people will think them impossible to achieve. When Dr Yunus first shared his ambition to build a commercial financial institution that would eliminate poverty in Bangladesh – forcing the need for a Museum of Poverty over time – everyone told him it was a project doomed to failure. Over time he built the number of those who believed by, through whatever means, bringing the doubters on board. He said his biggest challenge was to fight the mindset that prevented people from seeing what was possible, but he met the challenge by logging and recognizing each success – each 'island of achievement' – along the journey. The momentum became so strong that nothing has been able to stop Grameen's progress towards its ambition.

Notes

1 Figures from Grameen Bank Monthly Report, January 2016.

2 Amit K Kashyap (2014) *Indian Banking: Contemporary issues in law and challenges*, Allied Publishers, New Delhi.

3 The '16 decisions' of Grameen Bank are:

   1 We shall follow and advance the four principles of Grameen Bank – discipline, unity, courage and hard work – in all walks of our lives.

   2 Prosperity we shall bring to our families.

   3 We shall not live in a dilapidated house. We shall repair our houses and work towards constructing new houses at the earliest opportunity.

   4 We shall grow vegetables all year round. We shall eat plenty of them and sell the surplus.

   5 During the plantation seasons, we shall plant as many seedlings as possible.

   6 We shall plan to keep our families small. We shall minimize our expenditures. We shall look after our health.

   7 We shall educate our children and ensure that they can earn to pay for their education.

8 We shall always keep our children and the environment clean.

9 We shall build and use pit latrines.

10 We shall drink water from tube wells. If they are not available, we shall boil water or use alum to purify it.

11 We shall not take any dowry at our sons' weddings; neither shall we give any dowry at our daughters' weddings. We shall keep the centre free from the curse of dowry. We shall not practise child marriage.

12 We shall not commit any injustice, and we will oppose anyone who tries to do so.

13 We shall collectively undertake larger investments for higher incomes.

14 We shall always be ready to help each other. If anyone is in difficulty, we shall all help him or her.

15 If we come to know of any breach of discipline in any centre, we shall go there and help restore discipline.

16 We shall introduce physical exercises in all our centres. We shall take part in all social activities collectively.

4 Grameen Bank, after interviewing many borrowers about what a poverty-free life meant to them, developed a set of 10 indicators that could be used to assess whether a family in rural Bangladesh lived a poverty-free life. The indicators are:

- having a house with a roof;
- having beds or cots for all members of the family;
- having access to safe drinking water;
- having access to a sanitary latrine;
- having all school-age children attending school;
- having sufficient warm clothing for the winter;
- having mosquito nets;
- having a home vegetable garden;
- having no food shortages, even during the most difficult time of a very difficult year;
- having sufficient income-earning opportunities for all adult members of the family.

Médecins Sans Frontières   03

Témoignage: bearing witness to conflict and disaster

What makes Médecins Sans Frontières a performance powerhouse?

Médecins Sans Frontières (MSF) – or Doctors Without Borders – is one of the world's largest emergency aid organizations. In 2015, it sent out some 30,000 staff including doctors, nurses, logisticians, project managers and 'national' (or local) employees – approximately 90 per cent of MSF staff on any given mission are 'national' (or local) – to tackle some of the worst humanitarian crises brought about by natural disaster and conflict.

In 2015, MSF teams working in 69 countries around the world provided around 8.7 million outpatient consultations, admitted more than 598,000 patients for inpatient care, and helped deliver more than 243,000 babies. Teams also cared for more than 340,700 people living with HIV/AIDS; admitted more than 60,500 severely malnourished children to feeding programmes; vaccinated more than 1.5 million people in response to measles outbreaks and 326,100 in response to meningitis outbreaks. It performed more than 106,500 surgeries, and treated more than 2.3 million cases of malaria, more than 32,600 cases of cholera, nearly 20,100 for first- or second-line TB, and more than 11,100 victims of sexual violence. Staff also carried out more than 223,900 mental health consultations. In addition to all of this, MSF teams rescued and assisted 23,700 migrants and refugees at sea and, during the Ebola epidemic, treated more than 7,400 patients.[1]

MSF now has five operational centres in Europe and offices in 28 countries worldwide. It has treated in excess of 100 million patients since its foundation.

▶

Figure 3.1 Médecins Sans Frontières (MSF) Powerhouse Performance model

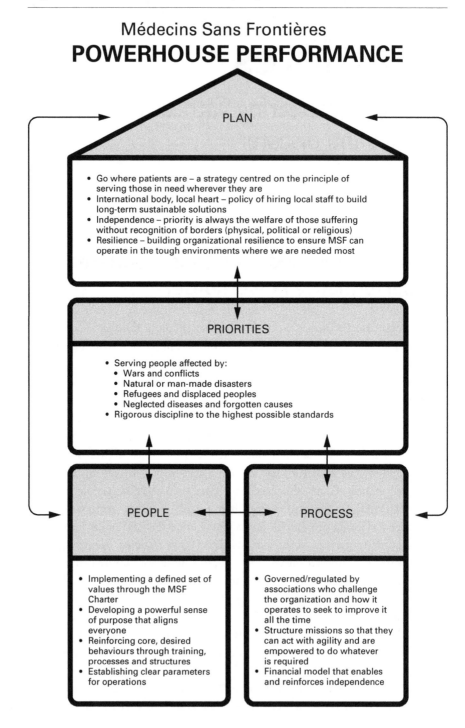

It has been involved in providing critical support in approximately 100 countries across Africa, the Americas, Asia and Europe.

In 1999, MSF was awarded the Nobel Peace Prize to honour its staff. This is one of only a handful of times when the prize has been awarded to an organization instead of an individual. The citation highlighted MSF's 'pioneering humanitarian work on several continents' and acknowledged its independent, neutral and impartial philosophy. The judges noted its role in 'calling public attention to humanitarian catastrophes' and highlighted how 'by pointing to the causes of such catastrophes, the organization helps to form bodies of public opinion opposed to violations and abuses of power'.

As the world teeters from one crisis to another – some natural, others brought on by conflict – time and again MSF is there to provide urgent care for those in desperation. The recent Ebola crisis has seen the organization yet again demonstrate its ability to overcome the political and structural obstacles that seem to halt others. An article in the *Wall Street Journal* in 2014 summed it up perfectly when it said: 'the humanitarian organization Doctors Without Borders is still the most functional outfit in a dysfunctional global health system'.[2]

Millions of people around the world rely on MSF. It is unquestionably a performance powerhouse.

The Médecins Sans Frontières powerhouse

Go where the patients are

Médecins Sans Frontières (MSF) was founded in 1971 by a group of disillusioned French doctors frustrated with the shortcomings of international relief organizations. The doctors were influenced by their experiences providing aid support during the civil war in Biafra in the late 1960s and then in the aftermath of a natural disaster in 1970 in eastern Pakistan, now Bangladesh. In each case, the doctors came away with a sense that the International Red Cross and other related aid agencies were excessively neutral and timid in their approaches to dealing with situations in which they were active. They would only intervene in crisis situations on invitation from or with the permission of local governments and they were duty-bound to stay silent despite anything they might witness during their service. Dr Bernard Kouchner, one of the founding members of MSF, observed first-hand what he believed was a lack of action on the parts of the aid agencies during the Biafran Civil War. Unwilling to stay silent, he and others spoke out about the genocide they believed they were witnessing during the conflict. To these doctors, not speaking out was unconscionable. They believed in more effective and questioning forms of humanitarianism and felt compelled to intervene based on need. They advocated ignoring boundaries – physical, political or religious – and emphasized that the real priority should always be the welfare of those who were suffering. A group of 13 like-minded individuals – doctors and journalists – decided it was time for action.[3] On 22 December 1971 they established a new humanitarian organization to provide emergency medical assistance in crisis zones. Dr Kouchner and his colleagues were determined that this new entity would not be restricted – either in where it could go or in what it could do to alleviate the suffering of those in need. Neither would it be influenced by gender, race, religion or political affiliation. As he put it: 'It's simple really: go where the patients are. It seems obvious, but at the time it was a revolutionary concept because borders got in the way. It's no coincidence that we called it Médecins Sans Frontières.'[4] This, in effect, is MSF's 'unreasonable ambition'.

From these humble beginnings in Paris in 1971, MSF has developed into the world's largest, and arguably most effective, humanitarian organization. MSF has never been afraid to challenge itself and how it operates. This is one of the core strengths of the movement. A seminal moment in its history occurred in 1979 during a robust and passionate debate at the General Assembly about the future direction of the organization. One camp firmly believed that they should continue to act as a band of quasi-guerilla doctors, while an opposing faction sought to develop a stronger organizational structure to grow MSF. The latter group won out and, from that moment, MSF flourished in scale and scope.

The MSF charter – more than rhetoric

The founding principles established by the original group of 13 have not changed over the 40-plus years that MSF has been in existence. At its core are five underlying values that form its raison d'être:

- *Medical ethics*: first and foremost, MSF is a medical organization providing the best possible care to those who need it most. It upholds patient autonomy, patient confidentiality and the right to informed consent.

- *Independence*: MSF has always maintained a strongly independent philosophy. The decision to offer support to any country or crisis situation is based purely on an assessment of need, carried out by the organization itself. It is critical to MSF that it has full and unhindered freedom in carrying out its role: 'MSF intervenes by choice – not obligation or conscription.'[5]

- *Impartiality and neutrality*: enshrined in the activities of MSF is the principle that assistance is provided to those in need irrespective of race, religion, gender or political affiliation. Priority is given to those in most serious and immediate danger, based on independent assessment, and they do not take sides or intervene according to the demands of governments or warring parties.

- *Bearing witness*: the silence of humanitarian organizations in the late 1960s was one of the main driving forces in the establishment of MSF. Whilst maintaining the principles of impartiality and neutrality, the organization will always speak out when it deems it necessary. This philosophy of *témoignage* ('witnessing') is a key part of how it operates, time and again in evidence in missions across the globe. Indeed this spirit of speaking out includes a level of transparency about its own organizational challenges and issues, which add further to its credibility.

- *Accountability*: in every mission it embarks on, MSF constantly reviews and evaluates the effectiveness of its activities to ensure that it does the best it can for the patients whose needs it is serving. MSF also feels a duty to be accountable to the millions of donors who contribute financially to its activities – who enable it to remain fiercely independent and unencumbered from obligation to governments or other entities.

These principles are enshrined in the MSF charter and every member explicitly agrees to uphold and honour them.

As we have seen, or will see, in the other performance powerhouses (eg Grameen Bank, Southwest Airlines, Tata Group and New Zealand All Blacks), a visceral and lived set of core values acts as a powerful reference point for high-performing organizations. Values are effective when they are lived in practice and demonstrated by act, as opposed to being the bland aspirational rhetoric that many similar value statements become in corporate entities.

The funding model that supports MSF's activities reflects and underpins these principles. In particular, by not relying on government donations but adopting a model of a large volume of private donations – in 2015, 92 per cent of MSF's income came from private sources, more than 5.7 million individual donors and private foundations worldwide made this possible – the organization can preserve its core independence, neutrality and impartiality. Financial independence means that MSF can go where it is needed most. Close to 90 per cent of all funds are spent on programme services around the globe. Less than 2 per cent are spent on management costs (including salaries) and general overheads. The remainder is focused on supporting fundraising activities. In 2015 MSF's total spend on its activities amounted to €1.28 billion. Its accounting practices are highly transparent. MSF publishes, annually, detailed analysis of where monetary resources are spent and is scrupulous in ensuring it holds itself accountable to its donors. MSF's level of accountability goes beyond financial transparency. There is a constant process of critique, review and analysis of operations at every level in order to guarantee that the founding principles are upheld and that resources are applied where they are needed most.

Serving those in most need

The work of MSF typically arises from one of four types of emergency situation:

- wars and conflicts;
- natural or man-made disasters;
- refugees and displaced peoples;
- neglected diseases and forgotten causes.

The first scenario involves providing urgent assistance in conflict zones or war situations. They have done this all over the world, including Vietnam, Rwanda, Lebanon, Bosnia, Afghanistan and Cambodia. In these situations MSF provides a range of medical support personnel including surgeons, anaesthetists, nursing staff and logisticians. They work in the most trying and dangerous circumstances to set up field hospitals and treatment centres with basic equipment to tend to the casualties of conflict, without prejudice. This type of work is not for the faint-hearted. War zones are obviously very dangerous, stressful and disturbing places and because of this only the very experienced and most highly trained staff are sent. Very strict security protocols are put in place and every effort is made to minimize the risk to staff. In some situations – for example in Somalia and Equatorial Guinea – MSF has been forced to take the decision to withdraw from the country to protect the safety of its people.

Figure 3.2 An expatriate health worker discusses problems with an armed soldier

SOURCE: Médecins Sans Frontières

The second scenario involves MSF responding to major natural or man-made disasters such as earthquakes, tsunamis, hurricanes or droughts. By their nature these events are catastrophic for the populations of people affected. MSF has developed the organizational capability to deploy rapidly in such crises and provide the urgent emergency response assistance needed. For example, when the devastating earthquake hit Haiti in 2010, MSF was treating its first patient within three minutes of the tremor. The experienced team of medical staff, logisticians, sanitation and water experts got to work rapidly to deal with the immediate after-effects of the disaster. Typically MSF support extends beyond the initial emergency response phase and shifts towards re-establishing longer-term infrastructure, systems and support.

A third area of support focuses on dealing with the aftermath of refugees or displaced peoples. Whether as a result of conflict or natural disaster, many of the poorest people in the world end up in refugee camps where diseases such as measles and cholera can spread rapidly. Basic standards of sanitation are lacking, and large numbers live in undignified conditions that are well below what any human being should endure. For example,

MSF works currently with refugees from places such as Somalia and Sudan, providing basic primary health care, immunization programmes, control of potentially epidemic diseases, provision of basic sanitation systems, nutrition advice and psychological care.

Finally, MSF also works in situations arising from neglected diseases such as multi-drug-resistant tuberculosis (MDR-TB, also known as Vank's disease), sleeping sickness etc, or forgotten crises – particularly where there is an absence of a health-care system, or there is exclusion from health care for certain groups of people.

The nature of the projects run by MSF are numerous and touch those with the most urgent needs, wherever they are. Whilst much of its most high-profile work is related to conflicts and large-scale disasters, some of which receives widespread publicity, a significant majority of its work impacts people in 'hidden emergencies'. MSF helps the marginalized and ostracized of society who, for many differing reasons, are neglected by authorities or other aid agencies.

Empowered to impact

Several factors go into the decision-making process to establish a mission in a country. First, most importantly, and as we have discussed already, intervention driven by need. An MSF team assesses the nature of each new humanitarian emergency and determines if assistance is required. The team evaluates precisely what type of medical aid can be provided and conducts a risk assessment to understand the security and safety profile of the situation. Every mission, by its nature, carries significant risks. However, MSF will not go to a crisis if it believes the level of risk to be unacceptably high. A recommendation is submitted to headquarters for decision and if approved the work of establishing a mission on the ground can begin.

Each mission has a small, tightly knit group of people coordinating activity. The Head of Mission is typically the most experienced member of the team, and has overall responsibility in overseeing the entire operation. He or she is supported by a range of medical and non-medical specialists. Each mission reports to and is linked directly to one of MSF's five operational centres (OC) – based in Belgium, France, Holland, Spain and Switzerland. These OCs make the key decisions about when, where and what medical care is provided by each mission. In turn there are currently 24 national associations around the world, which fundraise, recruit and employ MSF staff. Each national association is also linked directly to one of the five OCs. As missions become established in particular countries, the Head of Mission reports back regularly to the relevant OC on activity, issues and programmes, and looks for guidance on the future direction of the mission. The governance model has undergone a detailed review in recent years, culminating in the adoption of new statutes by MSF International and the establishment of an International General Assembly, which first met in Paris in 2011. These structures are designed to preserve the decentralized operational model critical to effective functioning, whilst simultaneously maximizing the organization's coherence and accountability in the face of the growth it has seen over its 40-plus years.

> This level of local autonomy is a repeating characteristic of performance powerhouses. The same principle is evident in the Finnish Education Model (Chapter 7) and all the other examples included in this book. Smart, motivated people empowered to make decisions with a clear framework for action characterizes these organizations. To be high performing, leaders in business need to enable their people to operate in this way.

Earning their MSF T-shirt

The process for joining an MSF mission is rigorous and the organization is very selective. Applicants are screened to assess the relevance of their qualifications, expertise and experience before being invited for interview. The interview process is used to determine fit for what will inevitably be very demanding working environments. MSF field work tests the most resilient of individuals. Many apply, few are accepted. It is critical to MSF that they ensure the highest standard of intake for its field missions. Once successful, new recruits are placed on the register and considered available to work for MSF. Field staff do not choose the locations to which they are matched. These decisions are based on operational requirements and where the needs are at any point in time. Once appointed to a mission it is likely that a new recruit to the field will be sent for a one-week, intensive preparation course called the Preparation for Primary Departure (PPD).

The PPD covers every aspect of life as an MSF worker in the field. First, recruits receive a detailed grounding in the fundamental values and principles of the organization. Every MSF staff member is deeply rooted in and driven by the MSF charter and core principles. The programme also covers the code of conduct in mission, and addresses topics such as how to deal with the media in crisis situations – maintaining neutrality and honouring the commitment to speak out. The scope of technical education is extensive and covers topics that include the basic structure of a field hospital; how to deal with an overwhelmed refugee camp where key decisions need to be made about prioritizing care; prevention of spreadable diseases such as cholera, malaria or TB; and amputation of limbs with limited equipment. The practical side of operating in the field is also addressed. There are briefings and lectures on security protocols, made real through tales from experienced veterans who have served in many different environments. Other briefings are given on critically important logistical support infrastructure so that recruits know how to ensure they have the necessary equipment and parts to provide medical care, and to access other support equipment. To be effective in the field, MSF workers, in addition to their medical knowledge, need to know how to get replacement parts for communications equipment and vehicles!

The PPD finishes with a symbolic and deeply personal moment for all the new recruits. Upon completion of the programme each person is presented with an MSF T-shirt. This is worn as a badge of honour by all staff. When working in the field the MSF logo carries special significance; the famous red-and-white logo earns instant respect. This is the result of over four decades of phenomenal service to the neediest in dire situations.

MSF mission in Haiti

To understand how MSF operates we decided to visit one of their missions. We travelled to Haiti to see the work being done there. The MSF mission in Haiti was established in 1991. Chronic underinvestment is a feature of the country's infrastructure and this was (and still is) most evident in its health system. When MSF first arrived, the hospitals and health facilities were in a bad state of repair, and standards of hygiene and medical care were low. The initial emphasis was on rehabilitation of these facilities and improving standards through training of health staff – surgeons, doctors, nurses and anaesthetists. In addition, water and sanitation programmes were introduced. In essence, MSF was providing critical support to a fragile and dysfunctional health system chronically lacking resources, expertise and standards of care. Compounding the problem were severe inequities in accessing the shambolic health system. Health care in Haiti is largely privatized and therefore out of reach for the vast majority of Haitians who simply cannot afford to pay for even basic health services. Some 25 years after MSF's arrival in Haiti that system is still woefully inadequate for its population.

Political unrest, high accident rates and an increasingly violent society hindered progress in addressing some of these challenges. MSF began to establish emergency trauma services to provide treatment for the many victims of accidents and violent encounters, as well as specialist maternity and obstetric care. To give a sense of the state of the nation at this time here are some startling statistics:[6]

- Haiti is the poorest country in the western hemisphere. It is ranked 168th of 187 countries in the United Nations (UN) Development Programme, Human Development Index.

- Haiti was ranked 145 out of 169 countries in the UN Human Development Index – the lowest of any western hemisphere nation.

- 70 per cent of Haitians lived on less than US$2 per day.

- 86 per cent of the citizens of Port-au-Prince were living in slum conditions.

- Half of the people living in the capital had no access to latrines and less than one-third had access to tap water.

A country in need

The fragility of the country's infrastructure left it extremely vulnerable to natural disasters such as tropical storms or hurricanes. When these events occurred MSF mobilized and provided crisis services to the desperate and needy. Nothing, however, could have prepared Haiti for what happened on 12 January 2010. A 7-magnitude earthquake struck near the capital Port-au-Prince. Its impact was catastrophic. An estimated 220,000 people died and another 300,000 were badly injured. Homes, schools, hospitals and other government buildings were destroyed; 1.5 million people were left homeless. The brittle economy was crushed. The estimated cost of the disaster ran to billions of dollars, and any chance Haiti had of building a sustainable future was crushed under the weight of rubble. Chris Herlinger and Paul Jeffrey, authors of *Rubble Nation: Haiti's pain, Haiti's promise*, estimated that 'removing all of the earthquake debris would require at least 1,000 trucks working 24 hours a day for five years'. As our initial drive from the airport evidenced, much of the rubble is still there.

The impact of the quake on the country's health system was inevitable. Apart from the physical damage to already rudimentary facilities – 60 per cent of Haiti's existing health facilities were destroyed – the cost in terms of personnel was crippling. Significant numbers of medical staff were killed in the disaster, many others decided to leave the country. A health system in a well-developed country would have struggled to cope – for one that was already in intensive care this situation was terminal. The scale of the crisis was unprecedented. The scale of the MSF response was equally enormous. This was simply the largest emergency response the organization has ever deployed. Over the 10-month period that followed the earthquake, MSF teams treated a staggering 360,000 patients, performed 16,570 surgeries, assisted at 15,100 births, distributed over 50,000 tents, half a million square litres of water per day and invested over US$125 million in the relief operation.

The curse of cholera

Inevitably, the next major crisis was prompted by living conditions, which pre-earthquake were shockingly poor and post-quake were rife for the spreading of disease. In October 2010, aided by poor hygiene standards and a large population lacking access to safe water supply, cholera – a water-borne disease that results in rapid dehydration and, untreated, leads to death as the organs fail – spread rapidly across the population. MSF quickly established cholera treatment centres (CTCs) in key locations. Notwithstanding this, within nine months, some 6,000 people tragically lost their lives due to the outbreak, while another 220,000 were infected. As the immediate intensity of the earthquake emergency response slowly abated, the cholera epidemic ensured that the herculean task facing the MSF staff intensified.

Figure 3.3 The challenge of dealing with a cholera outbreak, due to the fragile infrastructure in Haiti

SOURCE: Médecins Sans Frontières

MSF in Haiti today

Fast-forward six years from the earthquake and whilst the immediate crisis prompted by the disaster is over, the problems facing Haiti and the MSF mission in the country certainly are not. Much of the health infrastructure is still missing. Access to health care is still beyond a large proportion of the population and many rely for emergency care on MSF services, which are open 24 hours a day and available free of charge. Oliver Schulz, a German-born veteran of many MSF missions, is currently the Head of Mission in Haiti. He explains the key challenges facing MSF in Haiti today: 'The main problem we run into is a chronic lack of structure right across the system. There is simply no working central system to run the health system effectively and this creates a lot of obstacles to progress for the nation and for us. This, combined with a severe underinvestment in health makes our ongoing presence essential.'

The finger in the dike

The range of services provided by MSF in Haiti is vast. MSF runs Centre de Référence en Urgence Obstétricale (CRUO), a 130-bed maternity hospital that provides 24-hour care for pregnant women and a full range of services including family planning, postnatal care and prevention of mother-to-child transmission of HIV. Dr Rodnie Senat, the Haitian-born Medical Director, explains that 'our focus is on providing emergency support for complicated cases'. The hospital assisted in over 5,450 births in 2013. In September 2014 (the most recent figures at the time of our visit) CRUO triaged 1,670 cases in the month and assisted 572 deliveries.

The Drouillard hospital close to the Cité Soleil slum in Port-au-Prince houses an MSF specialist burns unit, the only one in the country. The high level of urban violence and major traffic-related accidents has led to a doubling of trauma deaths in the last decade. Yet there are virtually no traumatology services outside of those provided by the MSF-run hospitals. At the MSF Nap Kenbe hospital in Tabarre, opened in February 2012, the team treated 6,500 accidental trauma and 1,325 violent trauma cases in 2014 alone, including visceral surgery and orthopaedic care.[7] Surgeons performed on average 130 surgical interventions a month. The Drouillard hospital treated 13,200 trauma-related patients – one-third related to traffic accidents, one-fifth victims of violence and one-quarter injured in domestic accidents. There is only one (non-MSF) public hospital in Haiti offering orthopaedic surgical care but the Hôpital de l'Université d'Etat d'Haiti (HUEH) has not been fully rehabilitated since the 2010 quake and therefore is not running at full capacity. Whilst investment has seen new facilities built, some of these remain unused. For example, the new hospital built in Carrefour is unoccupied because of poor resource planning (see Figure 3.4). It is in this context that MSF emergency facilities such as the 160-bed temporary container hospital in the city of Léogâne, the CRUO, Drouillard and Tabarre hospitals are such an important component of the Haitian health system. They are critical in helping to overcome the shortcomings of the system overseen by the Ministère de la Santé Publique (the Ministry of Health). Effectively, MSF is operating like the little Dutch boy that saved his country by putting his finger in the dike.[8]

Figure 3.4 Carrefour, OCA surgery makeshift area outside the building of the Carrefour hospital, treating a patient with two broken legs

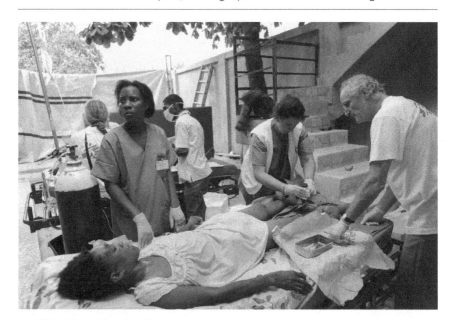

SOURCE: Médecins Sans Frontières

Aside from the traumatology services, the other major area of concern from a health perspective is the cholera situation. Given the poverty and social deprivation leading to very poor living conditions, it is an inevitability for some time to come that regular outbreaks will continue. Typically they are triggered by the rainy seasons, which usually arrive in late spring and autumn. For example, in 2014 MSF treated over 5,600 patients with symptoms of cholera, most of which happened in autumn. Despite the predictable pattern associated with the disease in Haiti, the levels of preparedness and response of the authorities are wholly inadequate. Again it falls on MSF to fill the void. They are effectively the first responders whenever cholera outbreaks occur – and they are very effective in treating the disease. A week before our arrival in Haiti in late October 2014 an outbreak occurred. Once it was established that the threat of an epidemic existed MSF mobilized rapidly. Within a mere six hours, they had established an emergency CTC in temporary facilities located behind the CRUO hospital in Port-au-Prince (see Figure 3.5).

Figure 3.5 An MSF cholera treatment centre in Port-au-Prince, Haiti

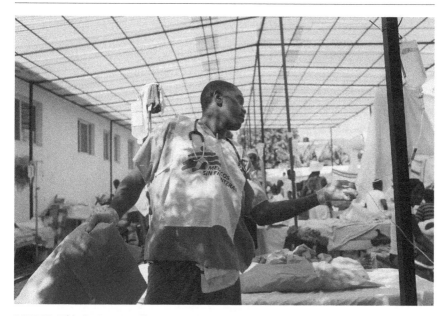

SOURCE: Médecins Sans Frontières

Since 2010 they have treated over 204,000 victims of cholera, achieving a mortality rate of less than 1 per cent. Without their expertise, the death toll in Haiti would be significantly higher.

International body, local heart

One of the strengths of the MSF mission in Haiti is the number of local people involved in its operation. Approximately 2,500 staff are employed by MSF in the country, of which 95 per cent are Haitian. This helps create a very strong bond between the organization and those they serve. It also represents a significant investment in the long-term capability of the medical system to become sustainable in the future. Training education and high standards of care are key skills that are being transferred from MSF to the Haitian health-care system. There is a poster on the wall of the staff canteen area in the CRUO hospital, the 'Charte du CRUO'. Massimo Ravasini, an Italian with five years' experience within MSF, is the project coordinator at CRUO. He explains that the Charte originated from another (non-MSF) hospital where a doctor was shot by one of the caretakers, who felt he had disrespected him. The staff at CRUO decided to develop their own charter to explicitly define how they wanted to behave as a team. The Charte is written in their own words and is something they take seriously. Every two months staff meetings are held and prizes awarded to staff members. One of the prizes relates to the staff member who best represents the embodiment of the Charte.

During our visit, outside the MSF house close to the CRUO hospital we came across a young woman of about 20 years of age, who we were told regularly stands outside the wrought-iron gates waiting for MSF people to emerge. We asked what she was doing. One of the MSF nurses explained to us: 'She is looking to get a job with MSF. She is here many days a week hoping that we will employ her. We have explained that she is one of many hundreds, if not thousands, looking for a job with us and that she should apply through the hospital administration staff. But she still appears regularly at our gate hoping that we will say yes.' It is not just a job she is looking for. She wants to be part of one of the few things that really works in Haiti.

Closing a mission

At some point a decision will be made to close down the mission in Haiti. However, this is unlikely to happen any time soon. The country is a long way from being capable of providing the primary and emergency care required for its citizens. Until such a time as the government demonstrates a stronger commitment of budget towards health care, MSF will be required to continue to operate as the finger in the dike within the system. The people are there – provided they are coordinated in the right way – but the money is not. It is important, however, that the health system in Haiti does not become permanently dependent on the presence of MSF. Oliver Schulz lays out the criteria he uses to determine when that time will come: 'When Haitians have the capacity and motivation to develop the system to meet the urgent need of the population then we will withdraw. We are working really hard to help them get there but unfortunately that point in time is still a long way down the road.'

Passion for making a difference

Throughout our time with the staff in Haiti we took the opportunity to ask them about their motivation for working with MSF. The responses were very consistent. First, they are all driven by a genuine desire to work for the good of others. They share a deep-rooted sense of purpose attached to their role. It is much more than just a job. Second, they are strongly committed to MSF. They have witnessed at first hand the many aid agencies active in the regions where they have been deployed and they say without either hesitation or arrogance that MSF is simply the best and most effective humanitarian organization in the field. The underlying values of independence, impartiality, providing medical care to where it is needed and acting as a witness on behalf of those in need create the foundation for this. The funding model further supports it. It means that things can get done. MSF is more nimble, responsive and agile. Outcomes are achieved. Those working within MSF feel as if they can change things. Decisions are not driven by donors but rather by need – and MSF is in control of these decisions. MSFers are trained to push for action and make things happen. Finally, there is a focus on ensuring quality on all levels. There is no compromise on standards, in spite of the very trying working conditions people are operating within. For example, at CRUO Massimo Ravasini tells me of how he maintains standards of care: 'We have strict medical protocols within MSF standards and we monitor these continuously. Those not conforming are warned and it is a three-strikes-and-out policy. This is supported through daily supervision and monitoring.' Across all operations in MSF, there is a shared commitment to not settling for second best. If it is not right then something is done to put it right.

Before we left Haiti we were invited to dinner with a group of the ex-pat staff. It was a rare, but enjoyable occasion and a chance for us all to unwind. Amidst the laughter and jovial atmosphere the conversation inevitably returned to some of the challenges facing the team in Haiti. The passion for making a difference never switches off.

MSF – a high-performance organization

That MSF is one of the most respected and effective non-governmental organizations in the world is indisputable. Since its foundation in 1971 it has developed an outstanding reputation for effectiveness across the globe. The organization has grown significantly and the scale of its activities is enormous. More importantly, the outcomes it delivers and the impact it has on the lives of millions of people are breathtaking. Our belief is that its organizational performance is driven by a number of factors:

- a values-centred approach;
- power of purpose;
- organizational agility driven by clarity of focus and supported by effective structures, processes and behaviours;
- commitment to high standards;
- resilience at an individual and institutional level.

Values-centred approach

The core principles of MSF were established by its founders in 1971. They were inextricably tied into its raison d'être. They are articulated in an explicit manner and are as relevant now as when they were originally developed. Everyone joining MSF is inculcated in these values from the outset. They permeate how everything is done. They are referenced with every decision that is made. Anything that is inconsistent with these values is clearly wrong and leaves a permanent mark on the DNA of the organization. Values are linked directly to the core purpose of MSF as an entity and each individual unit therein – whether at OC, country or project levels. Values are visibly linked to performance in the eyes of the organization. Every mission is judged on the extent to which in carrying out its function it has remained true to the underlying values of MSF. They permeate every aspect of the organization. They do not just influence behaviours, they are also central to the design of governance structures, the functioning of key processes – for example decision making at every level across MSF – and the nature and flow of information throughout the organization.

Power of purpose

A deep-rooted sense of purpose or meaning is a key driver of performance in teams and individuals. The motivations for working in MSF are intensely strong. Everyone who signs up does so out of a commitment to make a real difference in the lives of those who need it most. Financial rewards are not a driver – these highly qualified individuals could earn significantly more applying their expertise elsewhere. Risks are enormous. In many instances staff are literally endangering their lives. Many MSF staff have paid the ultimate price in carrying out their duties. Yet individuals still do it voluntarily. They endure great hardships on missions. They work ridiculously long hours. The reason they do so is because the power of purpose outweighs any other factor and motivates them to work well beyond the boundaries of what might otherwise be expected.

Organizational agility

Central to MSF's impact in the field are its nimbleness and agility. Time and again it has proven itself in reacting decisively to developing crises, more quickly than other actors in the environment and with greater impact. This agility is driven, in the first instance, by absolute clarity of focus. MSF exists for one purpose alone: to provide medical aid to those in crisis. The power of this sharp focus paves the way for rapid deployment. Once a need is identified the organization is empowered to mobilize. That, after all, is why it exists. This is further enhanced by its underlying structures. MSF's governance model is sufficiently decentralized at an operational level that people on the ground can act with haste. For example, how many other organizations would be able to establish a fully operational cholera treatment centre six hours after identifying the need? MSF's resource model makes it possible too. Its growth in scale has provided a financial resource base that enables quick deployment. Infrastructure supports the on-the-ground need. Finally, its independent philosophy eliminates the political considerations that often delay progress. MSF does not entangle itself in complex internal bureaucratic webs that make it difficult to move freely. Decisions are made quickly, they are enacted and there is an underlying culture of making things happen. If they don't, then people start asking why not. It provides for an empowering, highly motivating environment.

How effective would other organizations be if they were able to mirror this culture?

Commitment to high standards

Like many other high-performing organizations, MSF sweats about being the best it can be. Across all aspects of its operation it strives to achieve the highest standards. There is no compromise on quality. Enshrined in the value system is the idea of delivering the best standard of medical care possible. Underperformance is challenged. Staff, whether local or ex-pat, are expected to conform to MSF protocols. Recruitment of staff is rigorous. Not everyone is accepted. MSF is aware that if it allows the standard of intake to be relaxed, ultimately this will lead to a diminution of quality. It is not without reason that MSF is regarded as the best in its field.

Resilience

Given the circumstances within which MSF operates, it is not surprising to learn that at individual and organizational levels MSF demonstrates exceptional resilience. Resilience is often characterized as the ability to overcome difficulty, to remain tough in trying conditions or to bounce back when things do not go as planned. Resilient people do not wallow or dwell on these moments, rather they acknowledge them and quickly figure out how to move on. They do not get knocked off course when something goes against them. In fact, they become more determined to overcome the challenges and obstacles put in front of them.

Within MSF we see three areas where organizational resilience is cultivated. First, the powerful sense of purpose alluded to previously is relevant. Constantly strengthening this for everyone across the organization creates a more resilient culture.

Second, we see examples of conditioning for resilience. People are screened in advance of joining for how well they will fit within the structures of the various missions and how they will cope with the stress of operating in the field. Their emotional intelligence is just as important as their technical skills. Positive psychology plays a part too. Reinforcing a can-do attitude is central to developing resilience. The need for people to escape the intensity of the environment is also recognized. Recharge time between missions is important and not allowing people to become emotionally or physically exhausted is key to ensuring they remain effective.

Finally, we observed resilience practices in operation. Planning and preparation play major roles in anticipating issues before they arise, in managing risk and in scenario planning to prevent bad things from occurring in the first instance. The ability to think clearly under extreme pressure is increased with the clarity of focus highlighted previously. A willingness to openly question, to review what is working and not working, and discuss where learnings can be applied and effectiveness improved is ingrained in the DNA of the organization at macro and micro levels. These organizational strengths are central to making MSF what it is today.

Powerhouse Principle 2: purpose

In our discussion at the end of the last chapter, we talked about the need for ambition to capture the hearts and minds of those working within and around high-performance institutions. In our experience, and focusing in this instance on the lessons of MSF, we would argue that the means by which this is achieved is through clarity of purpose.

Clarity of purpose is important for two key reasons. First, purpose provides reasons for people to join and stay with an organization for the long term. Most people need to be convinced that what the organization wants for itself is aligned with what they want for themselves, and clarity of purpose is one key vehicle through which this is achieved. Where alignment is strong, people feel motivated and positive about being part of the journey – often becoming loyal and vocal ambassadors for the cause. By contrast, where purpose is ambiguous or weak those who have a choice tend to disengage and look for better, more aligned alternatives elsewhere.

Second, clarity of purpose is a prerequisite for those who are connected to the institution, in order to give the discretionary effort required for enduring high performance. Simply put, people give more of themselves when their efforts are connected to something that really matters to them. As a source of motivation, strong purpose always amplifies and in many instances – MSF being just one example – transcends simple financial reward. At the other extreme, our experience is that, absent of a clear purpose, people will only go so far. Our research shows that purpose comes particularly to the fore when pressure to perform intensifies – people in institutions with strong purpose respond positively, while those in institutions where purpose is weaker can flounder and tune out. When the heat comes on it becomes just a job, a means to an end, nothing more.

So how are clarity and power of purpose achieved in practice? In our view there are three key components:

- By defining it, explicitly, from the top. Leaders must always articulate the organization's raison d'être in such a way that everyone understands it. In MSF this was set from inception.

- By making it resonant and empowering for individuals. People need to see what they want for themselves in what the institution wants for itself – in effect, to imagine a win-win. In some instances the scope of the win-win needs to include a financial or economic dimension, while in others, including MSF, it is enough to align the vocational and developmental dimensions.

- By making it real and lived, and for everyone. Purpose must be real: it cannot be faked, and it must be believed and trusted. It is completely counterproductive to have something that looks good on paper but means little or nothing in reality. It must also be shared by leaders at all

▶

levels of the organization, from the top down. At MSF no one doubts for a second either the authenticity of the organization's purpose or the commitment of the leadership to it.

MSF is an organization with absolute clarity and strength of purpose – the provision of humanitarian aid to those most in need, without consideration for boundaries of geography, politics or religion. It was established by medics as an explicit reaction to the lack of effective support available to people in crisis situations, and its purpose is enshrined in its name – 'Doctors Without Borders'. Through the way the organization is resourced and operated, its purpose is also completely shared and lived every day, in the most demanding surroundings by staff at all levels of the organization, while its strength can be seen in the number of doctors who want to join and stay involved with the institution across the world.

Notes

1 http://www.doctorswithoutborders.org/about-us/faq.

2 *Wall Street Journal*, 28 November 2014, 'Ebola Crisis Stretches Doctors Without Borders' Means: Geneva-Based Organization Is Vital Resource in West Africa for Governments, NGOs', by David Gauthier Villars and Jeanne Whalen.

3 The original founders of MSF were Dr Jacques Beres, Phillippe Bernier, Raymond Borel, Dr Jean Cabrol, Dr Marcel Delcourt, Dr Xavier Emmanuelli, Dr Pascal Greletty-Bosviel, Gérard Illiouz, Dr Bernard Kouchner, Dr Gérard Pigeon, Vladan Radoman, Dr Max Recamier and Dr Jean-Michel Wild.

4 www.doctorswithoutborders.org.

5 The MSF La Mancha Agreement, Section 1.10, published 25 June 2006.

6 Disasters Emergency Committee – Haiti Earthquake Facts and Figures: www.dec.org.uk.

7 Nap Kenbe means 'staying well' in French Kreyòl.

8 Mary Mapes Dodge (1864) *Hans Brinker, or, the Silver Skates: A Story of Life in Holland*.

Southwest Airlines

04

Without a heart, it's just a machine

What makes Southwest Airlines a performance powerhouse?

Southwest Airlines can legitimately claim to be an airline that broke the mould, making air travel affordable for the mass market of US citizens and, in doing so, enabling new ways of living and working for residents and travellers in that country. It also changed the paradigm of air travel as a customer experience, bringing colour and fun to the traditionally monochrome process of travelling from A to B. Since it first took to the skies in 1971, Southwest has grown to become the largest scheduled carrier in the United States in terms of originating domestic passengers boarded, and the only airline in business today with 43 consecutive years of profitability.

In 2014 Southwest employed 46,000 people and operated a fleet of more than 650 Boeing 737 aircraft. It carried over 100 million passengers between 93 destinations across the Americas, and indeed it was the market leader in terms of passengers carried in 32 of the top-60 US metropolitan areas. In December 2014 it completed the integration of its 2011 acquisition of AirTran – rebranding and integrating its fleet and its routes into Southwest and, in doing so, giving the airline a greater geographical presence in key markets in the north-eastern United States, while for the first time bringing into its network international routes to Mexico and the Caribbean.

In an industry that is famous for its volatility and general economic underperformance, Southwest has been the consistently shining light. Despite the upheavals of the economic cycle – and even more distressing events, including the terrorist attacks of 11 September 2001 – and in complete contrast to its largest competitors, Southwest has made a profit in all but two years of its existence. Notwithstanding the volatility of the airline industry, and the capital required to build and maintain a fleet of aircraft, it

▶

Figure 4.1 Southwest Airlines Powerhouse Performance model

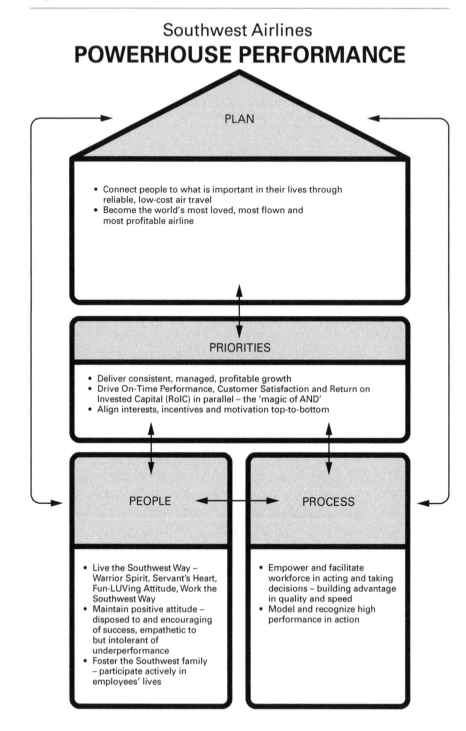

has maintained and steadily improved its industry-leading investment-grade debt rating, and from a shareholder's perspective Southwest has led the industry in delivering returns in excess of its cost of capital and in returning large fractions of the capital it has generated to shareholders.

By these standards, and many others, Southwest Airlines is truly a performance powerhouse.

The Southwest Airlines powerhouse

Flying across Texas

Texas is big and, by and large, Texas is flat. This reality is relevant in that Southwest Airlines was set up in the late 1960s to enable Texans to quickly traverse the large expanses separating the state's principal cities of Dallas, Houston and San Antonio. Air travel was highly regulated at that time, with routes and airfares across the United States tightly controlled by the Civil Aeronautics Board (CAB). Southwest's founders – Herb Kelleher and Rollin King, both of whom have achieved legendary status in the industry – determined that by flying within Texas rather than across state lines they could avoid regulation, disrupt industry operating models and offer a different service and lower fares to travellers as a result.

Southwest's initial offer, on becoming licensed to fly in 1971, was one-way travel from Dallas to Houston and Dallas to San Antonio for US$20. In addition to low fares, they offered a different experience that was more fun, as Southwest staffed their planes with attractive, extrovert, female flight attendants wearing hot pants and long boots, and offered free alcoholic drinks in-flight to their passengers. While clearly a proposition of its time, once the airline got going with regular flights between the city pairs – 6 to 12 round trips every day – its offer quickly captured the imagination of the market. Southwest grew from 108,000 passengers flown in its inaugural flying year of 1971 to 543,000 in 1973, before accelerating through the 1 million barrier in 1975, by which time it employed over 300 people and operated a fleet of four aircraft.

The origins of Southwest's high-performance model can be traced right back to these, the airline's earliest days and, as is the case with the other studies in this book, the airline's sustained advantage has arisen by design rather than by accident.

LUV is all around

All businesses – in particular all service businesses – are critically dependent on their organizations and people for their performance. However, right from the outset Southwest converted this dependence into its defining virtue. The days of provocatively dressed flight attendants pushing free cocktails on travellers are now distant memories – at one point Southwest was the largest distributor of liquor in the state of Texas! However, the idea of mobilizing a distinctive, high-quality workforce to deliver an advantaged customer proposition and experience remains live and central to the airline's success today.

For us this idea is best represented by the brightly coloured heart-shaped logo on the underside of the planes that are everywhere to be seen at Love Field – Southwest's business and spiritual home. The slogan that goes with the logo captures the sentiment at the core of Southwest's high-performance model, namely *'Without a heart, it's just a machine'*.

Figure 4.2 Southwest Airlines 'LUV' logo

SOURCE: Southwest Airlines

The notion of 'Love' (or in Southwest speak LUV) is ubiquitous at Southwest Airlines – originating from the coincidence of its primary location being at Dallas's Love Field Airport, and taking advantage of the connection between the concept of love and the airline's approach to high performance. The airline has adopted LUV for its stock market ticker symbol and, reflecting this and their focus on people, many Southwest initiatives have the language of LUV embedded in their titles.

Fixing the 'what', 'why' and – most importantly – the 'how'

Southwest is a distinctive and very particular organization – by design. Southwest set out from the start to provide a radically different, more appealing proposition to passengers – by challenging industry norms and conventions in every way possible – and to convert its proposition into a successful business venture. While the game has moved on massively – within Southwest and across the industry more broadly – from the airline's earliest days, the statements of *purpose* and *vision* in Figure 4.3 show that Southwest maintains the same absolute clarity of purpose and ambition that it had at the start.

Figure 4.3 Southwest Airlines' purpose and vision

Our Purpose

Connect people to what is important in their lives through friendly, reliable, and low-cost air travel.

Our Vision

To become the world's most loved, most flown and most profitable airline.

For us, each of Southwest's statements of purpose and vision is an exemplar of its type, and together they more than satisfy the 'acid tests' that we discussed in Chapter 2 on Grameen Bank. With regard to the statement of purpose, in addition to its basic sharpness we like its focus on the *benefit* Southwest aspires to provide to its customers and the *means* by which this benefit is delivered, which again defines a clear standard for the organization to achieve. We also like the effectiveness with which it removes any ambiguity – for all stakeholders in Southwest – as to exactly what business Southwest is in, namely the provision of air travel.

Southwest's vision statement is noteworthy for its simplicity, but even more for the attractiveness and unreasonableness of its challenge to deliver each of the three outcomes cited – most loved, most flown and most profitable – all at the same time. This was referred to on several occasions during our visit as 'the magic of AND', and it goes to the heart of Southwest's differentiation and sustained outperformance. There are inherent tensions between these three outcomes such that optimizing across them, on an ongoing basis, requires innovation driven out of real insight.

These statements respectively describe the 'why' and the 'what' of Southwest in ways that provide clarity, meaning and stretch for the organization. Southwest has gone further than this, though, and been equally clear and prescriptive about the 'how'. In this regard the airline has taken a generic desire for differentiation through people and translated it into a specific, highly accessible 'charter' that sets out the ways in which this differentiation should come through. It has then held this charter as 'law' when it comes to every aspect of the airline's organization and people models. The charter is known and documented as 'The Southwest Way', set out in Figure 4.4:

Figure 4.4 The Southwest Way

Live the Southwest Way

Warrior Spirit
- Work hard
- Desire to be the best
- Be courageous
- Display urgency
- Persevere
- Innovate

Servant's Heart
- Follow the Golden Rule
- Adhere to the principles
- Treat others with respect
- Put others first
- Be egalitarian
- Demonstrate proactive customer service
- Embrace the SWA family

Fun-LUVing Attitude
- Have FUN
- Don't take yourself too seriously
- Maintain perspective
- Celebrate successes
- Enjoy your work
- Be a passionate team player

Work the Southwest Way
- Safety and reliability
- Friendly customer service
- Low cost

As you can see, the Southwest Way is detailed and comprehensive. We see it as defining *both* sides of the essential people 'contract' at the core of the airline's high-performance model.

On one hand it sets expectations with regard to the attitudes and behaviours of each individual employee – what it means to be a member of the Southwest 'family' – and in this way it acts as the main yardstick for both recruitment and progression at the airline. On the other hand, though, it defines how the *whole* organization should work, and as such it articulates the 'north' at which the designs of Southwest's organizational and leadership approaches are pointed.

The Southwest Way reflects the values and convictions of Kelleher and King as Southwest's founders, and their insight as to how they wanted the airline to compete. It remains absolutely real today. The sensation of 'great service with a smile' was one that permeated from our flight, through our initial experience at reception to each of our discussions. We found Southwest people to be interested and interesting, and proud to the core of their association with their airline, and we left Dallas with the clear impression that the only way to survive at the airline is by becoming a fully committed member of the Southwest family.

Enabling the 'how' by finding and engaging the right people

Notwithstanding that the vast majority of Southwest's current workforce of over 50,000 is made up of permanent employees rather than contractors, it is *tough* to become a member of the Southwest family. In 2014 the airline received over 169,000 resumes to fill 4,000 jobs – a ratio of applications to hires of over 41:1 – as well as over 20,000 applications to fill 290 internship positions. The airline's workforce is highly diverse – covering a huge range of demographics and backgrounds, as well as technical, professional and other skill sets. Fit with the Southwest Way, rather than technical competence, is the main criterion used in evaluating candidates – the airline famously is said to 'hire for attitude and train for skill'.[1] Clearly the ability to pick and choose the best talent is a happy consequence of Southwest's long-standing industry leadership.

Having selected as employees those who it thinks will fit, the airline must mobilize that talent to deliver – in a manner that reflects and reinforces the Southwest Way – on a sustained basis for the business and, ultimately, its owners. This is Southwest's key, ongoing leadership challenge, and its approach forms the essence of its distinctive high-performance model.

Addressing the challenge starts right at the top of the organization. The airline's CEO is the designated employee champion and, with other senior leaders, is fully active and visible in putting the Southwest Way at the heart of the airline's advantage. This is achieved deliberately, using multiple, active, connected tools that cover both 'soft' and 'hard' – at individual, local and corporate levels.

In the first instance Southwest Airlines goes far beyond the norm in terms of *engaging* its employees – in ways that specifically reflect the Southwest Way. Engagement starts at the point of onboarding of new hires and continues for the duration of the individual's employment (and sometimes beyond). Engagement at Southwest is explicitly two-way – covering the employee's engagement with the airline and the airline's engagement with the employee. Reflecting the idea of 'Embracing the Southwest Airlines family', Karen Thrasher, of Southwest's People Department, said: 'We have a culture of knowing a lot about each other.' On one hand this helps everyone to maintain and manage work–life balance; on the other, however, it contributes to a Southwest environment that is sometimes described as intense.

Fun-LUVing attitude

Engagement happens in a variety of ways and styles, using a number of vehicles and channels, but always with a clear purpose in mind. At one end of the spectrum the airline is famous for running innovative, large-scale events that bring to life Southwest's 'Fun-LUVing Attitude'. Some events bring together groups of employees and connect them to each other and the business more broadly, while others facilitate employees in connecting with stakeholders, including passengers and communities. Examples of Southwest events include barbecues and fancy-dress parties, plane pulls and water fights, painting playgrounds and collecting debris. In 2014, 8,000 mostly Dallas-based employees attended the 'Spirit Party', held to mark the repeal of the much-maligned Wright Amendment, which up to that point had placed severe limitations on Southwest's route network to and from its home airport at Love Field.

At the other end of the spectrum comes more business- and performance-focused engagement, aimed at sharing information and involving employees (and their representatives) in the substance and development of the business. This too occurs in a multiplicity of ways, with examples including weekly broadcast briefings on performance and progress from the CEO; regular round-table discussions between groups of employees and senior leaders; quarterly briefings on Southwest performance, made to union leaders at the same time as to the financial analysts; one-to-one interactions between new employees and their mentors (or LUV guides as they are known); and formation of cross-business teams – the members of which may be asked to sign non-disclosure agreements (NDAs) – to progress specific initiatives relating to corporate, business and/or technology development.

A third type of engagement is aimed at reinforcing Southwest's egalitarian, respectful and open culture – again as prescribed in the Southwest Way. Typical here are 'blitzes' that occur periodically across the network every year. During these events, members of the leadership and culture teams turn up on location to 'share their LUV' with front-line staff, for example cooking food for maintenance crews, or meeting flight crews on arrival at the stand and inviting them to take a break while the blitz team cleans their plane.

> While engagement at Southwest overall is very carefully planned, much of it – the blitz is a good example – is presented at the point of delivery as impromptu. 'Surprise by design' is a key characteristic of engagement at the airline.

Engagement does not come cheap

Engagement is enabled by significant investment – in people, technology, and also in opportunity costs (Southwest employees and their dependants can fly for free if there are available seats on board). The level of this investment is noteworthy in an airline with Southwest's emphasis on cost minimization. Its investment includes a Culture Department – part of Southwest's broader People Department – which has a permanent staff of around 30 and further staff of approximately 120 operating on voluntary three-year assignments. As befits an organization as geographically dispersed as Southwest, the central team is further supported by over 140 local Culture Committees around the network. All of these resources have access to database technology, which allows Southwest to know and connect to its people, for example keeping track of life events and sending prompts as appropriate to ensure that milestones are marked.

The effectiveness of engagement at Southwest can be seen in the results of their 2014 employee engagement survey where, when asked how they felt about their work at Southwest, 71 per cent of respondents chose the description 'It is my calling'.

Mobilizing employees around the 'measures that matter'

Engagement on its own, however, is only a stepping stone to sustained high performance. Southwest builds on the commitment and energy that it creates by these efforts to mobilize its employees to perform at their best – by giving them absolute clarity of direction, by ensuring alignment of interest and then by empowering, equipping and expecting them to act as leaders.

As highlighted earlier, clarity of direction starts with the statements of purpose, vision and the Southwest Way. These set out the airline's ambition to win and, in a more tacit way, its strategy for winning. Southwest has operationalized these statements for its workforce by distilling from them the key performance 'measures that matter'. There are three of these, namely on-time performance, customer satisfaction (as measured by customer complaints and net promoter score) and return on invested capital.

'*The magic of AND*', as discussed earlier, is that winning means delivering on *all* of these 'measures that matter' at the same time, rather than on any at the expense of the others. Southwest employees, at all levels, understand and have ownership of these measures from the start.

Building understanding and ownership of metrics

This happens first through training. One element of the induction of all employees is training in business acumen, and part of this training covers the key performance measures highlighted above – explaining what they are and sharing how they link to the airline's vision and overall success. In addition, employees are educated about the drivers of each metric – big and small, corporate and local – and they learn specifically about how the drivers relate to their individual roles. Finally they are trained in 'the magic of AND', as outlined above, being shown how Southwest's sustainable performance advantage lies in driving all three measures in tandem. All of this sounds straightforward in theory, but in the context of a workforce as diverse and dispersed as Southwest's, the practice of getting 50,000 employees on the same page with regard to challenging operational and financial concepts – and the relationships between them – is quite complex.

Aligning employee and airline interests

Employees are also mobilized as a result of being explicitly invested – in the measures themselves and in 'the magic of AND'. They see them in their personal and team scorecards, and hitting pre-agreed targets against all three metrics together is the trigger for activating rewards and prizes through Southwest's employee recognition programmes. Southwest employees are also significant owners of the business – as of April 2016 they ranked collectively in the top-five shareholders in the business – and they share in a meaningful way in the airline's profitability. Southwest's contribution to employee profit-sharing amounted to US$228m in 2014, and US$620m in 2015 – equivalent to eight weeks' pay per head.

Act like owners

Having involved employees in the key measures that matter when it comes to creating value for its owners, and having created a clear and meaningful alignment of interest – Southwest then expects, encourages and facilitates its employees to act like owners all the time. Southwest's is an environment that fosters leadership at all levels. Clearly, in order to achieve economic success while bringing low fares to customers it has had to create a new, low-cost approach to operations and people. At the heart of this approach is a model of lean operation, which requires decision making to be devolved both safely and effectively throughout the organization.

Front-line staff, as much as senior leaders, are expected and encouraged to take decisions. On-the-ground targets are set for each of the key measures that reflect the magic of AND, *plus* the inherent tradeoffs that exist across them, and staff are expected to operate within and across these parameters day-to-day. For instance, the target for local on-time performance is set at 85 per cent – not higher – explicitly to allow a buffer for local judgement. This buffer allows, for example, flight dispatchers and gate crew, at their discretion, to hold a departure by up to 10 minutes past its scheduled time if, in doing so, they can deliver an improved customer experience – enabling, as one case in point, a large family or group to board the flight in comfort.

Information on performance against the key measures is rigorously tracked and made visible, both locally and at the level of the network as a whole, and processes exist at all levels to review and manage performance dynamically on an ongoing basis. For example, there are local team meetings at shift change to review team performance against the critical metrics and hand over any actions in train, while at the other end of the spectrum there is a daily conference call at 1 pm, attended by representatives of all stations in the network, which focuses on on-time performance and includes a review of the current and previous day's performance and trend data. As a result of this discussion, actions are identified and taken that address critical issues – to the extent possible by remediating the root causes.

Modelling and managing employee performance

Southwest mobilizes its workforce by managing – in a way that is positive and constructive but with an edge – to high standards. Key to this is how the airline *models* high performance. Modelling means capturing stories of actions carried out by employees and sharing them with broader audiences as examples of good or bad practice. Like the US Marines, New Zealand All Blacks, Mayo Clinic and most of the other examples in this book, Southwest views storytelling as an effective means for building its culture, reinforcing its standards and catalysing change. Through stories it makes the theory of the Southwest Way real and applied – and expected – of the airline's workforce.

The airline constantly collects, packages and shares stories of the Southwest Way in action. It has several sources including passengers, members of staff, and staff at partner organizations, including airports and other vendors. Stories are gathered verbally, in writing and – increasingly – through social media, and the airline packages these stories for relay to broad populations of employees. Stories are shared using a multiplicity of channels – for example through blogs, videos and news items on the airline's extensive intranet (called SWAlife), on the walls of their premises, or through the medium of the chief executive officer's (CEO's) weekly voicemail message to staff, which ends always with a 'shout out' of recognition to particular individuals and teams.

We were introduced to several stories during our visit – many of which showcased employees meeting the Southwest Way's standard of going beyond the norm in taking care of passengers. One example was that of the family of a military serviceman being invited airside to accompany their loved one for as long as possible before he departed for action, while another highlighted the effort made by a gate crew to reunite a child quickly and sensitively with a toy left behind. In addition to their resonance and value with internal audiences, some of these stories make it to the outside world and have the effect of reinforcing the ways in which the Southwest passenger experience is different. A video showing a flight attendant, Marty Cobb, 'interpreting' the safety briefing to make it funny and engaging, as well as accurate, went viral on social media and resulted in the attendant being invited to appear on the *Ellen Show* on national TV.[2]

Managing performance and making it consequential

While modelling is an important vehicle by which Southwest shares and reinforces high performance, key also is its approach to performance recognition and reward. This fits within Southwest's broader performance management model, which on the face of it is relatively mainstream, being built on annual goals and regular appraisals using a nine-box framework of performance versus potential. Performance recognition happens through a portfolio of interconnected programmes, which like other aspects of the airline's model are elegant in their clarity and simplicity. Recognition comes from multiple angles, being delivered by leaders (the previously mentioned 'shout out' that forms part of the CEO's weekly briefing is just one example of this), peers or by passengers – in particular frequent flyers. Recognition can be given on the spot, with no questions asked – for example, a 'Kick Tail'

Figure 4.5 Southwest Airlines employee recognition programmes

SOURCE: Southwest Airlines One Report, 2014

award from one employee to another in the moment to reflect a job well done – or following more considered review and evaluation, and much recognition is accompanied by rewards in the form of SWAG points (Southwest Airlines Gratitude) that can be accumulated and ultimately converted into cash or gifts.

Beyond material recognition of performance Southwest is also systematic in recognizing high performers by giving them the best access to new opportunities. The airline's performance calibration approach allows them to identify high performance and to create and manage a pool of high-potential employees systematically across their system. Unsurprisingly, given everything we have discussed so far, managing the talent pipeline is a key focus of senior management attention at Southwest.

Sharing examples of good practice in action – on a systematic and consistent basis – then recognizing, showcasing and rewarding those examples when they happen, is in our view an effective means of mobilizing high performance in large, diverse organizations. However, in order to maximize its impact, the organization's focus on the positive must be accompanied by an 'edge' of low tolerance for underperformance.

When it comes to its people, Southwest does place a relentless emphasis on the positive. However, clearly in an organization of the airline's size, its recruitment, deployment and development efforts do not always work out. In these situations, the airline defaults to another element of the Southwest Way and finds the courage to course-correct. Underperformers are addressed quickly and proactively – with a view in the first instance to understanding root causes and turning situations around, and a bias in doing this to be patient. However, in situations that ultimately prove beyond redemption, underperforming employees – in a beautiful example of Southwest language in action – are 'promoted to customers'.

Motivating innovation and rapid continuous improvement

The last area we would flag as being at the core of Southwest Airlines' high-performance model is its approach to managing and driving continuous improvement. The airline industry in the United States today is highly competitive and dynamic, such that small margins of advantage translate into big differences in performance outcomes. In that context it is one thing for Southwest to have got into the lead, but quite another to have retained this position on a consistent basis over several decades. This is particularly the case when many of the airline's biggest competitors have used bankruptcy and the Chapter 11 process to restructure their operating models and, in particular, their labour costs to the point where their wage rates, in many instances, are now lower than Southwest's. At the heart of Southwest's ability to maintain its leadership position is the airline's capacity to drive ongoing structural improvement in its capabilities, capacity and performance.

Continuous improvement at Southwest is a reflection of all the elements of its model that we have touched on through the course of this chapter – namely its culture (as defined by the Southwest Way), the behavioural norms and standards that arise from that culture, the ways in which that culture is enabled and maintained (processes, physical and information environments), the clarity of purpose/direction that exists across the airline, and the alignment of interests that has been created between what is good for the airline and good for the workforce.

Innovation in action

Examples and stories of innovation and continuous improvement are everywhere across Southwest. One transformational, but not atypical example relates to route network design and scheduling. Clearly delivering the 'magic of AND' across the measures that matter of on-time performance, customer satisfaction and return on invested capital requires competitive advantage with regard to the complex task of designing flight schedules across the airline's network. This job historically was carried out by hand; however, in the early 2000s, the airline made a breakthrough with the deployment of proprietary software known in Southwest legend as the 'Garage-O-Mizer'. Developed by one of Southwest's flight schedule planners working independently, on his own initiative and in his own time on his home PC, the platform allowed the efficiency of Southwest's schedules to be fundamentally re-engineered, unlocking the equivalent of several aircraft in additional capacity from the existing fleet. This benefit translated ultimately into hundreds of millions of dollars in extra annual revenues with low incremental costs.

Other initiatives show how continuous improvement is 'baked in' to Southwest's modus operandi. For example, office-based teams at Southwest, rather than simply hiring as their needs grow, default to thinking of new ways to do things – re-engineering and redistributing work to eliminate the need for additional personnel. Southwest staff who find themselves to be less busy will proactively 'Loan their LUV' to others who are more busy – minimizing the need for temporary or permanent recruitment.

As these examples of innovation and continuous improvement occur, they are captured, recognized and celebrated across the airline using the modelling approaches described earlier in this chapter. In this way, improvement becomes embedded as the norm and the standard for how things are done.

Driving better decisions

While the Garage-O-Mizer is a story of 'bootstrap' technology deployment giving rise to transformational performance improvement, the airline today is notable for using sophisticated technology deployment to drive performance and improvement. In essence, the airline uses technology to bring better information, faster and more consistently to the right place, where the right people, correctly empowered can act on that information to improve performance. Two live examples of this that we discussed during our visit are the Network Operations Control (NOC) and the Listening Centre, both of which are based in Dallas.

The NOC (see Figure 4.6 opposite) was opened in 2014 in a purpose-built, disaster-proof building beside Southwest's main headquarters. As the name suggests, it is a high-tech hub that is visually dominated by screens displaying the locations and status of the Southwest fleet in real time, together with every aspect of the fleet's performance. Southwest's breakthrough, in setting up the NOC, was to co-locate within it the key functions involved in managing ongoing fleet performance – namely flight operations, ground operations, maintenance operations and customer service – and to embed layouts, processes and behavioural standards that enable these groups to work effectively together all the time, taking advantage of the information at hand, to deliver 'the magic of AND'. The advent of the NOC has given rise to different decisions being taken in particular circumstances – for example with regard to the management of weather-driven cancellations of flights. Whereas, historically, rescheduling would have been carried out by the flight- and ground-operations teams, primarily with a view to minimizing operational disruption, it is now carried out by the broader group such that the passenger consequences of different alternatives are considered as well. Factoring in these new perspectives led to different decisions being taken with regard to cancellation, diversion and prioritization of flights. In addition, the presence in the room of the relevant functional resources means that any negative consequences of decisions can be communicated and managed quickly and proactively with the stakeholders concerned – whether passengers or Southwest staff.

Figure 4.6 Southwest Airlines Network Operations Centre (NOC), Dallas

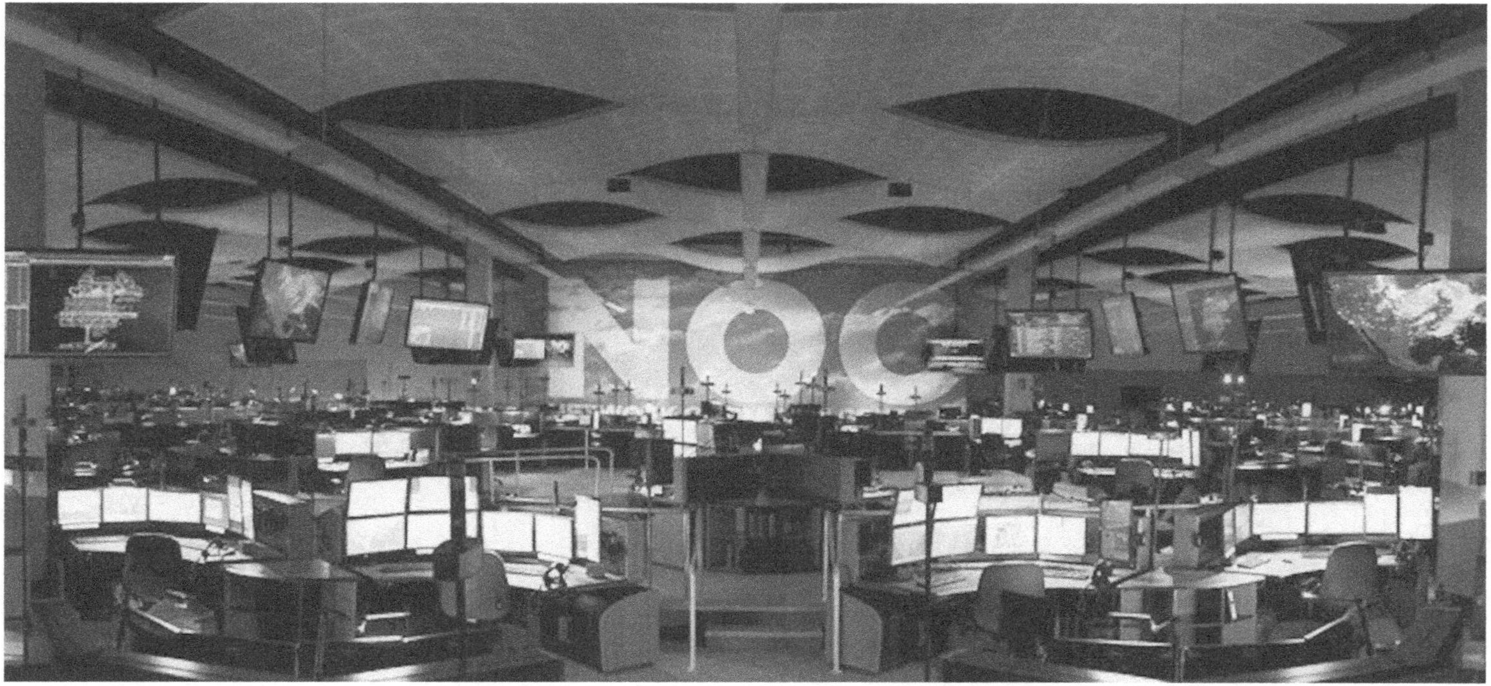

Building customer insight and intimacy

Figure 4.7 Southwest Airlines Listening Centre, Dallas

SOURCE: Southwest Airlines

Southwest's Listening Centre was also opened in 2014 and can be seen, in some respects, as the NOC's social media analogue. Smaller and physically less intimidating than the NOC, the principle is the same in that a group drawn from across several functions tracks social media traffic about and relevant to Southwest Airlines on a continuous basis on a panel of screens. The group is equipped and empowered to engage proactively as appropriate – taking advantage of positive discussions to reinforce the airline's brand and marketing messages, while intervening directly in negative discussions to address issues before they spiral out of control. In addition to its standalone role, the Listening Centre is integrated within the broader management infrastructure of the airline. In this way it acts as an effective vehicle for developing and testing new ideas, as well as for being aware and on top of relevant issues from elsewhere. For example, in November 2014 – just ahead of the Thanksgiving holiday – Southwest's competitor JetBlue announced that it would start charging customers for checked-in bags, leaving Southwest as the only major US carrier transporting checked-in bags for free. Insights gathered in the Listening Centre as to how JetBlue customers responded to the introduction of these charges played a large role in shaping the nature and timing of Southwest's product and marketing response, which was then in part reinforced through the Listening Centre's direct engagement with passengers.

Without a heart, it is just a machine

Southwest's CEO, Gary C Kelly, is on record as stating: 'Our people are our single greatest strength and most enduring long-term competitive advantage.' His statement mirrors similar statements made at one time or another by the CEOs of most of the world's leading businesses and organizations. Our sense is that Southwest is different to most organizations in the extent to which it has taken that statement to heart. It has, in effect, put its money where its mouth is and invested – because high performance, Southwest-style, is not free – to build a talented workforce, to motivate that workforce to perform at its best, to equip and facilitate them in achieving that outcome, and then to reward that outcome when it happens, before resetting its sights and pushing on again.

The idea of a business as dependent and focused on low cost as Southwest overinvesting in its people and organizational design as a path to high performance is counter-intuitive in some respects – sufficiently so to stop most of its competitors doing the same. However, the economic fruits of its investment are real and sufficient to have brought smiles to the faces of the most hardened investors.

The challenge of maintaining both the model and its success becomes ever more difficult as the competitive environment becomes more demanding and the scale, scope and complexity of Southwest's business continues to evolve – in particular with the integration of the AirTran business and its network, which for the first time includes international routes. Change fatigue – in particular with regard to front-line staff – was highlighted by Linda Rutherford, VP of Communication and Outreach, as a key risk on the horizon to be managed. However, she emphasized that Southwest's approach to managing the future reflects the successes of the past, namely:

- Set the bar high: 'We want to establish AirTran as the new standard for airline mergers.'
- Engage the workforce around the benefits the airline will provide for passengers: 'We will be heroes to Mexican travellers, bringing high service at low prices.'
- Retain Southwest's mission – the 'manic focus on bringing people along'.

Not surprising really, because 'without a heart, it's just a machine'.

Powerhouse Principle 3: measures

Effective measurement is at the heart of sustained high performance. In our view it is about two things – *selection* of metrics and *use* of those metrics to drive performance, achievement and further evolution of the organization's vision. While these elements are individually important and influential, designing each in the context of the other enables the performance measurement *system* as a whole to be greater than the sum of its parts.

Selection of metrics – landing on the 'measures that matter'

Our discussion of Southwest Airlines outlines how the airline focuses on and mobilizes all its staff around three 'measures that matter' – namely on-time performance (OTP), customer satisfaction and return on invested capital. Each of these metrics satisfies the well-known effectiveness criteria embedded in the acronym SMART (specific, measurable, achievable, relevant and time-bound), which in itself is a good thing. Much more important, however, in our view, is their alignment with the airline's statement of purpose – to 'connect people to what's important in their lives through friendly, reliable and low-cost air travel' and with its vision of becoming 'the world's most loved, most flown and most profitable airline'. By homing in on these three metrics Southwest eliminates ambiguity – for the workforce at all levels – as to what its statements of purpose and vision really *mean*, and as to what the airline is focused on in order to achieve its target outcomes.

Teams across Southwest Airlines, having absorbed these measures, home in on the key *leading* metrics that are relevant to their work and likely to give rise to winning on a sustained basis. Such leading metrics tend, in our experience, to fall into three broad categories – performance, progress and capability – and they are *situational* and *specific* to the roles of individual teams. For example, a leading indicator of on-time performance for a gate crew might be aircraft turnaround time, while for a maintenance crew it might be fulfilment of the agreed preventative maintenance schedule. For any team, the job of constructing the *right* performance scorecard – that enables a sharp focus on those measures most effective in driving its performance (in the context of the overall target outcome) – takes effort and, sometimes, creativity.

In this context, the simplicity and clarity of Southwest's approach is rare in our experience. We come across many organizations that fail to align definitions of their visions and strategies with those of their performance metrics, with the result that these are at best disconnected and at worst downright competing. In several instances – particularly in business situations – even when alignment is good, it is not understood by individuals and teams, such that they do not fundamentally 'get' how their organizations work and aim to win.

We also come across many organizations that misinterpret Kaplan and Norton's original concept of the balanced scorecard, creating extended sets of metrics that seek, in effect, to be all things to all people. A good scorecard *is* balanced, in that it goes beyond simply financial metrics to emphasize customer, operational and other drivers of financial performance. However, at the same time it maintains a *razor-sharp focus*, in that it links explicitly, unambiguously and unashamedly to the vision and strategy of the organization and the role of the team in question. It is much better, in our view, to work with a smaller portfolio of metrics and take the time, as Southwest does, to relate it to the specific activities of workers and teams than to take what is often the easier option of extending the scorecard to cater for all constituencies and circumstances.

Using measures to drive performance

In the first instance, performance metrics should be thought of and managed *as a set* – it is not about *any* of the measures, it is about *all* of them. Next, high performance in organizations is, by definition, a collective endeavour. As such, rather than assigning responsibility for individual metrics to individuals, members of leadership and other teams should *all own all of the performance* of their groups. Teams should be charged with recognizing and managing the *tradeoffs* that arise between metrics with a view to optimizing performance across the set. This is what Southwest leaders describe as 'the magic of AND', and its effect is to drive standards, team working and innovation across the organization.

Finally, for individuals and teams within an organization to own performance, they need to understand how performance is going all of the time. This requires information about performance against the scorecard metrics to be made available clearly and quickly (and reliably) for people and processes to use. The more that performance information is timely and visible, the greater the narrative and activity that exists around performance improvement. This is an area where combining the new world with the old gives rise to great solutions – using technology to facilitate rapid information gathering and processing, and using the physical environment to facilitate presentation, discussion and decision-making processes related to that information. Southwest's Network Operations Control (NOC) centre can

▶

be seen as a state-of-the-art example of just such a solution. However, we have also seen really effective lower-tech solutions using printed – or even manually completed – charts stuck to corridor and meeting-room walls.

Notes

1 Bill Taylor (2011) Hire for attitude, train for skill, *Harvard Business Review*, 1 February.

2 https://www.youtube.com/watch?v=07LFBydGjaM.

US Marine Corps

05

Semper fidelis: always faithful

What makes the US Marine Corps a performance powerhouse?

'Some people spend an entire lifetime wondering if they made a difference. Marines don't have that problem' – so said President Ronald Reagan of this unique fighting force that continues to play a key role in the evolution of the United States.[1]

Since it was born on 10 November 1775 (before the foundation of the United States) as a niche, expeditionary armed service, the United States Marine Corps has developed and consolidated its role as 'America's premier 911-rapid response force',[2] the first to fight in hostile situations, and capable of forced entry from the air, land or sea.

Marines have played significant roles in every major conflict in which the United States has been involved, with their skill and bravery in battle seen as central to securing crucial beach-heads in pursuit of US policy objectives. Examples cherished in the history of both country and Corps bridge from Fort Nassau in the Bahamas in 1776, to the Barbary Coast off North Africa in 1805, to the First World War Battle of Belleau Wood in France, and the Second World War battles of Guadalcanal, Okinawa and Iwo Jima – the last of which gave rise to the iconic, defining moment where Marines raised the US flag at the island's highest point. After the Second World War, the Corps was at the heart of the Korean War landings at Inchon, the Vietnam War Battle of Da Nang and, subsequently, Operation Urgent Fury in Grenada, Operation Desert Storm in Kuwait, and the Battle of Fallujah against the insurgency in Iraq. In 2012 they were deployed to East Africa to defeat Al-Shabaab militias linked to the terrorist force al-Qaeda, and to this day they remain on the ground supporting operations in Afghanistan and elsewhere in the Middle East.

▶

Figure 5.1 The US Marine Corps Powerhouse Performance model

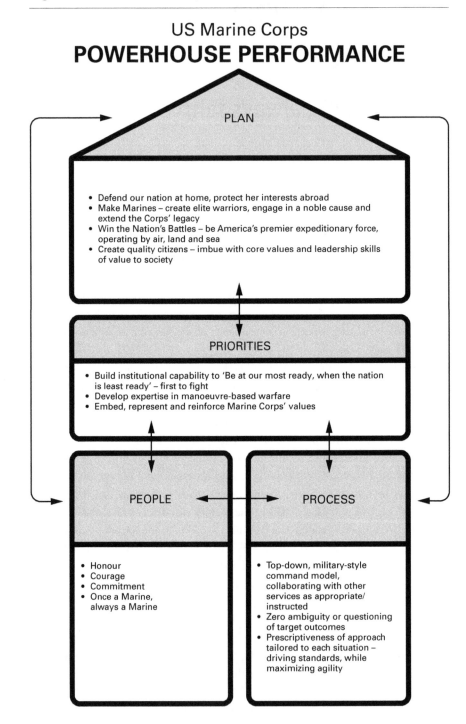

Marines have also been deployed on humanitarian missions – at home and overseas – providing support to displaced citizens in the aftermath of natural and other disasters. Notable examples of these include Operation Unified Response – a two-month deployment to support relief and recovery operations in Haiti following the earthquake there in 2010; Operation Tomodachi – supporting relief and clean-up in Japan after its earthquake in 2011; and deployment to support relief operations in New York and New Jersey after Hurricane Sandy in late 2012.

The Corps has a distinct identity within the US military services that reflects both its role and its history, and a distinct high-performance model that underpins its success. They have long been recognized by military and political leaders as one of the elite military organizations of the world. The famous US General MacArthur stated that there was 'not a finer fighting organization in the world!'[3] Even the wartime British Prime Minister Winston Churchill said: 'I am convinced that there is no smarter, handier or more adaptable body of troops in the world.'[4]

For these reasons, and many others, the United States Marine Corps is a performance powerhouse.

The US Marine Corps powerhouse

Becoming a Marine – Parris Island graduation day

It is Friday morning, 9 am on the Parade Deck at Parris Island in South Carolina, and 375 newly graduating Marines from the Recruit Training Regiment are resplendent as they march in perfect sequence at the command of their senior drill instructors (SDIs). Looking fit, energized and proud as they absorb the cheers of several thousand family members, veterans, current officers and other visitors, they are ready to move to the next stage of their training at the Marine Corps School of Infantry. If required, they could be deployed into combat within 3–4 months of this graduation day.

Their demeanour stands in sharp contrast to one week previously when they were in the middle of the famous Crucible exercise. This rite of passage for all Marine recruits involves 54 continuous hours in the field, spread over two days and three nights, during which they are given only limited quantities of food and only four hours of sleep. For the rest of the time they undertake a series of drills and exercises that bring together 12 weeks of training and test the limits of their physical, mental, moral and emotional capacity. At 7 am on Saturday morning, beside the

Figure 5.2 Marine Corps recruits during Crucible Exercise, Parris Island

SOURCE: Kotinos Partners

base's iconic Iwo Jima statue at the line marking the conclusion of the Crucible's final test – a nine-mile dawn hike – the successful recruits are presented by their DIs with the famous Eagle, Globe and Anchor emblem of the Corps, and with that they become Marines.

The role of the Marines – where they fit

The Marines have a unique role within the US military services. They are the military's expeditionary force; as such they tend to be the first ones deployed into combat situations and much of their action takes place at close quarters with the enemy. At its heart, the Corps is an infantry force – one of the Corps' defining characteristics is that 'every Marine is a rifleman'; however, it is more integrated and multidimensional than the other US armed services in that it has planes, helicopters, ships and boats – all within the Corps – that are used in combat to support Marines on the ground.

The basic unit of deployment is a Marine Air Ground Task Force (MAGTF), which includes ground- and air-combat Marines plus logistical support. MAGTFs range in scale – from the smallest, a mission-specific Special-purpose MAGTF, to a Marine Expeditionary Unit (MEU) comprising 2,200 Marines deployed amphibiously from the sea – to the biggest, a Marine Expeditionary

Force (MEF) of anything from 20,000–90,000 Marines. The MEF is the Corps' primary war-fighting force for larger operations. In general, the scale of Marine Corps deployments tend to be small relative to those of the other services, while the surroundings into which they are deployed tend to be highly ambiguous. Their combat approach, or doctrine, is based principally on warfare by manoeuvre as opposed to warfare by attrition. Success, as such, is typically a function of the adaptability, speed, ingenuity and cohesiveness of forces operating across an area and spectrum of conflict. Marines work in tandem with the US military's other services. However, the fact that they have air, sea and ground resources under their own command gives them a unique level of combat and logistical autonomy when needed.

The responsibility of the Corps, as explained by the senior officers and leaders that we met, is 'to be at its most ready when the nation is at its least ready, to provide flexible options and short response times without excessive cost, and to give options in times of crisis'.[5] Interestingly, the perspective of these leaders is that the United States does not *need* a Marine Corps, rather it *chooses* to have one, on the basis of its unique proposition and the value of that proposition to the nation. The Marine Corps operates with a level of institutional insecurity about its existence that keeps it permanently on its toes and operating at the limit of its capability.

Marine Corps recruit training, Parris Island

The Eastern Region Recruit Depot at Parris Island, South Carolina, is the bigger of two 'boot camps' (the other is in San Diego, California) where raw, civilian recruits – approximately 19,000 each year, both male and female and typically aged 17–26 – are transformed over 12 weeks into functioning, basically-trained Marines. Parris Island, in its modern incarnation, has featured in several well-known movies and songs; however, the island's notable role in US history dates back to 1521 – less than 30 years after Columbus's discovery of America – when the island and its surrounding area was claimed by seafarers in the name of the King of Spain. Over subsequent years it was the subject of battles involving Spanish and French colonial forces and Native Americans, before finally coming under British rule towards the end of the 16th century. The island gained its name from Colonel Alexander Parris, who purchased it in 1715, and from then to the time of the American Civil War its land was operated as a plantation. The island's US military history commenced in 1891, when its natural harbour became home to a US naval base. However, despite grand plans, and for political as much as practical reasons, it lost out to nearby Charleston for the construction of a new naval yard. The first Marine Corps barracks having been built in 1893, from 1909, Parris Island came under the full command of the Marines. It was initially used for officer training and, briefly, a military prison before, in October 1915, it became a permanent home for Marine Corps recruit training.

The base is big, occupying more than 8,000 acres, and unsurprisingly coastal and low-lying. In addition to its military residents, Parris Island is home to many species of plants, animals and insects – amongst which voracious sandflies are a particular occupational hazard. As we arrive at the base, we are greeted by a sign across its entrance stating starkly, 'We Make Marines', which as we will see is a core objective – not just of Parris Island but of the Corps overall. Parris Island can be said to epitomize what the US Marines are about and reflect the essence of the Corps as a high-performance institution.

There are many facets to the high-performance model of the US Marine Corps; however, through the remainder of this chapter we highlight three that, from our research and discussions, we would argue are at the heart of the Corps' effectiveness. These are:

1 clarity of direction, aligning institutional and individual aspirations;

2 relentlessly high standards – always moving up;

3 delegated, effective decision making – close to the action.

It is probably fair to say that these building blocks of the Marines' high-performance model are not unique among leading military organizations; however, the way that they come together to shape how the Corps works and performs is, we would argue, distinctive. In these, and other areas of high-performance model design, military organizations have – since the 6th century BC and the time of the Chinese philosopher Sun Tzu – driven thought leadership for institutions in other fields. Their concepts and practices – amongst them those we consider here – have been leveraged by many leading non-military institutions, including several of those showcased in this book.

Clarity of direction, aligning institutional and individual aspirations

Clarity of direction as a point of departure for institutional high performance is a recurring theme across the organizations discussed in this book. Clear, explicit articulation of what game we are in and what we aspire to achieve, with equivalent clarity of how we aim to win – that is anchored in the changing competitive and institutional context – is always a first point of mobilization of large diverse groups of people. Two recurring themes of our studies, however, are particularly evident with the Marines. The first of these is the effectiveness with which they engage around *why* – ensuring clarity and broad-based ownership of purpose. The second is the effectiveness with which the Corps aligns what the institution wants to achieve with what each individual Marine wants to achieve. In its articulation of direction, the Marine Corps explicitly targets a win-win.

At the institutional level, we discussed at the beginning of this chapter the conviction amongst US leaders that the United States has a Marine Corps because it wants, rather than needs it. At the individual level, Marine Corps recruits are enlisted on average for four years, to knowingly put their lives at risk in situations more extreme than most of the other institutions we consider. Deciding to have a Marine Corps – in the cases of the US Government and people – and/or to join the Marine Corps – in the cases of individual recruits, represent massive commitments for all involved, both within and around the Corps. Through developing and articulating a clear, holistic direction, leaders of the Corps, on one hand, create institutional space and support, while on the other they enable finding, attracting, motivating and retaining the best individual talent for whom the Corps is the right thing to do.

The Marine Corps' direction is summarized in Figure 5.3. Taken together as an example of a high-performance articulation of direction with the 'edge' required to inspire and mobilize diverse groups of people, this is both unambiguous and effective. It defines the Marines, and illustrates a standard at which leaders of non-military organizations with ambition to be the best should aim.

Figure 5.3 Marine Corps' clarity of direction

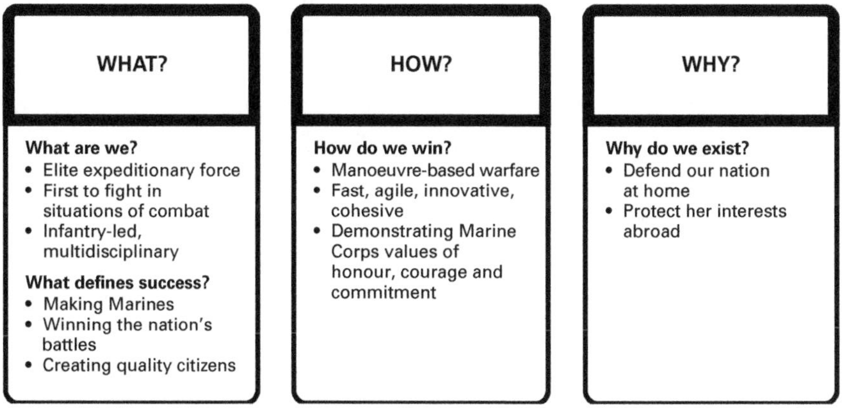

WHAT?	HOW?	WHY?
What are we? • Elite expeditionary force • First to fight in situations of combat • Infantry-led, multidisciplinary **What defines success?** • Making Marines • Winning the nation's battles • Creating quality citizens	**How do we win?** • Manoeuvre-based warfare • Fast, agile, innovative, cohesive • Demonstrating Marine Corps values of honour, courage and commitment	**Why do we exist?** • Defend our nation at home • Protect her interests abroad

The themes highlighted above of clarity of purpose and alignment of individual and shared interest can be seen in the Corps' definitions of why it exists and in its measures of success. Each of these presents the Corps – particularly when described in the context of its history and tradition – as a fundamentally patriotic cause worthy of the commitment it requires. Moreover, through its definitions of success, particularly when placed in the context of the long legacy of heroic Marines, the Corps aligns both individual and shared aspirations. As one officer put it to us during our visit, individual recruits can see what they want for themselves in what the institution is seeking to achieve overall.

> Key to mobilizing performance is getting to where people can see what they want for themselves in what the institution is seeking to achieve overall.

Notwithstanding the dramatic ways in which people and military combat have changed over the years, this direction – and the words used to describe it – has remained *constant*. This allows the Corps to leverage its history to add meaning and substance, to extend the connection to patriotism and national pride and maintain it – notwithstanding some wobbles along the way – as an innately 'noble' cause. Through it, the Corps presents itself to the world as an institution that is at the same time timeless and thoroughly contemporary.

A primary objective of boot camp, as explained during our visit, is to 'acculturate' new recruits, instructing them through practical- and classroom-based training in the history and traditions of the Corps, drilling (literally!) into them a sense of what it means to be a Marine, building commitment to owning and extending that tradition themselves, and preparing them for the next stages of their journeys. The clarity and consistency of the Corps' direction allows this three-step journey – from civilian to recruit to Marine – to be presented to recruits as a one-way trip. When we asked how the Corps, and boot camp, had evolved over the years to take account of the changing lives and experiences of teenagers and young adults, the simple response was: 'People come to join the Marines, we don't go to join them.'

This clarity of direction that exists for the Corps overall is maintained as a standard across the institution, to which leaders of other organizations should aspire. What differs, however, from one situation to another is the level of detail and specificity provided. At one end of the spectrum, direction for the senior commanding officers at Parris Island is provided through the Recruit Training Order (RTO), which documents the what, how and why of their brief in a detailed and highly prescriptive manner. Meanwhile, at the other end, similarly holistic templates exist and are used routinely (if not always with as much detail) for communicating battle orders to platoons and fire teams in combat situations. As we discuss later in this chapter, clarity of direction is a key enabler for effective, delegated high-performance decision making at all levels of the Corps.

Relentlessly high standards – embedded in the culture

The requirement for the Marine Corps to hold itself to consistently high standards follows as a necessary consequence of its role, its responsibilities and its purpose as a niche institution within the US military. The Marines must always be ready to go and, more to the point, be committed and ready to win, at short notice, in some of the world's most difficult and hostile situations.

While the necessity for high standards in this context might be obvious, two aspects of the Marines' model with regard to standards are particularly evident and interesting – how they are defined, and how they are achieved and extended over time.

Marine Corps standards – anchored in values

With regard to the first of these, Marine Corps standards are defined in terms both of effort and achievement, and linked explicitly to its values of honour, courage and commitment. This is different and, for recruits, often a stark change to their life experiences before they signed up. Simply put, living the values means maximum effort every time, and the consequences of falling short in this regard are every bit as severe as those for failing to meet the minimum levels of achievement. We observed this at first hand at Parris Island while watching a platoon of recruits, early in their training, completing a run. Some clearly strong athletes cruised through the finish at the head of the group, while others less strong finished just behind them at the point of complete exhaustion. The 'reward' from the DIs for those who finished first was, rather than praise, direct critical feedback with regard to their efforts and an order to complete a series of menial cleaning-up jobs while the rest of the group was still finishing the run. During the debrief that followed the exercise, those in the second group were held out by the DIs as exemplars – in terms both of effort and achievement – for the platoon as a whole.

> Marine Corps standards are defined in terms of both effort and achievement.

Second, Marine Corps standards deliberately emphasize collective as well as individual performance. While much of the training is about developing individual warrior skills and capacity, success in meeting these objectives is judged in the context of team performance. Indeed, contribution to team performance – practically and/or emotionally – is another key individual development criterion. Using notions like 'Once a Marine, always a Marine', 'Never Leave a Marine Behind', and even the famous Marine Corps motto of 'Semper Fidelis (Always Faithful)', the Corps goes out of its way to emphasize itself as a collective, and to reinforce its identity as a discrete, eternal brotherhood dependent on selflessness and taking care of each other.

How high standards are achieved – creating a culture

With regard to how standards are achieved and extended over time, we would highlight three aspects to this:

- equating the *idea* and language of the Marines with high standards – motivating and filtering in tandem;
- delivering rigorous, intense training – building skills and confidence at pace;
- using modelling, directly and through stories – reinforcing and raising the bar.

Building on the discussion above, the Corps is effective in making the very concept of the Marines absolutely synonymous with high standards. They are presented and recognized as two sides of the same coin and packaged like this for all the world to see. While the connection is obvious, it is reinforced in ways that add edge and meaning through the Corps' verbal and visual messaging. Recruitment advertisements use and reflect the Corps' strapline of 'The Few. The Proud', while news stories home in on images, quotes and stories of Marines living the values of honour, courage and commitment.

Figure 5.4 US Marines Corps' iconic Iwo Jima statue, Parris Island

SOURCE: Kotinos Partners

The legend over the doors – known as the 'Silver Hatches' – of the Receiving Building, which is the first point of processing newly arriving recruits, reads 'Through these portals pass prospects for America's finest fighting force' (see Figure 5.5 on page 91). Marine Corps' messaging is deliberately binary – aspirational and at the same time intimidating – to simultaneously attract, motivate, prepare and screen out amongst its audience of individuals and groups.

Next, standards are achieved through relentless, concentrated training, in a demanding environment, with particular focus on the basics and immediate, direct feedback and consequences for failure. The DIs who lead recruit training dominate the lives of their recruits over the course of their time in boot camp (and often beyond). From the moment of their arrival on base – usually in the dark of night – the standards associated with being a Marine are forcefully driven home by the DIs. Before they even get off the buses on which they arrive, new recruits are ordered to stand quickly to attention on closely grouped yellow footprints painted on the ground outside the door of the Receiving Building. They get immediate and direct 'feedback' from the DIs on the speed and intensity of their reaction to orders and on the quality of their formation before being marched inside the building. Once there they complete the enlistment process, receive their uniforms and equipment, have their hair shaved (male recruits only), make a short pre-scripted phone call to let their loved ones know they have arrived, and from there start their journey.

Recruit training is highly prescribed, and organized in three phases, with the primary focus of Phase 1 being instruction in core values, as well as basic standards and their achievement – how to stand, how to march, how to exercise, how to eat, how to dress and manage their personal hygiene, how to store their kit, how to address their superiors and peers, how to respond when being addressed, etc. In these and every other aspect of life as a Marine, the Corps maintains and enforces a standard, with the method of its enforcement in boot camp being constant, direct and intense. The intent is *transformation* (their word) to the point where the Corps' standards become the recruits' standards, and adherence to them is automatic, instinctive, consistent and demonstrated with conviction and confidence by all individuals in the group. Having institutionalized, dependably perfect basic skills that are completed automatically in practice is a real-world example of the idea of 'unconscious competence', from the field of psychology.[6] It provides confidence to the team, reduces risk of failure and frees up the minds of individuals and groups to think about more complex challenges.

The other points of focus of Phase 1 include classroom study of the theory and laws of warfare and on building basic fitness, confidence and competence in key disciplines (eg drilling, climbing, swimming, martial arts, etc) to meet the minimum requirements of the Corps. This latter objective is achieved through repeated intense training that culminates in a series of evaluations that the recruit has to pass as a condition for further progress. Despite the fact that sometimes many of these disciplines are completely new to Marine recruits, there is zero tolerance for failure to pass the tests. Indeed we listened to recruits describing at the point of tears how overcoming the fears associated with learning to swim and climbing to heights gave them their most memorable and transformational boot camp experiences.

As recruits move to Phases 2 and 3 of their training, the focus extends from basic disciplines, conditioning and capabilities to include new disciplines – in particular marksmanship. The focus also moves to the practical application of their skills and classroom learnings, in team environments, in situations that mimic combat. The style of training moderates as the programme progresses from one based on instruction to include more and more reflection and mentoring. Intensity and standards are maintained throughout, though, as is the extent of the physical and mental transformation and stretch demanded. Recruits' experience of boot camp – for the entirety of its duration – is 24/7, highly pressured and intense, with the mental challenge associated with achieving Marine Corps standards being every bit as demanding as the physical one. As we tour the base observing the activities of recruits at different stages of boot camp, two things are obvious – the degree to which recruits are being pushed to operate at their limits, and the extent of the transformation that is taking place as a result.

Finally, standards are established and reinforced by example – by having them modelled directly and indirectly all the time. As we pointed out above, part of being a Marine is living the standards, and transformation to where this is the case is the stated objective of recruit training. This reality is demonstrated explicitly by all involved in delivery and management of the programme. The standards to which DIs and officers hold themselves are higher than for recruits, by design. They are fitter, their uniforms and equipment are cleaner and better presented, they drill better, and their observance of protocols around communications are more complete and consistent. DIs are typically seasoned Marines, often with combat experience in lead roles, and they are selected for what is a three-year Special Duty Assignment based on their ability to showcase and foster really high standards with regard to how they live the Marine Corps values. If recruits want to see Marine Corps standards at first hand, all they have to do is look around.

When they do look around, however, in addition to other Marines and recruits, they will see statues, pictures, displays, flags and other icons relating to Marine Corps history. They will learn about Marine Corps history in the classroom and when they do exercises – most notably during the Crucible – they will find that the challenges to be overcome are presented with reference to actual combat situations, with formal and informal citations accompanying exercise briefings and debriefings. All through their time in boot camp, and to a degree greater than the other services, recruits are immersed in the history of the Corps. They learn in detail about where and how Marines have been deployed over time – the situations they encountered, the actions they took, and the consequences (positive and negative) that arose. On one hand this results in them becoming engaged in the traditions of the Corps, building connection, meaning and commitment to extending the legacy. On the other hand, the effect of using historical stories (or at least the positive ones) in this way is to reinforce – and subtly raise – performance standards over time. This is because the way in which much history is presented to recruits is with explicit reference to those standards – in particular to the values of honour, courage and commitment. The stories told illustrate again and again what it means to be a Marine, and to live (or not live) each of these values in different difficult situations. While the obvious effect is to underpin the performance expectations that exist, the practical effect is to incrementally raise the bar, as yesterday's heroism evolves to become tomorrow's norm.

Delegated, effective decision making – close to the action

Military conflict, in particular the types of conflict in which US Marines are engaged, is a human endeavour. It does not use long-range missiles, high-altitude aircraft or remotely controlled drones. Rather it involves Marines being inserted into the field to face enemy forces at close quarters. As we have discussed, being first to fight means being deployed into ambiguous situations where the lie of the land – either physically or from the perspective of the strength and hostility of enemy forces – is not clear, and having to work quickly and effectively to achieve an objective. It goes without saying, in this context, that effective decision making is key to success. At the heart of this capability in the Marine Corps is a concept known as *Commander's Intent*.

> Telling historical stories results in standards being subtly raised, as today's heroism translates to become tomorrow's expectation.

Commander's intent

For any given mission, the commander's intent describes the desired end state at the mission's conclusion. Reflecting the theme of clarity of direction, discussed earlier, it is a concise expression of the mission's purpose and target outcome that is explicitly communicated to the Marines at its outset as part of the briefing process. Once understood, Marines operating in the field are empowered – and expected – to adapt their pre-developed plans in real time to achieve the commander's intent while taking account of their specific, evolving circumstances. As such, commander's intent enables a rapid, delegated and contextualized process of planning and decision making by forces operating at significant organizational (and often geographical) remove from their leaders.

Commander's intent is practised across the US military; however, it is particularly relevant for the Marine Corps given its unique expeditionary role. Part of the appeal of commander's intent is its apparent simplicity. In practice, however, establishing fast, delegated planning and decision making as an organizational capability is anything but simple. We observed four key enablers of commander's intent as a source of Marine Corps advantage:

- stating the commander's intent using the principle of less (and clearer) is more;
- ensuring Marine Corps' values and norms are embedded;
- focusing constantly on communications;
- planning and practising alternative scenarios.

Articulating and communicating commander's intent is hard. Its statement needs to strike a balance between being comprehensive and, at the same time, absolutely clear and unambiguous. It needs to capture and prioritize complementary objectives while absolutely avoiding competing ones. Its job is to signpost the target outcome in a way that is constant and consistent, and as such to provide a clear reference point for in-the-field decisions. To that end, as we discussed earlier and observed in practice during the Crucible exercises, the Corps has standards and templates that it uses to write down and brief on the commander's intent.

Second, to the extent that the commander's intent specifies the 'what' and 'why' of a particular mission, the Marines' values represent an ultimate expression of the 'how'. As such, these must act both as motivators and constraints to action. The Marine Corps values of honour, courage and commitment effectively fulfil these briefs – in particular in the way that they are drilled and modelled into new recruits through the course of their training. Having diverse groups of Marines operating under acute pressure with poorly defined or ingrained codes of values would dilute the power of the collective and be counter-productive to the commander's intent being achieved.

Third, Marine Corps deployments are collective affairs where success depends on the choreography and coordination of actions across multiple individuals and groups. With this in mind, Marines are trained to bias towards overcommunicating and to ensure, when they take initiative to deviate from the pre-developed plan, that those around them are aware of what they are doing and why. This is both a behavioural and a process point that allows colleagues to adapt their actions to keep those of the whole group aligned. It is enabled in the field by their being equipped with multiple means of communication – ranging from sophisticated radios, cameras and GPS trackers, to simpler hand-signal codes. In debriefing with teams of recruits in the aftermath of Crucible exercises, we observed DIs focusing particularly on the level and quality of communication that was going on.

Finally, while they go into every mission with an agreed, preferred plan, Marines will also, as part of their preparation, have considered and – time and resources permitting – practised alternative approaches to achieving the commander's intent that allow for situations unfolding in different ways. This is an example of the idea of 'being strategic', discussed elsewhere in this book, and is a key high-performance concept for leaders of organizations of all types. Being strategic in the Marine Corps means managing the 'spectrum of improvisation', which means limiting plan changes solely to those elements that require adjustment – or, put another way, retaining the integrity of the plan at all times to the extent possible. However, within that context, they have a series of 'plays' that they have thought through that capture the actions of not only individual fire teams but the coordinated actions of the group as a whole in different circumstances.

You don't join the Marines, you become one

Another favourite Marine Corps saying is that 'you don't join the Marines, you become one'. Of all the institutions we study in this book, the Marine Corps is the one where sustained, institutional high performance is most dependent on the creation of shared vocation and personal commitment. Given that the Marine Corps' 'stage' is war which, as the famous Marine Corps General Krulak described, is 'among the greatest horrors known to humanity',[7] and that performance on that stage is literally a matter of life and death, the level of vocation required to pursue it seems obvious. However, it is striking that in marching through the silver hatches of the Receiving Building on that first evening at Parris Island, new recruits make an overt, explicit, one-way commitment to that vocation, to meeting and living the highest standards of effort, to pushing the limits of themselves, and to joining the brotherhood of the Corps in the name of defending and advancing the interests of the United States. The conditioning required for 'normal' young people to live this vocation is physical, mental and moral, and the recruit training programme at Parris Island is designed, and refined over many iterations, to meet these challenges. In this context, what we observe in train at boot camp is genuinely an *acculturation* process.

Figure 5.5 Committing to the Marines – Receiving Building entrance, Parris Island

THROUGH THESE PORTALS PASS PROSPECTS
FOR AMERICA'S FINEST FIGHTING FORCE
UNITED STATES MARINES

SOURCE: Kotinos Partners

The strength of the Marine Corps' high-performance model is its clarity, its alignment, its nobility to those involved, and the extent to which it really, obviously has been lived and discussed – in every corner of the organization, for a long time. When it comes to high performance, rather than being a case of 'The Marine Corps *does*...', we would suggest that it is a case of 'The Marine Corps *is*...', and boot camp is the first occasion where this reality is made tangible for new entrants. For all that most of its detail is public and available to be viewed on the web, the hands-on power of the model and the training is shocking to recruits in ways that are plainly visible to even the most disconnected outside observer.

For all its strength, however, the Marine Corps' model is also fragile, in that chinks in its alignment – in effect episodes where the model is not lived – risk undermining it and damaging the institution. Reflecting its role, and also its position in the hierarchy of the US military services, the Corps has always functioned at the limits of its physical and organizational capacity, being accustomed in particular to operating in difficult environments with constrained resources and information. Most of the time, the combination of difficult circumstances plus absolute commitment acts as a catalyst for innovation; however, there have been occasions where such circumstances have resulted in individuals and groups pushing too hard – compromising the values of honour, courage and commitment with devastating, and even fatal, consequences for Marines and recruits.

The Corps' leadership understands the model and the risks to which it is exposed and, as we have discussed, looks to hold itself to the same standards of honour, courage and commitment – doing the right thing, in the right way, for the right reasons – with regard to how it addresses its weaknesses. Having had difficulty recognizing and dealing with such incidences, evidence suggests that the Corps is now improving in this regard, in particular when it comes to taking steps to reinforce its standards and protect its people. For example, selection processes for DIs have been tightened over time as has DI training and the protocols that govern how they do their work. Resources – confidential and otherwise – have been established, with visible senior leadership support, to improve reporting, investigation and handling of issues, and the consequences of breaching the Corps' defined standards, regardless of the circumstances, are faster and more severe.

As high-performance institutions go, the US Marine Corps is an extreme case study. The definition of its high-performance model, and the vigour with which it is implemented and maintained, reflect to a certain extent the nature of war and the huge consequences of both winning and losing. That said, the people- and organization-centricity of the Corps' approach to high performance, together with the sustained outperformance its approach has delivered over a period of more than 240 years, means that it is also a rich case study, filled with learnings for other, civilian institutions with ambitions to hit the top of their game. *Semper fidelis!*

Powerhouse Principle 4: standards

Our discussion above highlighted a relentless focus on standards as being a core component of the Marine Corps' high-performance model. This focus is common to the other studies in this book and, we believe, has broader application in organizations with ambition to be the best.

The way in which high-performance organizations achieve sustained high standards is by having it ingrained in their DNA. High standards is not what they *do*, rather it is what they *are*, and as such it is intrinsically *cultural*. Maintaining this level of cultural association in institutions that, in some instances, are made up of thousands of diverse, dispersed people is both a huge challenge and a huge source of competitive advantage. The means by which it is achieved is complex, and as much intangible as tangible. However, drawing from our experience of the Marine Corps, we can identify some key elements of the 'formula' for success:

- *Establish high standards as an organizational value*
  Values reflect an organization's sense of right and wrong or what 'ought' to be. By embedding high standards – explicitly or implicitly – in an organization's values, we create a platform for it to pervade across every aspect of the institution – from recruitment to definition of structures and roles, to design and execution of processes and information flows, to behavioural expectations for people at all levels, and so on. High standards are absolutely implicit in the Marine Corps' values of honour, courage and commitment, the relevance and impact of which covers the totality of the institution. This facilitates the creation of a standards and performance *edge* that is both constant and enduring.

- *Message them – communicate the commitment*
  High standards is not something for which organizations aspiring to be the best should apologize or feel shy about. Rather they should make their commitment visible and transparent – to internal and external audiences. In this way they attract and set expectations for those who share the standards and the ambition, and screen out those for whom these institutions might not be the right choice. The Marine Corps uses messaging like 'The Few. The Proud' and 'America's elite', supported by visual imagery of Marines in action at the tops of their games, in order to emphasize its commitment and its culture.

- *Really live them – at all levels, all the time*
  In order to be convincing and sustainable, high standards must be the only standard – for everyone, all the time. Leaders must 'walk the talk' with, if anything, the standards 'bar' getting higher as they progress to more senior levels within their organizations. The Marine Corps uses modelling as a key vehicle for demonstrating standards to boot camp recruits and for reinforcing their central importance in what it means to be a Marine.

- *Identify and manage failure fast – in doing so reinforcing the standards*
  High standards as a source of institutional advantage is game-changingly powerful but at the same time fragile. Unaddressed failures in standards risk undermining the reputation and the confidence of the organization, with potentially catastrophic consequences for performance in both the short and long term. Leaders in high-standards organizations should embrace trust, while avoiding complacency, and establish processes that

▶

allow identification and addressing of failures quickly and effectively – in a manner that itself reflects high standards – when they occur. This is possibly the hardest element of the formula to implement and is an area where the Marines have been significantly challenged over time. In this chapter we discussed several initiatives currently in train that improve both identification and response to failures in meeting the Corps' people and operating standards.

High-performance organizations that have cultures of high standards are demanding by definition. They set themselves up to attract skilled individuals and challenge themselves to maximize the potential at their disposal in order to achieve an institutional ambition. Doing this consistently over time means, however, being all about people. As such, even institutions operating in circumstances as extreme as those in which the Marine Corps finds itself need to think and take steps to meet individual objectives as well as institutional ones, and to foster a consistent environment of respect, empathy and mutual support.

- *Culture is strategy*

Finally, for all that the Marine Corps' culture of high standards has been 240 years in the making, each newly arriving company of recruits absorbs this culture from scratch over a period of just 12 weeks. This, for us, is a great example of culture as an *outcome* of the processes, systems, values and behaviours that are deployed by the people within the Corps rather than, as it is sometimes considered, an amorphous 'thing' that is inherited, mysterious and inflexible.

We often hear business leaders describing culture in these terms and attributing performance credit or blame to it after the fact, in the process throwing out the old saw that 'culture eats strategy for breakfast'.

For us, in a high-performance world, culture is dynamic, transparent and flexible, and something to be designed and managed *proactively* to enable the performance outcomes that we want. Rather than being *eaten* by strategy, culture *is* strategy; rather than being *born*, in a high-performance world culture is *made*.

Notes

1   United States President Ronald Reagan, 1985 [Online] www.marines.com.
2   Colonel Daniel Haas, Commanding Officer, Marine Corps Eastern Recruit Depot, Parris Island.

3 General Douglas MacArthur, US Army, outskirts of Seoul, Korea, 21 September 1950.

4 Winston Churchill, 1917 [Online] www.marines.com/history-heritage.

5 Colonel Daniel Haas, Commanding Officer, Marine Corps Eastern Recruit Depot, Parris Island.

6 Learning Stages Model, Gordon Training International.

7 General C C Krulak, Commandant of the Marine Corps, 'Warfighting' – US Marine Corps MCDP 1, 1997.

Curtis Institute of Music   06

What makes the Curtis Institute of Music a performance powerhouse?

The Curtis Institute of Music is widely regarded as one of the best music conservatories in the world. The list of 4,000 alumni includes renowned composers, conductors, musicians and vocalists such as Leonard Bernstein, Gian Carlo Menotti, Jaime Laredo, Samuel Barber, Alan Gilbert, Lang Lang, Gary Graffman, Alan Morrison and Juan Diego Flórez.

Curtis musicians occupy principal chairs in every major US symphony orchestra. Alumni have received coveted awards including Pulitzer Prizes and Guggenheim Fellowships. The major opera houses of the world in New York, London and Milan regularly feature Curtis alumni as lead vocalists.

The rigorous music education received by its students ensures that Curtis graduates go on to highly successful musical careers. More importantly they are recognized as leaders in change, bringing their art form to new levels and making a profound impact through their art. It is one of the most difficult colleges to get into in the United States, with lower acceptance rates than the Ivy League colleges such as Harvard and Yale.[1]

In the world of music and the arts, the Curtis Institute is unquestionably a performance powerhouse.

The Curtis Institute powerhouse

An inspirational setting

On the corner of a Philadelphia street on any given day, the hustle and bustle of modern life may be interrupted by the melodious strains of great music. The sounds of pianists, violists, cellists, trombonists and opera singers

Figure 6.1 The Curtis Institute Powerhouse Performance model

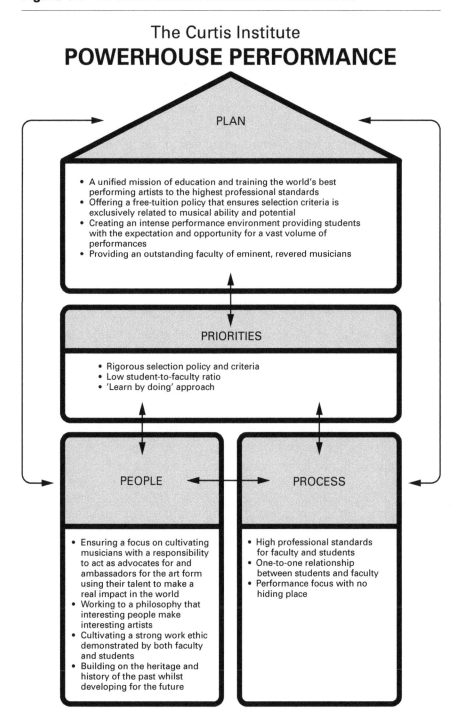

The Curtis Institute
POWERHOUSE PERFORMANCE

PLAN

- A unified mission of education and training the world's best performing artists to the highest professional standards
- Offering a free-tuition policy that ensures selection criteria is exclusively related to musical ability and potential
- Creating an intense performance environment providing students with the expectation and opportunity for a vast volume of performances
- Providing an outstanding faculty of eminent, revered musicians

PRIORITIES

- Rigorous selection policy and criteria
- Low student-to-faculty ratio
- 'Learn by doing' approach

PEOPLE

- Ensuring a focus on cultivating musicians with a responsibility to act as advocates for and ambassadors for the art form using their talent to make a real impact in the world
- Working to a philosophy that interesting people make interesting artists
- Cultivating a strong work ethic demonstrated by both faculty and students
- Building on the heritage and history of the past whilst developing for the future

PROCESS

- High professional standards for faculty and students
- One-to-one relationship between students and faculty
- Performance focus with no hiding place

float through the air from a cluster of period buildings in the heart of the city. There are no ostentatious signs heralding what is within their walls. On the contrary, their understated facades belie the wonderment within. As you enter you realize immediately that this is a very special place.

A case in the foyer displays memorabilia from the past, including a letter from Curtis founder Mary Louise Curtis Bok. The letter outlines her vision for a music conservatory with rigorous standards of teaching and performance that will train the next generation of musical artists. The vision that she set out has, 90 years later, delivered generations of the world's most gifted performers – and the traditions, philosophy and impeccable standards of the school are stronger than ever before.

We are greeted by the school's President, Roberto Díaz. With a warm smile and gentle handshake he welcomes us to Curtis. As we stroll towards his office on the ground floor he notices we are still absorbing our surroundings. With a nod he remarks, 'It is an inspirational place, isn't it?' It certainly is.

The birth of a great institution

The Curtis Institute of Music was the brainchild of Mary Louise Curtis Bok, the only child of wealthy publishers Louisa Knapp and Cyrus Curtis, whose Curtis Publishing Company produced popular American magazines such as *Ladies Home Journal* and *The Saturday Evening Post*. Inspired by her work at the Settlement Music School in South Philadelphia, where she worked with culturally and financially deprived children, many of whom were talented enough for professional careers, Mrs Bok decided to establish a music conservatory with rigorous standards of teaching and performance to train the next generation of musical artists. She and her husband Edward purchased three buildings on Rittenhouse Square at Locust Street: the Romanesque home of the Drexel family, the adjoining Sibley House and the Beaux Arts-style Cramp mansion. The Commonwealth of Pennsylvania chartered the Curtis Institute of Music in April 1924 'to train exceptionally gifted musicians for careers as performing artists on the highest professional level'. With the artistic guidance of conductor Leopold Stokowski and renowned pianist Josef Hofmann, Mrs Bok put together a faculty and developed a philosophy that would attract, inspire, develop and train the most promising students, preparing them for stellar musical careers. Leopold Stokowski predicted that Curtis 'will become the most important musical institution of our country, perhaps the world'. On 13 October 1924 the Curtis Institute of Music opened its doors for the first time.

In its 90-year history, Curtis has remained true to the vision of its founder. The philosophy set out by Mary Louise Curtis Bok – enshrining rigorous standards, personalized attention from a celebrated faculty and a distinctive 'Learn by Doing' approach – is at the heart of the success of this famous institute. However, it was a decision taken four years into its existence that was to have the most profound impact on creating the performance culture that underpins Curtis's reputation. In 1928, at the urging of Josef Hofmann, the school's then Director, Mrs Bok agreed to establish a merit-based full tuition scholarship for all students. To facilitate this, she added a staggering US$12 million to the existing US$500,000 endowment fund. The consequences of this decision still impact today. The establishment of this unique free-tuition policy meant that, from that moment onwards, the Curtis Institute of Music was able to base all admission decisions on one simple criterion – artistic promise. No other factor comes into the equation.

Free-tuition policy

Roberto Díaz explains that this decision was so profound for the school because it allowed all admission decisions to be entirely merit-based. The ability of students to pay tuition fees is never considered – if it was, it might compromise the exacting standards required of their student intake. Instead, the process is exclusively centred on the artistic talent and potential of the student.

Elizabeth Warshawer is the Executive Vice President, Chief Operating Officer and Chief Financial Officer of Curtis.[2] She is certain that the free-tuition policy is at the heart of the success of the institute: 'The full free merit-based scholarship scheme fuels everything that happens here from a high-performance perspective. We accept students purely on artistic merit – you can't buy your way into Curtis – and we are uncompromising on this policy and principle.' She describes the decision taken in 1928 to implement this policy as 'monumental' and wonders to what extent Mary Louise Curtis Bok realized just what it would lead to 90 years later. Mrs Bok undoubtedly would be very pleased to observe the ongoing impact made by her decision. The free-tuition policy is another example of how clarity of focus helps drive performance. It is central to the Curtis strategy.

Time and again, we have seen how the performance powerhouses such as Southwest Airlines, Toyota, Grameen Bank and Tata establish this razor-like sharp focus strategically to set them up for success.

Petri dish of talent

The free-tuition policy ensures that admission is exclusively based on artistic promise. However, getting into the Curtis Institute of Music is no easy achievement. Curtis is consistently ranked one of the most selective institutions of higher education in the United States, with an annual acceptance rate between 3 and 5 per cent.[3] In light of the fact that the baseline criteria for application are rigorous in the first instance, this statistic is even more impressive. On the assumption that only very talented musicians apply to the Curtis, its acceptance rate ensures that only the *crème de la crème* of musical potential enters the doors each year. Other world-famous academic institutions such as the Ivy League colleges, the US Naval Academy, and Massachusetts Institute of Technology (MIT) are easier, statistically, to get into.

As a result, Curtis becomes a melting pot of talent where there is a baseline of excellence from the outset, and where it is virtually impossible not to improve dramatically and quickly – even accounting for the exceptionally high standard of intake. No matter how good you are when you arrive, by being surrounded on a daily basis with the outstanding talent at Curtis it is inevitable that you will leave a far better, more accomplished performer. As Elizabeth Warshawer phrased it, 'Put all this talent in a petri dish and organically amazing stuff happens.'

High entry standards

The admission process ensures that the *performance gap*, or 'distance' between the highest- and lowest-performing students in the class, is narrow. The process is, as we might expect, rigorous and testing. Curtis posts audition requirements for all instruments, and auditions are usually scheduled for February or March in Philadelphia. Prospective students play for up to 30 minutes to the entire faculty for their chosen instrument. For example, about 100 violinists were heard at audition by the violin faculty in 2013. Based on this audition a shortlist of applicants will be invited to play a second, longer audition. Faculty rank the musicians in order and, depending on the number of places available for that instrument, will offer places to candidates. If there are five places available for violinists, for example, they will offer the top five auditionees a place at Curtis. However, if in the view of the faculty the standard of candidate is not high enough to fill the available places, only those meeting the required standard will be offered a place, even if this means places go unfilled.

Roberto Díaz describes how Curtis maintains its high standards by not inviting any applicant to attend who does not meet those standards. He cites a recent example of a year where there was one place available for a tuba player. Having gone through the auditions, faculty members were undecided about whether anyone had met the standard. Some felt one candidate had, but others were unsure. The decision they took was to leave the place unfilled. Instead, they invited a tuba alumnus to join the Curtis Symphony Orchestra for a year, who used the opportunity to improve further and gain valuable experience. The following year a different applicant met the standard and was admitted as a student of the school.

A narrow *performance gap* is a key element of an effective high-performance model. The same principle is evident in virtually all of the examples we studied. It is explored in more depth as a Powerhouse Principle at the end of this chapter.

Uniquely low student–faculty ratio

The student to faculty ratio is incredibly low. The 174 students are supported by an outstandingly qualified faculty of 113 top-tier musical artists and highly credentialled classroom teachers in musical studies, liberal arts and career studies. That is a student to faculty ratio of less than 1.55 to 1 – a ratio virtually unheard of in any other educational institution. A high proportion of the faculty at Curtis are eminent performing musicians and there are no teaching assistants employed within the school. In addition, Curtis frequently hosts world-renowned visiting artists to work with its students in masterclasses, chamber music coachings and residencies. When applicants are successful in the audition process and are offered a place to study at Curtis, they are given a list of faculty members for their instruments. Typically, they will have a choice of several. Students select the faculty members that they want to work with on a one-to-one basis.

The uniquely low student to faculty ratio provides an opportunity for intense, personalized attention and the already highly talented musicians thrive under this close mentorship. Is it any wonder that the output from Curtis – in terms of musical influence and impact – is so great?

Figure 6.2 Ren Martin-Doike in a lesson with Joseph de Pasquale

SOURCE: Pete Checchia

Advocates for the art form

Curtis mission is to 'educate and train exceptionally gifted young musicians to engage a local and global community through the highest level of artistry'. Previously, the mission statement mentioned only the word 'train' but that has since been replaced with the phrase 'educate and train'. This is a critical distinction. The essence of Curtis is to develop students with exceptional musical talent and help them to use that talent to make an impact in the world. As Roberto Díaz puts it: 'Part of the responsibility of a successful artist is to be an advocate for the art form. Ultimately that is at the heart of what we are doing here.' That means that the school consciously works on opening the minds of the students, developing the curiosity element of the artist and helping them to utilize their musical talent to explore and create new developments.

By setting out to do more than just train musicians, the Curtis ensures that its '*ambition*' is linked to its mission of ensuring its students make a lasting difference to the art form. As we explained in Chapter 2 (Powerhouse Principle – ambition) this is a key feature of how ambition is used to drive performance.

Interesting people make interesting artists

One area that Curtis concentrates on heavily with its students is developing intellectual curiosity. In most cases, students have been playing their respective instruments from an early age. This can lead to a one-dimensional world view. The senior administrative leadership sees a key part of its role as opening their students' minds and broadening their scopes of interest in order to be more aware of connecting their musical talent to the outside world. Díaz observes: 'Interesting people make interesting artists.' One mechanism for achieving this is the 'all-school project' introduced in recent years. The school selects a topic for the students to explore; for example, in 2013 it was 'Russia: A land and its influence'. Students are encouraged to explore this topic in detail, and in so doing become better-educated artists while fostering their curiosity. These projects are taken very seriously. Díaz points out that with more open minds these gifted musicians will make a greater impact on the world. The more successful they are at achieving this, the more the students will be capable of translating the skills and talent they possess into meaningful impact beyond their time at Curtis.

It means, too, that the school itself prides itself on its ability to evolve, adapt and remain relevant, without losing its focus on its primary mission. This is something that the leadership group at Curtis is constantly evaluating. It demands a delicate balancing act of maintaining the rich heritage and history of the organization while reacting to the ever-changing environment in which it operates. Students with ambition to use their talent to serve, influence, make the most of their ability and develop to the fullest will thrive at Curtis. They are encouraged to take risks, experiment and develop broad perspectives on how they achieve their goals. 'Ultimately we want our students to make a difference in the world of music', Díaz says.

Learn by doing

A critical philosophy within Curtis is 'Learn by Doing'. Everyone we talk to cites this as one of the factors that sets Curtis apart. All students are encouraged to perform frequently and the typical student will perform countless times per year. For example, it is common for students in their first week at Curtis to be cast in an opera, and be expected to perform publicly less than six weeks later. In total, the Curtis Institute of Music students present in excess of 200 public performances each year. The reason for this is simple, according to Díaz: 'Our job is to make some of the world's greatest performers, and artist citizens. As performers, how people behave on stage is the ultimate measure – there is no substitute.' He reflects on his own experiences. He spent two years studying at Curtis as a violist and throughout that period he performed constantly. All told, he believes he performed close to 100 times while at Curtis. At the school he attended before Curtis, his only solo performance in a four-year period was his senior recital, and he remembers this as one of the most daunting experiences of his life. 'You could be the best soccer player in the world', he explains, 'but if you can't handle the pressure of a big game then you will not perform at your best. We help our students learn to cope with performance pressure by ensuring that they are constantly performing.'

Figure 6.3 Student recital series

SOURCE: Pete Checchia

No hiding place

Dr David Ludwig is part of the Curtis family. He is a descendant of several generations of eminent musicians, including the pianist Rudolf Serkin (his grandfather and also a former Curtis Director). He is currently on the composition faculty at Curtis and serves as the Dean of Artistic Programmes and Gie and Lisa Liem Artistic Chair of the Department of Performance Studies. Ludwig is a perfect example of the calibre of faculty at Curtis. He is an esteemed composer, regularly producing critically acclaimed works, and is prolific in his musical output while maintaining his role among Curtis staff. He is a graduate of Curtis himself, and also attended three of the other top conservatories in the United States. He is well placed to offer perspectives on what makes Curtis unique from other schools with excellent reputations. In his view the biggest difference is the philosophy of 'Learn by Doing'.

At Curtis, for student composers, there is an expectation that they compose copiously and have their compositions performed. For example, he expects his students to deliver one full orchestra piece, a chamber piece (lasting approximately 15 minutes) and many other pieces over the course of a single year. It means his students compose music all year round. He demands that the quality of these works is 'Curtis standard'. He contrasts this with his experience as a student elsewhere: 'At one of the schools I attended, you could get away with doing a little composing and there was little or no expectation of your material being performed.' Likewise, his experience at another school contrasts with that of Curtis. He observed: 'It is easier to be anonymous at a bigger school; it is possible to hide a little there if you really want to.' That is impossible at Curtis.

Performance focus

Ludwig also does several residencies at other schools around the world. A notable difference he sees between Curtis students and students elsewhere is how they prepare for performances: 'A Curtis student will not go on stage unless they are 100 per cent prepared and they are constantly challenging themselves to play at the top of their abilities. This comes from the focus of our "Learn by Doing" philosophy. We have a very focused and intense performance programme and it needs to be if we are to remain as good as we can be.' When one considers this ethos combined with the sheer number of performances presented by a Curtis student in any given year, it becomes clear as to why graduates from this school reach world-class standards.

To illustrate commitment to the philosophy, Dr Ludwig cites the example of a student who won a very prestigious prize while studying at Curtis. As a consequence of winning the prize, the student had the opportunity to perform in over 100 concerts at various international venues. Under normal circumstances, the student would have been faced with a very difficult dilemma: complete his studies at Curtis and forgo the opportunity to perform with the associated exposure that came with the prize, or take the performance opportunities provided and drop out of the Curtis programme. However, with the encouragement and support of the faculty, the student was facilitated to do both and a schedule of continued study was built around the performance and touring demands that came with the prize. While the logistics of this solution were challenging for the school, it made perfect sense because it was fully aligned with the 'Learn by Doing' philosophy. The student benefited enormously from the challenge of performing so frequently while maintaining his ongoing musical education with the support of his tutors at Curtis. Other schools are more rigid with their attendance requirements. Without the flexible approach adopted at Curtis that creates room to expose students to intense performance pressure on a very frequent basis, the 'Learn by Doing' philosophy simply would not be possible.

The constant drive to perfect performance is similar to what we found elsewhere, for example at Toyota, the Mayo Clinic, Tata and the New Zealand All Blacks. At Curtis this is delivered through the 'Learn by Doing' philosophy. The pressure to always improve is a feature of performance powerhouses.

'Curtis on Tour'

A recent development that reinforces the 'Learn by Doing' philosophy is the introduction of the 'Curtis on Tour' initiative. This programme provides students with a host of performance opportunities in professional settings to both national and international audiences. The existing students are joined by celebrated Curtis alumni and faculty on tour. It is a wonderful development opportunity for the students and it reinforces the underlying performance philosophy that is so central to the ethos of the school. Since Curtis on Tour was launched in 2008, ensembles have travelled to 50 destinations worldwide, including countries in Europe, Asia and North and South America, with new venues added each year. Highlights include a 2012 tour to Europe, where the Curtis Symphony Orchestra gave the opening night performance at the Dresden Music Festival. This growing schedule of international performances reflects the global nature of Curtis, with alumni found in orchestras worldwide and on the rosters of the Metropolitan Opera, La Scala, Covent Garden, the Vienna Staatsoper, and the San Francisco Opera, among others.

Continual self-learning

Curtis is a continuous learning environment. Typically students will have a minimum of one major intense tutoring session per week with their chosen faculty member, and some students have more than one principal teacher. It is an intimate, supportive and constructive relationship that develops with their faculty mentors. Outside of the weekly sessions, assessment of students is a daily event. Essentially, this boils down to two key areas. First, they are assessed on the technical aspects of how well they play their instrument. Second, and just as importantly, they are assessed on how well they 'perform' – this includes stage presence, expression, ability to connect to the audience and so on. Assessment is constant and is carried out in a nurturing manner. Combining performances with intense mentoring by faculty and the weekly schedule of lessons and ensemble rehearsals means that the workload of a Curtis student is heavy. It also means that learning is constant.

When it comes to formal assessment of students, ultimately they are graded with respect to their potential and their accomplishment. This is the same at audition phase and throughout their time at the school. Each student possesses exceptional talent; they would not be admitted to Curtis without this in the first instance. However, their grading reflects what they do with their latent potential. How accomplished is their performance and how well developed is the talent that they possess? The best students are the ones who develop their talent to the maximum.

When working with students, faculty members focus on cultivating the ability to self-teach. As Díaz notes: 'Our job is not to teach these kids how to play. Our job is to teach them to be self-reliant, as this is key to being able to continually learn.'

This helps create the feedback-rich culture that we have identified as a driver of better performance. See Chapter 11 (New Zealand rugby) for more detail of the characteristics of this type of culture.

Summerfest masterclass

During our visit we were able to see the learning style of the Curtis in action. Roberto Díaz delivered a masterclass to a group of students attending one of several programmes offered as part of Curtis Summerfest, the Young Artist Summer Programme. This programme is an opportunity for young musicians to get a taste for Curtis during the summer term when the regular students are not at the school. The three-week residential programme is targeted at 14- to 19-year-olds for instrumentalists and composers and 14- to 22-year-olds for vocalists and conductors who have studied privately at the intermediate to advanced level. It offers these young artists the chance to experience conservatory life, with a rigorous musical schedule and opportunities to perform with their peers in an intimate, challenging and supportive environment.

The masterclass involved students performing selected pieces to the room. It is daunting and they are clearly nervous. Díaz probes them when finished. 'Do you practise dealing with the nerves that come with performing publicly?' His first key point for the students is that they must learn to cope with the pressures of performing. 'You don't need to go to Carnegie Hall to get nervous. Playing publicly for anyone teaches you how to practise coping with that nervous energy. All of you should seek as many opportunities to practise this as possible, as it will have a profound influence on your ability as a performer.'

The art of practice

Díaz then focuses on the art of practising. He invites the students to reflect on how they practise. 'Learning how to practise efficiently is critical to improving performance. Ask yourself for every practice session, "Why am I going to practise, and what am I going to fix?"' Díaz offers the insight that 'playing music is not about playing notes; it is about connecting them'. He gets one student to repeat a passage and demonstrates the difference between playing notes versus connecting them. In a short space of time – less than 10 minutes – we can see how the student dramatically improves how he plays. Díaz concludes by observing that 'No teacher will teach you how to play. Ultimately you teach yourself. It is this ability that we are trying to cultivate in you to maximize your potential.' It is a very practical demonstration of the underlying philosophy of how the Curtis faculty work with their students.

Later that day, we encounter three of the students who performed for Díaz as they rehearse in one of the many practice rooms overlooking Gould Rehearsal Hall. The trio – a violinist, cellist and pianist – all hail from Canada. Their dream is one day to attend Curtis as students and they are relishing the taste of the unique environment that Summerfest offers. We ask them about the masterclass. One of them observes, 'I have been playing this instrument for nearly 15 years and in 15 minutes Professor Díaz profoundly changed my perspective on how I play it. I can be technically very good but there is so much more to delivering a performance. He just asked some very simple, probing questions and I have come away with so much to reflect on and I can see how I can really improve. It was amazing.'

One of the keys to developing a feedback-rich culture is helping people to analyse their own performance. Adopting a questioning style – in the way Roberto Díaz did with the Summerfest students – helps create the environment where people can quickly self-diagnose. This in turn allows them to take corrective action and rapidly improve.

Strong work ethic

Getting into Curtis is a privilege. Every student recognizes this. They take personal responsibility for maximizing the opportunity they have been afforded. As a result students have a strong work ethic and the discipline to practise and self-learn. They egg each other on to excel. As a consequence students at Curtis are 'on' all the time. It is not the sort of environment where they can coast. Unlike other academic environments, students cannot pull an all-nighter to learn a piece! There is a lot of communication with the faculty about students and how they are getting on – especially in their early stages at Curtis. Staff will go through the full roster of students and review their progress on an ongoing basis to ensure they receive the right level of support. In the very rare occurrence where it becomes obvious that Curtis does not suit a student, a great deal of respect and care is offered to support the student in taking what can be a tough decision, that of not continuing at the school. It would not be their talent that is in question; they would not have been offered a place in the first instance if it were. Rather it is their ability to cope with the demands of the schedule of classes, tutoring, rehearsals and performance that are the daily life of a Curtis student.

It might be expected that this would create a very intense competitive environment among the students. However, this is not the case. Of course, in the early days an element of competition prevails, but very quickly the students realize that the biggest pressure they face is from themselves and not their peers. In this initial phase at the school some students experience a degree of insecurity. They arrive having spent most of their lives to that point knowing they are exceptionally talented compared to their peer group and, in some cases, are surprised to learn that there are others just as good as they are. However, they quickly transition through this phase and embrace their new environment. In a short space of time they settle in and any internal competition dissipates once the students come to terms with life at Curtis. The small size of the student body helps greatly towards eliminating this. As David Ludwig notes, 'Once you get into Curtis, being better than everyone else no longer is a big deal; it becomes more like you are a part of a very small, very accomplished family.' After this settling in period is negotiated, the students quickly adopt a vibrant peer-to-peer learning culture, which is encouraged by the faculty.

With only 165 students it is impossible to get lost in the crowd and strong, deep, supportive relationships develop between students, reinforced by the familial culture that has been a feature of the school from its foundation. The narrow *'performance gap'* principle we have highlighted helps drive this culture. Without it the work ethic and pressure to perform would not be as intense.

> Business leaders can learn a valuable lesson from Curtis. By keeping performance levels tight and to high standards within a team, a natural performance improvement imperative is created. Members of such a team know they must pay attention to standards and always strive for better or they will stand out amongst their peers. In every high-performing team we have studied, this feature is a constant. Business managers need to work hard to ensure they never let the performance gap within their teams widen.

Never standing still

The organization cannot stand still. It must look at how it balances the challenges of maintaining its heritage with responding to the changing needs of modern society. There are several examples of new developments at Curtis that show how it achieves this tricky juggling act. For example, the newest facility, Lenfest Hall, was opened in September 2011. The building is named in honour of Curtis board chairman H F 'Gerry' Lenfest and Curtis overseer Marguerite Lenfest, who spearheaded the campaign to fund the building's construction with a transformational US$30 million challenge.

While many traditionalists expressed concern at the project to build the facility – fearing that the proud traditions and core values of Curtis would be jeopardized by becoming too big – the reality is that the opposite has happened. Lenfest Hall has created not just world-class facilities for the students to work in but also a vibrant social space in which magic happens. The students mix comfortably and it has fostered a collegiate atmosphere amongst the student body. As we wander through the building we see and hear students interacting, practising and learning from each other, energized by the dynamic new space. As one faculty member observed, 'Great things happen here now at 2 am!'

Another example of Curtis' modern outlook can be seen in its foray into the digital era. Curtis Performs (www.curtis.edu/CurtisPerforms) has been developed as an online platform that showcases performances from faculty, alumni and students and allows anyone, anywhere, to enjoy a Curtis concert. As Roberto Díaz says: 'Just as a concert hall is built for a great orchestra, we have designed an incredible online space to watch our performances.' The online presence is further enhanced by the launch of innovative internet-based courses. During our visit we were invited to attend a recording session for an online course in Beethoven's piano sonatas by pianist Jonathan Biss. A small group of approximately 15 people sat in Field Concert Hall in the main Curtis building as Jonathan delivered his insightful analysis of Beethoven's masterpieces. This free course – available through Coursera, a leading provider of online open courses – attracted over 35,000 students, even before any content was posted online. To put this in context, in its 90-year history Curtis has just over 4,000 alumni! In one fell swoop the online programme launch opened Curtis teaching to multiples of those privileged to attend as full-time students. This experiment represents potentially the tip of the iceberg for Curtis and may in the future open up channels for connecting to the outside world in even more prolific ways.

> The theme of continual improvement is ever present in all our case studies. Unsurprisingly it is a non-negotiable for any aspiring high-performance organization. How it is delivered varies from example to example. What does not change is the constant striving for perfection and an endless quest to get better, all the time.

At Curtis, Elizabeth Warshawer sums this up succinctly: 'You can't be great if you stop growing as an organization.'

Cherishing Curtis Institute of Music's heritage

While the steps outlined above are tangible examples of how Curtis is evolving over time, the balance is maintained by upholding some of the cherished traditions of the past. Each December the annual Holiday Party is hosted in Field Concert Hall. Timed to provide a relaxing interlude ahead of exam week, everyone participates in seasonal entertainment, dancing and refreshment. Every Wednesday at 3 pm throughout the school year, the Curtis family – students, faculty, staff and special guests – gather for afternoon tea in the Gary and Naomi Graffman Common Room. This tradition dates back to the founding days of the school and is one of the mechanisms used to ensure that the close-knit, familial atmosphere is preserved.

Each of the beautifully ornate and spectacular practice rooms in the old mansions on 1726 Locust Street is named after a celebrated artist of the past. Whether in the Mieczyslaw Horszowski or Efrem Zimbalist rooms or elsewhere, the history of Curtis is celebrated and practising students are reminded of those who have preceded them. Each room contains artefacts and memorabilia of these great artists, including the desks they worked at in their time at Curtis and some of the instruments they played. In the Zimbalist Room a document hangs on the wall that brings the lineage of the Curtis vividly to life. The document is like a family tree and traces the lineage of the violin faculty from 1928, when it was led by Auer, the famous Hungarian violinist, to the present day. It shows how Zimbalist and all subsequent faculty link back to Auer. Every member of the faculty from 1928 to date has studied under Auer or one of his protégés, maintaining the links from the past to present for all to see.

By maintaining its proud traditions and cherishing the history of the past, while continually focusing on developing into the future, the Curtis Institute of Music is set to continue to shape the musical landscape for generations to come.

Powerhouse Principle 5: gap

The Curtis Institute of Music highlights a very important concept when it comes to high-performing organizations – namely the 'performance gap'. This has a profound impact on the dynamics of performance within teams or institutions. Let us explain why this is the case.

If the performance levels of members of a team are ranked from best to worst, the performance gap within that team is the difference between the scores of the best- and worst-performing individuals on that team. When ranked on an ascending 1 to 10 scale of performance, the most common gap we encounter in teams is of the order of 9 to 3. In other words, the best performer on the team scores 9 out of 10 while the worst scores 3.

Over time, if that gap is allowed to remain, our experience says that top performers get frustrated with the lower standards of those around them and choose to leave. Alternatively, they become complacent and drop their standards – in many cases without being aware that it is happening. Without intense pressure from within the team to maintain their status we find that these individuals can ease up and accept 'good enough' as their new standard.

Meanwhile, the likelihood for average performers is that nothing will change dramatically. They are protected by those with lower scores from negative comparisons on performance, while the gap to the best performers seems too large and too much effort to be worthwhile. So in the absence of strong impetus for change from either direction they continue to perform at an 'average' level.

Finally, the fact that scores of 3 out of 10 persist signals an environment where the poorest performers are not challenged strongly by those managing them. Often, in our experience low performance is either ignored or – worse still – ducked, with those individuals receiving soft feedback regarding effort or potential, which leaves them thinking they are better than they actually are. While poor performers may experience occasional moments of discomfort or 'heat' from their bosses, these instances are not enough to shift them up the performance curve to any significant degree.

The prevailing wind, therefore, in teams where the performance gap is large is in one direction. The better performers are slowly but surely pulled back to the pack, while the performance of the pack itself drops off.

By contrast, for teams where the performance gap is small, the prevailing wind blows in the opposite direction. In these situations, there is significant pressure to perform and improve at every point within the team. Individuals wishing to maintain or improve their positions in the team need to be on their games all the time, and there is no room for complacency.

At the Curtis Institute, the performance gap between students is very small, as a result pressurizing and incentivizing them to continually improve. If a student eases up on effort for even a short period of time they stand out compared to their peers.

To build a high-performing team it is essential to manage the performance gap so that it remains as small as possible. There are a number of steps that leaders can take to do this:

1 Define clearly what represents unacceptable performance: very few managers define explicitly what represents a standard of 'not good enough', and without this definition people set their own standards. High performers set the bar high, but poor performers have a much lower threshold for what they deem to be unacceptable. Our experience is that when a clear definition of the range of acceptable performance is provided – at team or individual levels – it enables people to deliver within that range. Equally, clear definition from the outset allows performance below the minimum threshold to be visible and actioned quickly.

2 Maintain rigorous selection criteria when bringing new people into teams: high-performing organizations sweat over who they allow into the

▶

fold. They adopt strict entry criteria or demanding selection processes to ensure only those join who will maintain or improve the team. Rather than compromising their standards, they will leave positions vacant until they find the right fit.

3 Make relative performance transparent across the team: in any performance culture there needs to be the right amount of pressure to perform. Too much leads to negative behaviours – but not enough is equally damaging. Making relative performance transparent creates a peer pressure that sustains performance improvement. It also exposes any weaknesses amongst leadership teams in addressing under-performance. The more that relative performance is transparent, the harder it is to ignore relative disparities in levels.

4 Ensure the performance environment includes clear consequences for good and bad performance – such that performance *matters*. People must see that good things happen to those who perform well and that sustained underperformance is not tolerated.

The Curtis Institute of Music is an example of an institution that is proactive in keeping the performance gap within its student group as narrow as possible. They know that this is a critical enabler of the culture within the institute and one of the mainstays of its position as a performance powerhouse.

Notes

1 StartClass, a higher-education research organization, ranked it as number 1 in terms of the most selective colleges in the United States in 2015 [Online] http://colleges.startclass.com/stories/10128/most-selective-colleges.

2 Elizabeth Warshawer stepped down from her role at the Curtis Institute of Music in May 2015, having helped establish a new strategic direction to propel Curtis towards its centenary in 2024. With a new 10-year strategic plan approved by the board she decided to allow her successor, Rauli Garcia, to oversee its implementation.

3 'Best Colleges: Top 100 — Lowest Acceptance Rates' (as of 'Fall 2011 Acceptance rate'), U.S. News & World Report (2012) [Online] http://www.usnews.com/rankings.

The Finnish state school education system

07

Candles of the nation

What makes the Finnish state school education system a performance powerhouse?

Finland breaks many of the rules of conventional wisdom in school systems, especially those of developed countries. Finnish children start formal education later than in most of the rest of the world, entering school at the age of seven. These children have shorter school days and receive less homework than their counterparts internationally. They do not sit standardized exams until the very end of their time in the school system. Moreover, the state has long abandoned the school inspections beloved of other nations. Teaching professionals are afforded autonomy to determine how to deliver the national curriculum guidelines. There are no published league tables indicating the best and worst schools in the system, and virtually no private tuition or private schools in the country.[1] Despite all of this they consistently top the rankings of international education performance.

The Programme for International Student Assessment (PISA) is a worldwide study carried out by the Organization for Economic Co-operation and Development (OECD). It is designed to assess the performance of 15-year-old students in mathematics, science and reading across 65 participating countries and is conducted every three years. Since the first PISA results were published in 2001, Finland has consistently ranked in the top echelon of

▶

Figure 7.1 The Finland school Powerhouse Performance model

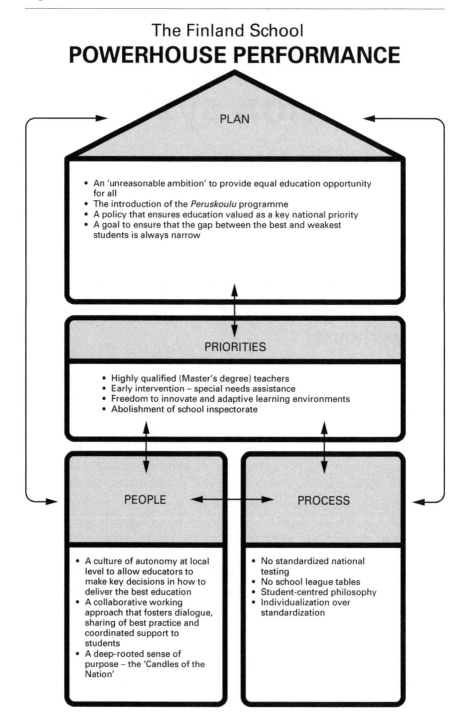

The Finland School
POWERHOUSE PERFORMANCE

PLAN

- An 'unreasonable ambition' to provide equal education opportunity for all
- The introduction of the *Peruskoulu* programme
- A policy that ensures education valued as a key national priority
- A goal to ensure that the gap between the best and weakest students is always narrow

PRIORITIES

- Highly qualified (Master's degree) teachers
- Early intervention – special needs assistance
- Freedom to innovate and adaptive learning environments
- Abolishment of school inspectorate

PEOPLE

- A culture of autonomy at local level to allow educators to make key decisions in how to deliver the best education
- A collaborative working approach that fosters dialogue, sharing of best practice and coordinated support to students
- A deep-rooted sense of purpose – the 'Candles of the Nation'

PROCESS

- No standardized national testing
- No school league tables
- Student-centred philosophy
- Individualization over standardization

nations along with the South-East Asian countries such as China, Japan, Singapore and South Korea. More impressively, analysis of PISA data reveals that the gap between the highest- and lowest-performing students is smaller in Finnish schools than anywhere else in the world. While the Asian countries focus on intense academic work, Finland delivers top results with no standardized exam regime, no after-school tutoring and with lots of arts and crafts built into their curriculum. Finnish educators would not have it any other way. As the PISA test becomes more established – heading into its sixth cycle – many educators suspect that nations may amend their school curricula to maximize their chances of success on the test. The Finns will never alter their approach to 'engineer' better PISA scores.

The Finnish school system can truly be described as a performance powerhouse.

The Finnish education powerhouse

'Peruskoulu' – *the big dream*

Modern Finnish society is deeply egalitarian. Ingrained in the national psyche is the notion that equality for all is paramount. It is particularly reflected in social policies in the areas of welfare, health and education. One of the basic principles of Finnish education policy is that all people are guaranteed equal access to high-quality education and training. The same opportunities of access to education should be available to all citizens irrespective of their ethnic origin, age, wealth or where they live.

As we outlined earlier, PISA studies confirm that Finland leads the world in terms of overall education effectiveness and – more importantly for those involved – the gap in attainment between the highest- and lowest-performing students. Taken together, these outcomes demonstrate successful achievement of their core educational objective: equal opportunity for all.

It was in the 1960s that education took centre stage in the economic development of Finland. In a country with little more than timber as a natural resource, the leaders of the day recognized that they had to have great human capital in order to develop a competitive economy. They made a brave and bold decision. To compete internationally, Finland had to focus heavily on its most abundant natural resource – its people. The major reform came with the introduction in the 1970s of *peruskoulu*, which loosely translates as 'basic school'. *Peruskoulu* captured an ambition to provide a higher level of education to all. At its heart was the notion that all children from the age of 7 to 16 – regardless of socioeconomic or ethnic backgrounds, or where they lived – should enrol in the same nine-year basic school programme. Private schools should be eliminated and every child given an equal opportunity in education. This was revolutionary. Pasi Sahlberg, author of the definitive book on the Finnish education system, *Finnish Lessons: What can the world learn from educational change in Finland?*, describes the introduction of *peruskoulu* as the 'big dream of Finnish education'. Many were opposed to the move, fearing that standards would have to be dumbed down to accommodate less able students. They argued that not everyone could learn at the same level and that the ability to learn was not evenly spread across the population. *Peruskoulu* challenged this narrative. It painted a vision of a more just society with equal – and higher – education levels available to all. Indeed, dissenters remained vocal until late 2001, when the PISA studies were first published. Finland outperformed almost all other OECD countries, ranking first in reading, fifth in mathematics and fourth in science. Even more importantly, it ranked first in terms of the performance gap between its strongest and weakest students. Finland had achieved its goal to provide a high standard of education for all – not just a privileged few or those perceived to be the most talented. *Peruskoulu* was vindicated!

The objective of equal education to the highest possible standard was, and remains, Finland's 'unreasonable ambition', in the same way that Muhammad Yunus set the ambition when founding Grameen Bank of using micro-credit to eradicate poverty. By accepting the challenge, those in charge of policy forced themselves to think differently.

It is this 'ambition' dynamic in a performance environment that leads to people challenging the status quo and introducing new ideas that other 'competitors' simply don't even contemplate, never mind implement.

Policymakers committed to deliver on this ambition and they designed strategies that were equal to the challenge. Since the launch of *peruskoulu* this objective has been realized through the introduction of an aligned series of reforms, including the requirement for all teachers to hold a master's degree; the abolition of ability grouping or streaming; and the disbanding of the inspectorate of schools.

Finnish educators continually challenge themselves to review the system and amend it to ensure it delivers into the future. For example, the national curriculum is under review at present and a revised version is planned for launch in 2016. Both at national and local levels, there is no sense of complacency, rather a questioning mindset that seeks to identify the next steps required to keep the 'big dream' alive.

'Kansan kynttila' – *candles of the nation*

Dating back to the 1800s, teachers in Finland have enjoyed a special status in society. In the rural, agrarian economy of the early 20th century, education standards and literacy rates were modest. In the immediate aftermath of independence from Russia, the 1921 Primary School Compulsory Education Act ensured that primary schools were established in every village. Society looked to teachers to educate the nation and ensure that literacy rates improved. They were often responsible for other cultural activities in their local villages such as organizing plays, music recitals, choirs and adult education. They were afforded great respect and trust. In most Finns' eyes, teaching came to be seen as a noble and prestigious career on a par with other professions such as medicine and the law. The phrase *kansan kynttila,* which means 'candles of the nation', was coined to describe their roles. In modern-day Finland, teachers are still held in the same high regard. Pasi Sahlberg noted: 'Teaching as a profession is closely tied to sustaining Finnish national culture and building an open and multicultural society.' Teachers see their mission as bringing light to the nation and creating a better society through education. Throughout our visit we asked many teachers the same question: 'Why do you do what you do?' In every case they alluded to this deeper sense of purpose and meaning in their role. Would the same, consistent responses come from teachers in other countries?

A key principle of any high-performance culture is that the organization's employees must feel valued and respected. Performance powerhouses focus on ensuring this is the case by design. Aspiring leaders need to think carefully about how they can create the same sense of value for their people.

The teachers of Finland are made to feel that they matter. They are celebrated for the contributions they make. They are trusted to deliver what is best for their students. They operate in an environment that acknowledges the role they play and makes it easy for them to feel special about what they do. This pattern is repeated time and again across each of the case studies we visited. The employees of Southwest Airlines, the staff in Grameen Bank and the professionals working for Médecins Sans Frontières all enjoy the same sense of worth that is cultivated by the environment they operate in. In the Finnish case it is the spirit of *kansan kynttila*.

Feedback-rich culture despite limited 'formal' testing

In the Finnish education system, standardized tests – beloved of many nations performing well below the standards of Finland – are avoided. Visitors will not find school league tables or rankings. They are redundant, as the quality of education offered across the system within *peruskoulu* is consistently high. Indeed, even the much heralded PISA tests, which have awakened the world to the success of Finnish education, are given little focus by the teaching profession. Yes, they are proud that Finland scores so well, but, in the grand scheme of things, they are not overly concerned about these results.

In Finland the first opportunity to sit a standardized test occurs in sixth grade – when pupils are 12–13 years of age. At this point there is the option of a district-wide exam. Participation is voluntary and the decision as to whether or not students take the test sits with the teacher. Many do so out of curiosity, but the results are not published. Rather, they are used privately to provide a sense-check on how students are progressing. The one and only national standardized examination comes at the very end of a student's time within the secondary school system. The National Matriculation Examination was first introduced in 1852 as an entrance exam for the University of Helsinki. The exam is used to discover if students have assimilated the knowledge and skills required of the national core curriculum. Finnish teachers are not under pressure to prepare students for high-stakes standardized tests. Rather they can concentrate on teaching, learning and knowledge acquisition. Finnish teachers would be aghast at the thought of being judged on the performance of their students in standardized state exams, as is the case in many other countries.

It would be wrong to assume that because there is minimal standardized testing that Finnish students are not assessed. Quite the contrary, teachers carry out classroom-based assessments on an ongoing basis. Responsibility lies solely with the teachers to carry out these assessments and it is a major part of their out-of-class working time. In addition, every semester a comprehensive review of each student's progress is carried out and a report card completed. This review includes feedback from all teachers and allows decisions on interventions to be made should they be required. The methodology used for this review is the responsibility of each individual school – again avoiding the temptation present in other nations' education systems to 'teach for the test'. Optional district-wide testing is available from sixth grade and is another mechanism for tracking student progress.

Just as in every other example we review in this book, the Finnish model demonstrates what we call a 'feedback-rich culture'. The perception may be that with little or no national standardized testing the feedback environment is soft, but we found the reality to be the opposite. With their focus on continual performance feedback for both students and teachers we find the 'performance' focus to be much sharper than in other educational systems.

Give good people autonomy to make decisions

In Finland, educational administration is organized at two levels – national and local. At national level, the Ministry of Education and Culture is responsible for setting education policy with the Finnish National Board of Education, which itself is responsible for implementation of policy aims. At local levels, local authorities and individual schools take responsibility for decisions such as allocation of funding, design of local curricula – based on the broad national guidelines – and recruitment of teachers and support staff. It creates a flat organizational structure with little hierarchy or bureaucracy and a great deal of local autonomy.

Dr Peter Johnson is Director of Education for the city of Kokkola. He is responsible for overseeing the general education school system within the local area, which includes 32 *peruskoulu* (schools for Grades 1–6 or 7–9) and four *lukio* (upper secondary schools). He also has responsibility for six other service areas of education and culture, including early childhood education, library, culture, museum, youth and sport services. Peter explains how the curriculum is planned at local levels across the country: 'The national core curriculum is determined by the Finnish National Board of Education. It includes the objectives and core contents of different subjects, as well as the principles of pupil assessment, special needs education, pupil welfare and educational guidance. The principles of a good learning environment, working approaches as well as the concept of learning are also addressed in the core curriculum.' Within the framework of the national core curriculum, local education authorities and the schools themselves outline their own curricula. The local curriculum defines values and general educational and teaching objectives, and addresses specific issues such as lesson-hour distributions to be observed locally, cooperation between home and school, and instruction of pupils who require special support or belong to different language and cultural groups. The dialogue created in establishing the local curriculum is meaningful and enriching for principals, teachers, parents and even pupils, and it builds a strong commitment to the curriculum. As Peter suggests: 'This kind of curriculum planning process is unique in the world... It is one of the cornerstones of Finnish education.'

A major factor in the success of this model is the fact that all administrators, such as Peter, are educators themselves. They are not business people, academics, career civil servants or politicians, but rather practitioners. They all have field experience. As a result, key decision makers understand education. They have the confidence of the principals and teachers. They can communicate with each other on the same level.

Finland has not been immune from the economic pressures experienced elsewhere in the world. In fact, they have been hit hard. The financial crisis of the early 1990s placed severe pressure on all elements of the public purse, including education. However, due to the local autonomy afforded to the municipalities and school principals, critical decisions for how to maximize the shrinking budget lay in the hands of the right people – educators. Peter Johnson and others in similar positions in local authorities across Finland were best placed to determine how to manage the resources at their disposal without compromising educational standards and aspirations. Together with the school principals in their areas, they were free to make decisions based on the needs of teachers, students and society. As Peter notes: 'Finland has for the most part succeeded in creating sustainable leadership and education reforms because policies have been based on firm long-term vision, consensus and respect for the professionals at local and school level.'

The workforce is highly qualified, especially in the art of education itself. Teachers are fully engaged in their profession. They are focused on constantly developing their skills and have freedom to apply their expertise in whatever way they believe is in the best interests of their students. They operate in a spirit of collaboration with colleagues – both internally within their own schools and externally with other schools right across the system.

Time and again we found the same pattern in our case studies. Give good people autonomy and a clear framework for action and then let them go. The Powerhouse Principle at the end of this chapter explains this concept in more detail.

Freedom to innovate

To see Finnish education in action, we visited two schools – the Kirkkojärvi School in Espoo and the Hollihaka Primary School in the northern city of Kokkola. The principals, Kari Louhivuori and Pertti Kuosmanen, kindly allowed us access to their schools, affording us the chance to move between classes, meet teachers and students, observe lessons in progress and really get a feel for the culture of the Finnish system. We discovered a vibrant, creative learning environment and countless examples of innovative ways to teach kids.

For example, in Hollihaka Primary School, we went into what we thought was an art class. The 10-year-old children were busy painting. It turns out that what we had joined was a history class. The kids were painting figures from ancient China to reinforce the history work they had been doing in studying this era. In another room a woodwork class was in progress. The students were making wooden periscopes. Again the class was covering more than one discipline. The craft skills of woodwork were being taught in tandem with the physics of reflection. In another room we found a first-grade English class under way. Amongst the seven-year-olds were four grandparents. The class was focused on the contrast between life today and when their grandparents were children. Pupils had been asked to draw up 30 questions in English that would give them an insight into the world as it was some 40 years ago. What toys did you play with? What type of house did

Figure 7.2 Students inside the Kirkkojärvi School in Espoo

SOURCE: Kari Louhivuori

Figure 7.3 Students leaving the Kirkkojärvi School in Espoo

SOURCE: Kari Louhivuori

you live in? How did you get to school? The primary subject for the class was English – the questions were testing the children's ability to work with the language – however, they were simultaneously assimilating a history lesson from their grandparents. Both children and grandparents were hugely enjoying the class.

Each classroom we visited showcased creative ways for students to reinforce their learning that typified innovative Finnish teaching methods. It was dynamic and stimulating for the children. Creating active learning environments is a recurring theme. As we spoke to the teachers in charge of the classes, they explained the latitude they have to be innovative in their approaches to teaching: 'We have free rein to experiment with how best to teach our lessons. It provides us with endless options for making lessons work.'

Special needs: the norm not the exception

The most important objective of the education reform that came with *peruskoulu* was the achievement of social equality. The ambition said that every child should have the same opportunity to get a high-quality education, that socioeconomic status should be irrelevant, and that where children live should not be a factor in maximizing their potential to learn. From the outset it was understood that achieving this would require a system that identified early any learning difficulties or other issues impeding educational achievement. To achieve the objective, special education support was established as an integral part of the school curriculum and adequate resources – in the form of experts trained to support students with special needs – were made available throughout the school system. This strategy has worked spectacularly well, and is a major reason for Finland having the smallest performance gap between best and worst performers in the PISA studies.

Both Kari Louhivuori and Pertti Kuosmanen illustrated how the school system has achieved this. Their schools are well resourced with specially trained teachers. Each school has a student welfare group that includes a psychologist, social worker, nurse and study counsellor as well as the principal and teachers within the school. The group meets weekly to discuss each student cohort. They immediately identify any students who require special assistance and plans are put in place to address any issues and ensure that students do not fall behind. Both Kari and Pertti indicated that over 50 per cent of their students would receive extra individual educational support at some point during their schooling. They highlighted that because it formed such a fundamental part of the system, there was no stigma attached to requiring this special needs support; it was seen as perfectly normal. Special needs classes are capped at a maximum of 10 students. In most cases they are much smaller than this.

The Basic Education Act 2011 enshrined this process in law. The legislation dictates that teachers must immediately react when student problems become apparent. Needs can be identified by teachers, support staff or parents and the school must react to that need. Every student has the right to educational support. The law has simply reinforced what was already common practice across the country's schools. Pertti Kuosmanen summed it up perfectly when he said: 'We will do whatever it takes to give every student the best chance to achieve their full potential. It is a fundamental part of our philosophy.' Early, effective intervention is the recipe that delivers the most equitable education system in the world.

A narrow performance gap is a trademark of high-performing organizations. Time and again we have found this phenomenon. Our study of the Curtis Institute of Music describes in more detail why this is so important in helping drive its performance. In Finland the means through which the system ensures the performance gap is the smallest in the world is early intervention and overinvestment – compared to other countries – of special education resources. Aspiring high-performing organizations can learn from this.

Intervene at the earliest opportunity to address performance gaps. If leaders allow wide variations in performance across their teams this will have a negative impact on group performance over time.

Continual teacher education

Teachers in Finland spend a significant proportion of their time on improving their educational skills. A large national budget (in excess of US$30 million) is allocated to ongoing professional development and plans are in place to double this funding pool in the coming years. It is expected that teachers should reflect on their own work, improve and learn more all the time. Each year, teachers are required to partake of in-service training. It is included in their agreement on salaries. The agreement mandates that they spend three days a year on professional development. This is coordinated by local education authorities and combines national educational development needs identified centrally with assessment of needs as determined by local municipalities. A 2007 study carried out by the University of Jyväskylä found that teachers devoted about seven working days – or 50 hours – per annum to professional development. This means that over half of this investment came from teachers' personal time. Teachers in Finland regard the three days' in-service training as a privilege and participate enthusiastically. The hours – mandated and voluntary – devoted by teachers to their continued development allows them to spend time with other teachers from other schools – sharing ideas, discussing best practice and exploring new methods that will improve their abilities. For example, Kari Louhivuori described how, in Kirkkojärvi School, he conducts a yearly review with every member of staff and sets development goals for them. Training sessions are organized outside of core school time to meet with other teachers in Espoo and engage in how they can improve. These sessions are voluntary; however, the take-up rate from his staff is very high.

Three factors combine to ensure that the focus on improvement is constant. First, the allocation of a large state budget and mandatory three days' development means that the system is set up to ensure that improvement happens. Second, the ethos of collaboration across schools encourages teachers to share ideas with a view to everyone improving. It is a win-win philosophy; we all get better at what we do rather than individuals looking for an edge on the competition. Finally, and importantly, teachers themselves are inducted into a culture of continuous development, which starts from their first days in teacher training and continues throughout their careers. It is a fundamental part of their mindset and of any high-performing institution.

There is no room for complacency. Any business aspiring to high performance must maintain a questioning and challenging mindset.

None of our case study examples allow themselves to stand still. The New Zealand All Blacks search constantly for the perfect game, the Kirov Ballet for the perfect performance, Southwest Airlines for ever more efficient operations.

Results achieved with modest investment

As part of our research into the Finnish school education system we were intrigued to assess the extent to which its outstanding results might be achieved by overinvestment by the state in the school system relative to other countries. The OECD report 'Education at a glance 2013' compares the relative spend across OECD and other G20 countries and shows clearly that the Finnish approach does not involve, to any excessive degree, throwing money at the problem. For example, the report shows that annual expenditure per student in primary education in Finland in 2010 was US$7,624 – less than the OECD average of US$7,974, and the EU21 average of US$8,277. Finland ranked 18th out of 34 countries. Similarly, for spend on secondary education Finland ranked 16th out of 34 countries with an annual spend per student of US$9,162, just above the OECD average of US$9,014 but below the EU21 average of US$9,471. Tellingly, due to the structure of the education system, Finland ranks as one of the lowest across the comparator countries (29th out of 31) in share of private expenditure on educational institutions, with a mere 0.8 per cent of private funding going into primary, secondary and post-secondary non-tertiary education. In terms of teacher salaries Finland lies in the middle of the group of comparator nations (primary teachers ranking 10th out of 23 countries, lower secondary-school teachers 14th of 22 and upper secondary-school teachers 11th of 22) in an index of salaries for teachers with 15 years of experience/training.

These statistics clearly illustrate that Finland is not an outlier in terms of its national spend on primary and secondary education. Finland lies very much in the middle of the pack on key spend measures as outlined above. This makes the country's consistently high performance and education standards all the more impressive.

The tradition of penkkarit

As our visit to Finland comes to an end we are given one final reminder of the status of education in Finnish society. It is mid-afternoon in Kokkola. In the distance we hear the loud horns of trucks and notice crowds gathering on the street corners. The local offices are emptying and workers stand on the side of the street. Dr Peter Johnson fills us in on what is happening: 'This is the tradition of *penkkarit*. The students in the local school are finishing school tomorrow before they prepare for their final matriculation exam.

They stand on the backs of the trucks and parade through the town to mark the occasion. Wait for a few moments and you will get some candy!'

The celebration of the *penkkarit* varies from school to school. Typically the school-leaving students organize pranks such as interrupting teachers and replacing lessons with parody classes. The antics usually end with the school leavers riding away from the school on trucks decorated for the purpose. In larger towns, *penkkarit* festivities culminate in parades where trucks drive across the city at a slow speed with final-year students on top shouting slogans and throwing candy at passers-by.

With that, the first of the trucks turns the corner and heads in our direction. The students are all in fancy dress and are singing and cheering as the vehicle approaches. In turn, the by-standers wave and cheer at the students and collect the candy that they throw. It is a significant event in the lives of the students. They are marking the end of their time within the school education system. *Penkkarit* means that the students are 'pushing back the seats for the last time and are getting up and out of school'. It is a moment that is shared by everyone in the town. The message is clear. Education is valued. It is at the heart of Finnish culture. It is something to be celebrated. It marked a fitting end to our visit to Finland.

Powerhouse Principle 6: decisions

A key theme of the high-performance model of Finnish education is the importance of giving good people autonomy for decision making. Smart people – equipped, enabled and trusted to make smart decisions. There are a lot of smart people working in organizations who do not enjoy the same level of autonomy for decision making. Our belief is that this is an important principle for high performance. So how should leaders ensure that their organizations are set up to leverage high-calibre people and empower them with responsibility to do their jobs well?

Business organizations are becoming increasingly complex. As a result, the way that businesses are managed is becoming more complex. In particular, it is no longer always obvious – even from inside the organization – where control lies for matters of either strategy development or execution. We subscribe to the view that 'strategy happens' – that strategy is what businesses do, rather than what they say they do. Strategy (and therefore performance) is the amalgam of many individual insights, decisions and events occurring throughout a business over long periods of time.

▶

Control confusion: who is in charge?

In a world where fresh insights emerge every day and decisions are constantly there to be taken, confusion around control – coupled with confusion around how to deal with this confusion – creates real challenges when it comes to delivering sustained high performance. Phil Rosenzweig, professor of strategy and international business at IMD, Switzerland, highlights the value of doing things at the right time in his book *Left Brain, Right Stuff: How leaders make winning decisions*.

Unless managers are certain that they have control over a particular strategy or decision, typically they default to perceiving that they have no control, and effectively look to refer or delegate particular decisions elsewhere (Figure 7.4). Sometimes this approach is entirely appropriate, particularly if the decision-making 'receiver' is geared up and ready to step into the breach. More often, however, our experience is that decisions referred become decisions untaken. As a result, unnecessary issues crop up, performance-enhancing ideas remain untapped, performance 'stalemate' ensues and managers become increasingly frustrated and disengaged.

Figure 7.4 Strategy and decision making – who has control?

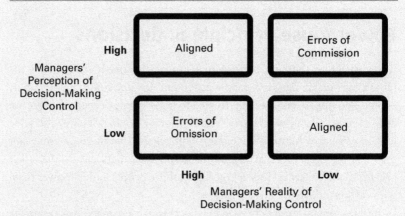

SOURCE: Kotinos Partners

Day-to-day remedy: change the default

Confusion over who has control can be addressed by pushing teams to switch their default to the opposite setting – assuming that they *have* control unless it is completely obvious that they don't, and to being proactive in filling any strategic or decision-making vacuums they observe. The focus then shifts to making sure that environments and working models within their teams maximize the performance outcomes they deliver. This, in effect, is what the Finnish education model has achieved. Local administrators, school principals and teachers are allowed to assume control for key decisions in how they will implement the national curriculum. It unlocks the creativity of the workforce and the level of responsibility they take for the outcomes they are trying to achieve.

A key to high performance: control by (organizational) design

While this approach occasionally leads to conflict in large organizations between middle and senior management, or in a multinational corporation between local and central management teams, in practice such conflict is rare. Moreover, if managed professionally and collaboratively, such conflict often gives rise to even better decisions and outcomes for the business. We believe that biasing towards too much ownership for performance, and therefore looking to err on the side of *commission* (doing too much) rather than *omission* (doing too little), leads to better and more sustained business and organizational outcomes.

This principle is maintained more structurally through effective organizational design. Leaders should look to design ownership for strategy and performance as far down into their organizations as they can get, and to the maximum extent that they can achieve – albeit within an overarching business or corporate framework. Rather than strategy and decision-making control having to be assumed, high-performing businesses design organizations based on capability, empowerment and trust, where these are routinely given. The advantages of pace, engagement and leverage delivered by this approach convert seamlessly into sustained outperformance of these businesses over time.

The Finnish education model has this dynamic right. The strategy has been set at a national level – equal education opportunity for all based on the *peruskoulu* concept and other aligned reforms. Local educators are then equipped, empowered and expected to determine how best to deliver to the students. The default setting is control at the local level – and the quality of decision making and delivery of outcomes shows how effective this is.

Note

1 The few private schools that exist in Finland are granted the same government
   funds as public schools. They are required to use the same admissions standards
   and provide the same services as public schools. The majority of the private
   schools are faith-based.

Tata Group

08

Nation builders

What makes the Tata Group a performance powerhouse?

Founded by Jamsetji Tata in 1868 and headquartered in India, the Tata Group is a global enterprise comprising over 100 independent operating companies. With a mission 'To improve the quality of life of the communities we serve globally, through long-term stakeholder value creation based on leadership with trust', it operates today in more than 100 countries across six continents.

Tata is an enormous and fast-growing conglomerate. Taken together, Tata companies employ over 600,000 people, and in 2014–15 their total revenue was US$109 billion – representing a sevenfold increase in turnover in just 10 years. 29 publicly listed Tata enterprises had a cumulative market capitalization greater than US$116 billion on 31 March 2016 – representing year-on-year growth of 15 per cent over 10 years. The list of largest Tata companies – many of which have achieved global industry and brand leadership in their fields – includes Tata Steel, Tata Motors, Tata Consultancy Services, Tata Power, Tata Chemicals, Tata Global Beverages, Tata Teleservices, Titan, Tata Communications and Taj Hotel Resorts and Palaces.

Tata Sons is the principal investment holding company for Tata companies. 66 per cent of Tata Sons' equity capital is held by philanthropic trusts that support education, health, livelihood generation, and art and culture. The Tata Trusts have endowed institutions for science and technology, medical research, social studies and the performing arts. The Tata Trusts also provide aid and assistance to non-government organizations working in the areas of education, health care and livelihoods. Tata companies themselves undertake a wide range of social welfare activities, especially at the locations of their operations, and also deploy sustainable business practices.

As a highly diversified, profitable and growing conglomerate with a powerful philanthropic purpose to improve the lives of the communities it serves, Tata Group is undoubtedly a performance powerhouse.

Figure 8.1 The Tata Group Powerhouse Performance model

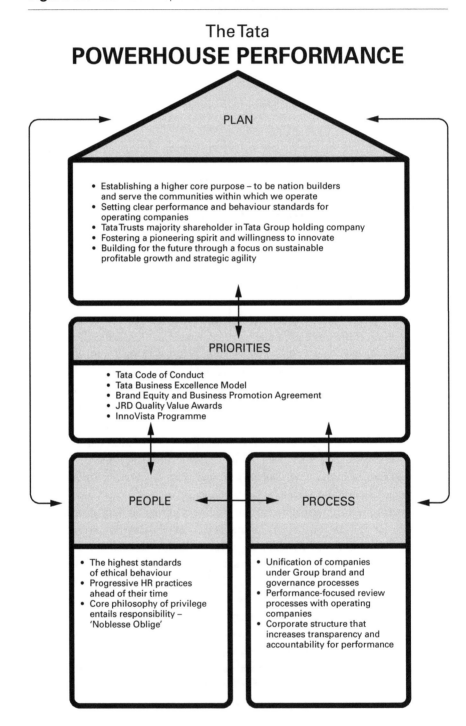

The Tata
POWERHOUSE PERFORMANCE

PLAN

- Establishing a higher core purpose – to be nation builders and serve the communities within which we operate
- Setting clear performance and behaviour standards for operating companies
- Tata Trusts majority shareholder in Tata Group holding company
- Fostering a pioneering spirit and willingness to innovate
- Building for the future through a focus on sustainable profitable growth and strategic agility

PRIORITIES

- Tata Code of Conduct
- Tata Business Excellence Model
- Brand Equity and Business Promotion Agreement
- JRD Quality Value Awards
- InnoVista Programme

PEOPLE

- The highest standards of ethical behaviour
- Progressive HR practices ahead of their time
- Core philosophy of privilege entails responsibility – 'Noblesse Oblige'

PROCESS

- Unification of companies under Group brand and governance processes
- Performance-focused review processes with operating companies
- Corporate structure that increases transparency and accountability for performance

The Tata Group powerhouse

Tata – a corporation with a difference

Tata is unique amongst the large business institutions of the world and even those high-performance institutions discussed in detail in this book. First, it has successfully swum against the conventional business tide flowing from West to East, extending from its home in Mumbai, in the developing society that is India, to establish itself as a true global player on a par with some of the world's greatest corporations. Second, it has done so by evolving a commercial business model that is fundamentally and explicitly anchored in a moral, principled and philanthropic approach. Tata exists to deliver its mission by executing in keeping with its values. Improving the quality and consistency of its leaders' execution aligned to those values represents the main focus of the organization's most senior executives. As such, in order to understand the business, we must first understand and discuss its values.

A value-centred corporation

Tata has five core values that underpin its business. These are as follows:

- integrity;
- understanding;
- excellence;
- unity;
- responsibility.

At first glance, Tata's values look similar to those of most other major business corporations across the world. However, unlike most of its peers, for Tata its values are both the glue that holds the conglomerate together and the single, true starting point for decisions, performance and progress.

The origin of Tata's values go back to the Group's founder, Jamsetji Tata. When he established the business in the late 19th century his philosophy reflected his upbringing in the Parsi religion – and its belief in the mission of lifting others from suffering and improving their lives to become righteous – and his travels in Europe at the time of the Industrial Revolution. These formed the basis for his pioneering thinking and the powerful sense of purpose he brought to his business. Tata's commitment to ethical behaviours dates back to these earliest days; however, in 1998 it was decided to formalize the Group's values in a documented Code of Conduct. The code focuses on honourable behaviour in business and encourages all individuals in their professional and personal capacities to internalize its beliefs. The code has remained largely unaltered in its essence, but it undergoes occasional updates to keep up with changing regulatory norms and the nuances of working in different parts of the world. It runs to over 30 pages and addresses core values and principles, codes of conduct relating to employees, customers, communities and the environment, value-chain partners, financial stakeholders, governments and group companies.[1]

All employees and businesses within the Tata Group must comply with every aspect of the Code of Conduct. It is included in the Brand Equity and Business Promotion Agreement that each company within the Group signs, along with a commitment to participating in the Tata Business Excellence Model (see below for more detail on this). Compliance is monitored on an annual basis and any issues at odds with the code are dealt with quickly and decisively. The privilege of being an employee of Tata carries with it a responsibility for upholding its Code of Conduct. Expectations for behaviour and business conduct are clear from the outset for new arrivals to Tata.

Integrity in action – 100 per cent or 0 per cent!

Tata's first value of 'integrity' demands that leaders 'must conduct business fairly, with honesty and transparency. Everything must stand the test of public scrutiny.' In Tata, integrity happens. From the company's inception in 1868 this has always been the case.

In 1947 the Indian Government, having achieved independence from British rule, sought to manage all aspects of economic activity through licensing. It introduced the License Rāj system, whereby, in order for a business to set up and produce goods, it had to pass through a complex, convoluted system of regulations and permissions to get a licence.[2] This system created a bureaucratic minefield of red tape and was open to widespread corruption. The Tata Group aspired to grow, yet it was unwilling to compromise its core value of integrity to do this. J R D Tata had once observed: 'What we have sacrificed is a 100 per cent growth. But we wouldn't want it any other way.'[3] The same sentiment was echoed by Gurcharan Das in his book *India Unbound*, when he observed that the Tatas made over 100 proposals for investment in projects relating to existing or new business in the period from 1970 to 1990 – and every single one of them was rejected.[4] As explained by Member Group Executive Council and Group Chief Human Resources Officer Dr N S Rajan: 'We were willing to let go of commercial gain but not willing to forsake our core ethos.'

There is no question that this stance stunted Tata's growth at the time. However, from the moment the License Rāj system was dismantled in 1992 there was no holding back the Group. From then until now, the business has expanded and grown at an astonishing rate both in its domestic market and overseas, without any recourse to corruption. As Dr N S Rajan explains: 'When you embrace values you may not always win in the short term. But you will most certainly not lose in the long term. Our Group Chairman, Mr Cyrus Mistry, has also highlighted the need to have zero tolerance even in the face of competition and tough regulatory conditions. According to him, you cannot be 99 per cent trustful or adherent to values. You are either there or not: 100 per cent or 0 per cent.'

Integrity issues addressed – the Tata Finance crisis

The other side of integrity that happens at Tata can be seen in how the company deals with internal issues. For example, the case of Tata Finance, which was an investment arm of the Tata Group and in 2001–02 appeared to be performing well. However, an internal audit of the business found widespread irregularities, including evidence of insider trading and false paperwork. The company's capital adequacy ratio was found to have been propped up by dubious means, and a stock market crash led to huge losses and a hole in Tata Finance's balance sheet. The response of the Tata Group was fast, principled and unequivocal. Ratan Tata, the then chairman, addressed the crisis at a shareholders' meeting, explaining that there was a major issue and a big hole in Tata Finance's accounts, and he committed to getting to grips with the scale of the issue as quickly as possible. In the same meeting he went further, to make it clear that no matter how big the investor losses from the irregularities turned out to be, Tata would be responsible for covering them. 'The losses are our moral responsibility and we will make them good', he said. Most particularly he was adamant that – having put trust in Tata because of its name and its reputation for integrity – every depositor would be fully protected.

Tata followed through on that commitment and the Group ultimately had to pump in approximately Rs700 crore (or US$70 million) to cover the losses. Governance processes and systems were strengthened and the painful lessons to ensure that it would not happen again were assimilated. The cost of the Tata Finance crisis in the short term was high. However, the payoff in the long term has more than covered that 'investment'. The reputational value generated by how it handled this episode has strengthened the brand and consumer confidence in the Group. Investors were retained and grew in numbers; trust in the Tata name was enhanced not diminished and the Group emerged from the crisis stronger than before in terms of reputation and business performance.

Understanding – building a city not just a company

The second value is 'understanding'. By this Tata means 'showing respect, compassion and humanity for colleagues and customers and always working for the benefit of the communities they serve'.

Figure 8.2 Jamsetji Nusserwanji (J N) Tata (1839–1904)

SOURCE: Tata Central Archives

Again, the practice of this value dates back to the very foundation of the Group. During its earliest days, Jamsetji Tata attended a lecture given by philosopher and historian Thomas Carlyle in Manchester, England. During the lecture Carlyle proclaimed: 'the nation that gains control of iron soon acquires the control of gold'. From this Jamsetji understood the link between economic power and prosperity on the one hand, and the iron and steel industry on the other. He committed to establishing a steel industry in India and immediately went about trying to find the best location. When geologists found significant iron ore deposits in the village of Sakchi in the Central Provinces of India, Jamsetji knew he had the perfect site for a steel mill. He also, however, committed to learning from the other societal lessons he picked up on his travels to Europe. He observed that the industrial towns of north-west England had been unable to cope with the rapid expansion brought about by the Industrial Revolution, with the result that many steelworkers were forced to live in slum conditions. If Tata was to catalyse the development of a steel town in India it would be one in which the steelworkers were looked after properly. As such, in addition to building accommodation for his workers Jamsetji committed to building a community in which they could live a comfortable life. He wrote to his son Dorab and laid out clear instructions: 'Be sure to lay wide streets planted with shady trees, every other of a quick-growing variety. Be sure that there is plenty of space for lawns and gardens. Reserve large areas for football, hockey and parks. Earmark areas for Hindu temples, Mohammedan mosques and Christian churches.'[5]

The result is the city of Jamshedpur – renamed from Sakchi in 1919 in honour of Jamsetji. Jamshedpur is administered by Tata and held up to this day as an example of enlightened capitalism. It is the only city in India with a population over 1 million people without a municipal corporation. The state has proposed on a few occasions to end Tata's administration and bring it under the control of a municipality; however, the move has been resisted consistently by local residents – an indicator of their regard for the influence of the Tata Group.

Ahead of their time

The fruit of Jamsetji Tata's labours is the Tata Iron and Steel Company (TISCO). Following Jamsetji's death in 1904, his sons Dorab and Ratan took over and – reflecting their father's values – put in place some of the most innovative human resource (HR) practices long before they became workplace law. For example, the brothers introduced an eight-hour working day in 1912 – a long time before this became a legal requirement in India. They put in place an accident and injuries compensation scheme in 1895; provided for paid leave and free medical aid for workers and their families in 1915; maternity benefits for women in 1921; profit-sharing schemes in 1934; and they created a pension fund for their workers as early as 1877. These practices were not only the first of their kind in India, they were amongst the most progressive HR policies of any corporation in the world.

Safety first

The 'understanding' value also translates through to present-day Tata. In the early 2000s – acutely conscious and troubled by the safety issues associated

Figure 8.3 Empress Mills crèche circa late 1800s

SOURCE: Tata Central Archives

with Indian families weaving through crowded city streets on motor scooters – Tata Motors announced plans to develop a safe, reliable and affordable car, the Nano. The car was pitched at an initial price point of US$1,500 and aimed at the domestic mass-market in India. As it turned out, however, a major issue arose with regard to the manufacturing of the Nano. The original site selected for manufacturing was in Singur, West Bengal, where the local government, keen to attract investment, made land available to Tata. However, the plan was met by protests from local displaced farmers, which were fuelled by opposition government leaders. As plant construction continued the protests became increasingly violent. The Tata Group made a difficult decision. In the interests of the safety of their workers they decided not to continue building at Singur, but rather to relocate the production facility to Sanand in Gujarat, some 2,000 kilometres away. At the point in the project where the decision was made, the implications for Tata and its suppliers were significant. Tata was forced to write off its heavy investment in initial plant construction, and delay the Nano's launch date by a year. Added to this, 70–80 suppliers also suffered losses as a result of having themselves established facilities in Singur to support the new factory. However, Tata stepped in to compensate them, covering 75–80 per cent of their losses. In the new location, and enabled by the goodwill generated with workers and suppliers, they managed to build the factory from scratch to production-ready in just 14 months and the first Nanos rolled off the line. In spite of the huge cost of relocating, the decision to do so was done out of concern for their employees. The safety of their workers came well before the financial and marketing considerations. If compassion and humanity are core values, tough decisions like this become easier to make.

The Nano project demonstrates more than a value-centred approach to business. It also highlights a pioneering philosophy coupled with a sharp focus on business excellence. By committing to building an affordable, safe car a new market was forged. The engineers responsible were challenged to rethink the car design and manufacturing process. Every part of the supply chain had to be designed to keep costs low, without compromising reliability and safety. When the first Nano car rolled off the production lines in 2008 it provided further proof of Tata's ability to balance values and business acumen seamlessly in one organization.

Excellence – swimming with the big fish

The third Tata corporate value is 'excellence'. The meaning of this value is self-evident. However, the spirit of excellence is at the heart of the institution's enduring success. Tata's moment of truth in this regard came in 1991 with the advent of the Indian Government's wide-ranging programme of economic reform and liberalization. Overnight many parts of the economy were opened to overseas players, who salivated at the enormous size and potential of the newly presented opportunities. Previously sheltered Indian companies, in order to survive, would have to compete toe-to-toe with the best international competitors.

Equally, the reforms opened the door for ambitious Indian companies to expand overseas. Ratan Tata, taking over as Group Chairman, understood what was going to happen – 'We are moving into a highly competitive environment, the India of tomorrow' – and he prepared Tata for the heightened competitive landscape. He was determined that Tata should be able to capitalize on the new developments as an opportunity. He saw that this required the establishment of excellence as a norm in Tata, and took a number of steps to make this the case.

He took steps to establish excellence as a manufacturing standard for the Group. He did this by pioneering the adoption by indigenous Indian companies of a globally recognized standard approach – in Tata's case it was the Malcolm Baldrige National Quality Award. This is an internationally recognized quality framework, which has been successfully used by US companies seeking to compete with Japanese and European competitors. The Baldrige model includes a diagnostic tool that tells companies how well they function in their business practices. In Tata's case it served as a benchmarking tool that allowed the Group to assess how close (or far away) they were from world class in their business processes and management practices.

Having introduced the standard, he then launched the JRD Quality Value (QV) Award (named after the former chairman J R D Tata) to recognize those businesses scoring highest on the Baldrige diagnostic. The diagnostic produces an overall score out of 1,000 with anything over 850 regarded as world class. Initially the Group companies were lower on the scale; however, with the additional focus brought by the diagnostic and benchmarking processes, scores improved very quickly. Soon, company after company within the Group started to win the JRD QV Award – Tata Steel in 2000, Tata Consultancy Services (TCS) in 2004, Tata Motors in 2005 and so on – such that what was formerly viewed by Indian companies as an unattainable global standard became Tata's norm.

A model of excellence

As the benchmarking process has matured, the Malcolm Baldrige framework has been adapted to be more specific to Tata and renamed as the Tata Business Excellence Model (TBEM). The TBEM has seven core components – leadership; strategic planning; customer focus; measurement, analysis and knowledge management; workforce analysis; operations focus; and business results. The model has three primary purposes within the Group:

1 help identify and improve business excellence practices, capabilities and results;

2 facilitate communication with a common language of excellence and the sharing of best practices amongst the Tata companies;

3 serve as a working tool for understanding and managing performance, for providing planning guidance and for identifying learning opportunities.

Every company within the Tata Group must participate in TBEM. It places a focused demand on ongoing performance delivery and quality improvement. Evaluations are carried out every year on every company – involving intense one- to two-week exercises that are taken very seriously by all involved. This is not a soft process aimed at delivering merit awards, rather it is a hard, performance-focused process that demands continuous improvement and achievement of the highest international standards. Where companies score low, corrective actions are identified and the expectation is that situations will improve quickly. Ultimately, if this does not happen, Tata Sons can decide to revoke the use of 'Tata' from the company's name.

The end result is that business excellence has become a way of life. It is embedded in the business operations of every Tata company as the route through which they drive performance. It has been responsible for the transformation of many of the companies in the Group – helping to eliminate waste, boost efficiency, improve employee engagement and drive customer focus. TBEM assessors act as internal business consultants, ensuring compliance to the highest standards and advising on improvement projects. Tata's internal commitment to quality and business excellence is fundamental to its external market success – both in India and overseas. Dr Mukund Rajan, the Tata Brand custodian and a member of the Group Executive Council, reflects on this situation with pride: 'Tata is the only Indian group that has survived and been in the top 10 brands for every decade since inception. This is an incredible achievement, especially in the post 1991–92 reform period. InterBrand places Tata as the number one brand in India, well ahead of everyone else.'

Excellence, ethics and performance

Tata's definition and practice of business excellence are the vehicles by which it marries its commitments to moral and ethical values with its commitments to economic success. These commitments, contrary to how some might think, are not mutually incompatible. Rather in Tata's case we would argue that they are fundamental to its success. As commented by Peter Casey, author of an excellent book on Tata, *The Greatest Company in the World? The Story of Tata*: 'The spectacle of an enterprise as highly moral as it is profitable is rare in society. They reformulated the criteria of business success, and made humanity, philanthropy and ethics not adjuncts to profit but its very core.'[6]

Tata's focus is long term. They believe strongly that an exclusively short-term focus can contribute to unethical corporate behaviours that run counter to the core values of the Group. However, despite Tata's commitment to the long term, there are scenarios where it becomes difficult to achieve its core economic business objectives. In these situations the Group will shed or divest the partner company. Under the chairmanship of Ratan Tata the key business performance metrics and investment criteria became more focused and could be tracked through TBEM. For example, returns should be greater than the cost of capital; each company should occupy a top-three position in its sector and benchmark with the best in the world; the business should have potential for high growth and global competitiveness.

Ratan Tata also oversaw a consolidation of Group companies. The decision was made to exit pharmaceuticals, cosmetics, cement and other areas in favour of expansion or entry into higher growth-potential sectors such as retailing, power, insurance and passenger cars. This helped bring the Group closer together and facilitated development of best practice and sharing of information across businesses. It also helped the individual businesses to think more as elements of an integrated Group rather than as a loose confederation.

> One outcome of a performance focus is to be clear where success can be achieved or where these standards could not be met.

When Tata does decide to withdraw from a business or market, its values – and particularly that of excellence – again govern its approach. Its standard is to do so in a way that is graceful and humane, in particular in how it deals with people, with its recent exit from the UK steel-making industry being a good example. In April 2016 Tata Steel announced its withdrawal from steel making in the UK and, in particular, the possible closure of plants, including notably the Port Talbot plant in Wales. Employment at the Port Talbot site totals 4,000; however, it loses approximately £1 million per day and needs massive investment to make it viable. Whilst the announcement has caused shockwaves in both the struggling UK steel industry and the declining industrial heartland of South Wales, neither business nor government commentators have placed blame at Tata's door. If anything, they have praised Tata's efforts in handling the difficulties, and acknowledged that Tata has gone to great lengths to turn around plant performance in the face of a perfect storm of worldwide recession, falling prices, the flooding of the market with cheap imports and a major, inherited pensions deficit. They have spoken of the lengthy negotiations in which Tata has engaged with local management, the UK Government and other stakeholders to find a solution in the best interests of those impacted. UK Business Secretary Sajid Javid described his talks with Tata as 'constructive and positive', while the general secretary of the steelworkers' union, Roy Rickhuss, highlighted how: 'Tata Steel has honoured its commitment to be a responsible seller of the business.'[7] As we write, Tata remains fully engaged in the process to find a buyer for the business that will provide certainty for the future of UK steelworkers and their families.

Dare to try

Tata's value of excellence also captures its long-standing commitment to being pioneering, enterprising and innovative. The story – and indeed the business model – of Tata is all about identifying and pursuing new market opportunities, and indeed about creating new markets in areas previously considered inaccessible. Our earlier story of the Nano, as the world's most affordable car, is one practical illustration of Tata's pioneering spirit. However, the history of the Group is littered with many others – for example, the initial setting up of a steel plant in the jungles of Bihar; the foundation of India's first national airline; or Tata's leadership in the building of power stations based on clean energy.

Maintaining and sustaining this pioneering spirit is recognized by Tata's leaders as a prerequisite for ongoing outperformance and, to that end, it has taken steps to institutionalize innovation across its companies. It has created a Tata Group Innovation Forum to foster and enable new ideas and positive change, with Tata InnoVista – a pan-Tata innovation competition – launched as a key vehicle for change. The scope of InnoVista covers four categories, as follows:

- *promising innovations*: for successful products, service, core process, support process innovations;
- *the leading edge*: for promising business ideas with proven technology, yet to be commercialized;
- *design honours*: for designers thinking about addressing latent customer needs;
- *dare to try*: for the most novel, daring and seriously attempted ideas that did not achieve the desired results.

The Dare to Try Award is the one that captures our imagination most. The award lauds bold attempts at innovation that did not succeed. It celebrates the spirit that propels individuals and teams to try to innovate and is a reward for the risk-taking that is necessary for path-breaking innovation. In 2015, for example, Tata Consultancy Services won the award for an insurance fraud-detection solution. The project was targeted at large insurers and was unsuccessful due to their reluctance to partner with an unproven partner. The project has now relaunched with a focus on partnering with an industry-recognized fraud investigation firm and is showing signs of potential success with the mid-tier insurers.

> For disruptive innovation to flourish people must be encouraged to take risks. Fear of failure will stifle real innovation at source.

Continuity and quality of leadership

Tata's value of excellence finally manifests itself in the Group's commitment to enduring, high-quality leadership. Since its foundation in 1868 – almost 150 years ago – the Group has had six chairpeople. Each of the six is lauded for the roles they played in defining and preserving Tata's culture. Each oversaw major achievements and milestones in the history of the Group. However, the fact that there has been only six in total has allowed Tata's long-term focus and commitment to values to survive. Each leader has come through the ranks, been rooted in the heritage of the institution, and committed totally to the Tata culture. None has felt compelled to fundamentally reform the organization, rather they have viewed their roles in more evolutionary terms as guardians of Tata's heritage. Tata recognized many years ago that as the Group grew, it would need all its leaders to adopt similar principles and operate to the highest standards in consistent ways.

To that end, in the 1950s J R D Tata set up Tata Administrative Services (TAS). In its current incarnation, the TAS programme oversees recruitment of talented graduates from leading business schools and puts them through an intensive 12-month programme to prepare them for general management. Through their participation in the TAS programme, they gain a thorough grounding in the Tata Business Excellence Model, in Tata's core values, and in how these combine to deliver superior, enduring performance. Alongside other similar leadership development programmes, this consistency of approach, when combined with longevity of tenure, contributes to management at every level of the organization understanding and becoming invested in the Tata way. This has been a key organizational strength. Harish Bhat, a member of the Group Executive Council and author of the book *Tata Log*, sums it up succinctly: 'our culture is built on continuity not discontinuity'.

Excellence of group governance

The Tata way of managing is reflected in the Group's governance oversight practices. With over 600,000 employees worldwide in hundreds of operating companies, spanning multiple industries, the challenge of maintaining control over the Group's activities is a complex one. Indeed, during his tenure as chairman, Ratan Tata understood that this was an area where the Group was exposed to risk – if he did not change the governance model there was a danger that as the Group continued its expansion and growth the core fabric of Tata might be threatened. The model he established has become embedded as the norm for how the company is run today.

The first component of the model involves establishing a legal agreement – the 'brand equity and business promotion' agreement – between each member company under the Tata umbrella and the Group. This specifies two key requirements – first, the Tata Code of Conduct that must be adopted uniformly across all member companies and their employees, and second, the Tata Business Excellence Model, which enables the Group to measure and improve organizational performance. This agreement ensures a level of cohesiveness, control and visibility across the Group and those entities operating under Tata's control.

The second component of the model relates to how the Group is set up. In an approach that is the opposite of that pursued by many other conglomerates, many of Tata's operating companies are publicly quoted and listed on stock exchanges, while the Tata Group entity is unlisted.

The result of this, in essence, is to give leaders of Tata companies a level of 'controlled autonomy' which ensures performance while keeping the scale and complexity of Group governance manageable, despite the rate of Tata's growth. Management decision making and performance is *bounded* by the legal agreement, *guided* by the training they receive through TAS and other leadership development programmes, and *exposed* through openness of the ownership structures in place. As recognized by Harish Bhat, Tata's culture of excellence is appreciated by international partners and stakeholders: 'Internationally the Tata brand is seen as one that does business in a good manner, is benign, delivers good products and services, with a strong performance focus.'

Unity – powering global expansion

The fourth Tata corporate value is '*unity*'. This captures Tata's enduring commitment to creating and working in partnership with leaders, employees and the communities they serve – to building strong relationships based on tolerance, understanding and mutual cooperation. This value is best illustrated by reflecting on the story of Tata's international expansion. Consistent with Jamsetji Tata's dream to become a global player, this has been a major focus of Tata's efforts since the early 2000s, with the company driving its international presence through organic growth and a stream of high-profile acquisitions. Notable amongst these were the acquisitions by Tata Global Beverages (formerly Tata Tea) of the Tetley group in the UK (2000) and the Eight O'Clock Coffee Company in the United States (2006); Tata Motors' acquisitions of the Daewoo Commercial Vehicle Company in Korea (2004) and Jaguar Land Rover in the UK (2008); Tata Consultancy Services' purchase of Citigroup Global Services in the United States (2008); and Tata Steel's acquisitions of NatSteel Asia in Singapore (2005), Millennium Steel in Thailand (2005) and Corus Steel in the UK (2007). As a result of these and other transactions over the period, Tata has achieved its current position as a truly global player – with over 70 per cent of group revenues coming from outside of India.

We are not conquering a kingdom

The most striking thing about these acquisitions, however, is neither their quantity nor their scale but rather the manner in which they have been implemented. Tata's approach to post-acquisition integration – reflecting the Group's commitment to the long term – is deliberately respectful and measured. Rather than changing everything overnight in newly purchased entities, they take time to work in sync with existing ownership and staff to ensure that Tata becomes embedded in a manner consistent with its code. In particular, despite assuming ownership, Tata is careful to respect the history and heritage of the brands it buys, and the connections between those brands and their home countries and communities. In fact, in many countries in which Tata has acquired major household brands, the Tata name remains under-recognized in brand awareness surveys. Tata Motors is a good example of this in that it has retained and continued to support the Daewoo Commercial and Jaguar Land Rover brands post-acquisition.

There are several reasons for Tata to adopt this strategy. One is the opportunity afforded to leverage known and respected brands in existing and new markets – clearly important in the cases of Daewoo Commercial and Jaguar Land Rover – while undoubtedly another relates to a nervousness with regard to how a quintessentially Indian brand might be perceived in developed countries. The biggest reason, however, according to Tata's leaders, is the Group's commitment to its value of unity, or working in partnership. For Tata this is an issue of respect, of operating without ego, and of focusing on what is best for the long-term future of the business. This approach is well summarized again by Dr N S Rajan: 'When we acquire a business, we see the employees of that entity as our own. We do not view Tata as a conquering kingdom, instead we are in the business of harnessing inherent synergies and creating winning and lasting relationships. Therefore, we truly believe that we need to be mindful and treat people with dignity.' Tata's approach undoubtedly informs how acquisitions are received by leaders in acquired companies, where the initial fear of the unknown becomes quickly replaced by optimism at the opportunity offered by Tata's strong culture and supportive influence.

Responsibility – nation builders

The fifth and final Tata corporate value is 'responsibility'. This relates to Tata's commitment to be a force for good. Again the heritage of this value goes back to Tata's founder, Jamsetji Tata. Amongst the many artefacts on display in Tata Central Archives in Pune is the following quote from Jamsetji: 'In a free enterprise the community is not just another stakeholder in business, but is in fact the very purpose of its existence.'

Jamsetji was determined that the business he founded should see its mission not as maximizing profit but rather as building a nation. The business goal of creating profit was, in his eyes, simply a means to a greater end. He saw the primary purpose of the organization as creating jobs and income to enrich local communities and the nation as a whole. In this respect the philanthropic ethos of Jamsetji and the Group he founded set it apart from others. There are many examples of successful businesspeople who have used their wealth for the greater good. Andrew Carnegie and John D Rockefeller are names from the past. Bill Gates and Mark Zuckerberg are more contemporary examples. However, there is a crucial difference between these individuals and Jamsetji Tata. The others became philanthropists *after* amassing vast wealth; Jamsetji on the other hand set out *from the outset* to build his business to serve the less fortunate – and this ethos has remained at the core of the Tata Group ever since.

There have been two strands to Tata's nation-building role. The first was to establish under its umbrella the key infrastructural businesses that would help India to develop as a modern economic power. Jamsetji Tata started by building a textile mill and ventured into the interiors of the country to source cotton. He then established its first steel plant in the guise of TISCO – later known as Tata Steel. The pioneering nature of that initial Tata Group continued after his death with the establishment of India's first national airline, Tata Airlines. Almost single-handedly throughout the period from the early 1900s to the economic reform in 1991, the Tatas built much of Indian industry. The second strand related to how the wealth generated through its enterprises was used for the greater good of the nation. These strands are maintained in the modern-day Tata organization and in many respects set it apart from other major corporations.

Noblesse oblige

The core philosophy of putting wealth to use for a greater common cause underpins the philanthropic ethos that defines Tata today. From the start, as soon as his business ventures became profitable, Jamsetji sought ways to put those profits to good use. He established an endowment fund to enable bright Indian students to attend some of the best universities in the world. To date some 3,500 scholars have benefited from this scheme. He subsequently set aside the majority of his personal wealth to create the Indian Institute of Science, which opened in 1911, several years after his death. His sons took up the mantle from there. They established Tata Trusts, which now control two-thirds of the shares of the holding company. The wealth accrued annually from these trust funds is significant and is invested in an array of projects for the benefit of others. For example, the trusts have funded the establishment of the Tata Institute of Social Sciences, the Tata Memorial Centre, the National Centre for the Performing Arts, the National Institute of Advanced Studies, and many other institutions and causes in education, research, community development, disaster relief and social welfare projects.

The Tata Trusts – remember these own 66 per cent of total group equity – invest huge amounts of money. Their trustees are careful to direct the monies to enable and effect positive change. As the leadership of the Tata Group has changed hands over the years the commitment to serving a higher purpose has remained intact. J R D Tata, the fourth of six chairmen, proudly stated that the wealth created by the Tata Group was merely a fraction of the amount by which it enriched the nation. Placing that wealth in trust in such large quantities for the benefit of the people ensures it is exclusively used for that purpose. As the responsibility value demands: 'what comes from the people goes back to the people many times over'.

Enshrined in the beliefs of the founder and every subsequent leader in Tata is the notion that privilege entails responsibility. '*Noblesse oblige*' is a French phrase that literally translates as 'nobility obliges'. It asserts that nobility extends beyond mere entitlement and requires the person who holds such status to fulfil social responsibilities, especially in leadership roles. This goes to the very core of what Tata is about. This spirit of responsibility is deeply ingrained in the DNA of the organization. Dr Mukund Rajan is unequivocal as to the importance of purpose for employees: 'this has a major impact on why people work for Tata and what it means to be part of the Tata Group'. Harish Bhat affirms this viewpoint: 'many are proud to work in Tata because our profits go in large parts to the Tata Trusts, which do so much good in the community'.

When it comes to upholding the values of the organization, Tata literally puts its money where its mouth is. No other modern-day conglomerate can make this claim with as much conviction as Tata. The organization has stuck rigidly to its principles for almost 150 years. These values have remained unaltered through recessions, financial crises, economic and regulatory challenges, generations of leadership, and lapses in individual behaviour. They are stronger today than they ever were.

Jamsetji Tata famously said: 'What advances a nation or a community is not so much to prop up its weakest and most helpless members, but to lift up the best and most gifted, so as to make them of the greatest service to the country.'[8] Values lived!

Powerhouse Principle 7: code

The term 'governance' captures the model by which an institution is run. Thinking about governance is, at the same time, the 'stuff' of management and one of the tasks to which leaders look forward the least. In a high-performance context, however, governance is where the rubber hits the road as, in designing an institution's governance model, its leaders go much further even than they might think in creating the high-performance environment that underpins sustained performance.

High-performance institutions are busy by definition – with activity ongoing all the time either delivering performance today or enabling better performance tomorrow. As such, one characteristic of high-performance governance is that there should be 'just enough of it'. Governance should free up – and trust – leaders to lead, and people to actually do what they need to get done. This is achieved by better understanding the relationship between the way that leaders of institutions behave, and the nature and need for governance process in that institution.

Leading business thinker Stephen Covey, in his 2006 book *The Speed of Trust*, argued that absence of trust in leadership teams acted as a 'tax' on their performance, while the presence of trust gave rise to positive performance multipliers.[9] We view this as a specific example of a broader point, which is that the amount of process *required* in an institution is *inversely proportional* to the quality and effectiveness of the leadership behaviours in place (where our definition of leadership behaviours includes, but extends beyond, 'just' trust). Better behaviours should equate to less 'volume' of governance process and vice versa. Figure 8.4 summarizes the relationship.

Figure 8.4 Relationship between leadership behaviours and volume of governance

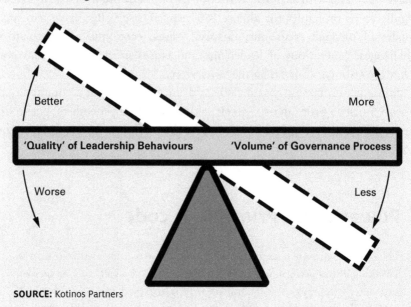

SOURCE: Kotinos Partners

Understanding the interdependency between governance processes and leadership behaviour is critical to unlocking enduring high performance. In particular, leaders need to understand that the interdependency is *two-way* and, at least in part, *causal*.

In practice, to minimize risk, governance processes *must* always align with the lowest common denominator of leadership behaviours – in fact we believe that if left unmanaged over time, governance models will evolve 'on their own' to the point where this equilibrium is reached. If we want, therefore, to reduce the volume of process, for example to unlock time for leaders to lead and take on broader roles, then at the same time as we re-engineer the processes, we *must* enable this transition by implementing improved leadership behaviours. This is both a design challenge – identifying and articulating the required 'behaviours to win' – and also a development/ enforcement challenge. It is one, however, that one way or another must be directly taken on. Organizations like Tata, Netflix, Southwest Airlines and the US Marines, which use their values as key enablers of their competitive advantage, 'get' this linkage and push for high standards of behaviour in everything they do, in part as a means to reducing the need for process.[10]

The other side of this causal relationship, which we must also understand, is the capacity of governance process design – either inadvertently or by design – to *influence and promote* particular behaviours. In short, if the governance processes in place are consistent with *poor* standards of behaviour, then over time, in another example of the system drifting to its lowest point, poor standards of behaviour is exactly what will transpire. We have come across several examples where the well-intentioned implementation of detailed, prescriptive governance processes has brought the unintended, counterproductive consequence of diluted accountability and broken trust.

As a result, governance processes must be explicitly 'aimed' to align with a defined standard of leadership behaviour and, within that context, to meet the standard of 'just enough process', as discussed earlier. Those involved in overseeing the implementation of governance models need then to work *both* the process *and* the behavioural angles in parallel. In practice this is hard, in particular because it raises the bar on feedback, performance management and leadership to ensure behavioural issues are met with behavioural solutions rather than with the imposition of more process.

Notes

1 Tata Code of Conduct [Online] http://www.tata.com/ebook/tcoc/index.html.

2 Rāj is the Hindi word for 'rule'.

3 Harish Bhat (2012) *Tatalog*, Penguin Books, India.

4 Gurcharan Das (2002) *India Unbound: The social and economic revolution from independence to the global information*, Penguin Books, India.

5 Tata Central Archives, Jamsetji Tata in a letter to his son Dorab in 1902 about his vision for the township that would eventually become Jamshedpur.

6 Peter Casey (2014) *The Greatest Company in the World? The story of Tata*, Penguin Books, India.

7 R Mazumdar (2016) Tatas have been responsible seller, *The Economic Times*, India, 11 April.

8 Tata (2008) [accessed 15 June 2016] The Quotable Jamsetji Tata [Online] http://www.tata.com/aboutus/articlesinside/The-quotable-Jamsetji-Tata.

9 Stephen M R Covey (2006) *The Speed of Trust: The one thing that changes everything*, Free Press, New York.

10 See Kotinos article (2014) [accessed 15 June 2016] Values-Based Management [Online] www.kotinospartners.com.

St Louis Cardinals

09

The birds on the bat

What makes the St Louis Cardinals a performance powerhouse?

Walk into any sports bar, anywhere in the United States and ask which is the best-run baseball franchise in the country. Chances are, once local allegiances are set aside, that the consensus will be the St Louis Cardinals. Ask the same question of those with in-depth knowledge of the 30 baseball teams in the Major Leagues and the vast majority will confirm this. What is it about the Cardinals that places them in such high esteem? Let's look at the evidence:

- The St Louis Cardinals have the second best record, after the New York Yankees, in baseball history – they have won 11 World Series titles and 19 Championship Pennants.

- They qualify consistently for post-season action[1] – in recent years more than any other team in the Major Leagues, making the playoffs in 12 out of the last 16 seasons.

- They have had just one losing season (below .500 record) in the 21st century.

- They keep winning in spite of the fact that the Cardinals' payroll is smaller than those of many of their rivals. In 2015 they were ranked 11th of the 30 franchises in terms of size of payroll, at just under US$121 million – less than half that of the most expensive team in the league (LA Dodgers at US$273 million).[2]

- They operate in a relatively small market – the city of St Louis has a population of approximately 2.8 million, ranking it 22 of the 30 Major League Baseball (MLB) cities by population size – yet they have the second-highest total attendance.

Figure 9.1 St Louis Cardinals Powerhouse Performance model

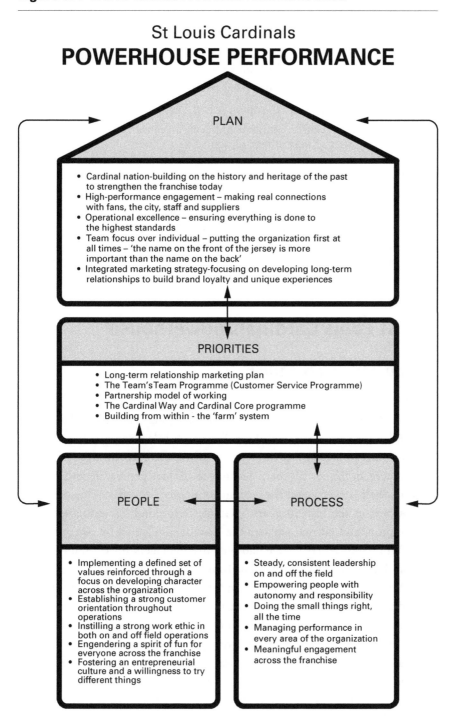

St Louis Cardinals
POWERHOUSE PERFORMANCE

PLAN

- Cardinal nation-building on the history and heritage of the past to strengthen the franchise today
- High-performance engagement – making real connections with fans, the city, staff and suppliers
- Operational excellence – ensuring everything is done to the highest standards
- Team focus over individual – putting the organization first at all times – 'the name on the front of the jersey is more important than the name on the back'
- Integrated marketing strategy-focusing on developing long-term relationships to build brand loyalty and unique experiences

PRIORITIES

- Long-term relationship marketing plan
- The Team's Team Programme (Customer Service Programme)
- Partnership model of working
- The Cardinal Way and Cardinal Core programme
- Building from within - the 'farm' system

PEOPLE

- Implementing a defined set of values reinforced through a focus on developing character across the organization
- Establishing a strong customer orientation throughout operations
- Instilling a strong work ethic in both on and off field operations
- Engendering a spirit of fun for everyone across the franchise
- Fostering an entrepreneurial culture and a willingness to try different things

PROCESS

- Steady, consistent leadership on and off the field
- Empowering people with autonomy and responsibility
- Doing the small things right, all the time
- Managing performance in every area of the organization
- Meaningful engagement across the franchise

- They fill the stadium day in, day out – in 2015 total attendance was over 3.5 million fans and an average attendance of 43,468 – close to 100 per cent capacity.
- The Cardinals are the only team in baseball to finish in the top three in local TV audience share in each of the last 10 years.
- As of March 2015, the Cardinals had the highest operating income of all 30 teams at US$73.6 million and, with revenues of US$294 million, the franchise is valued at US$1.4 billion.[3]

The St Louis Cardinals' consistent success comes from shrewd and steady leadership, astute baseball development, operational excellence in the front office, and outstanding fan and staff engagement. In essence they do far more with far less financial might than their rivals. This results in consistent winning, which is what makes the Cardinals the best-run sports franchise in baseball.

The St Louis Cardinals powerhouse

Steady hand on the tiller

The sports business can be fickle. Fans are demanding and the pressure to produce results is constant. This leads to regular changes in leadership positions. However, at St Louis, this rollercoaster ride is smooth. In particular, the revolving-door policy at the top of many sports franchises just does not happen here. In the last 30 years they have had three general managers – Dal Maxvill, Walt Jocketty and the current John 'Mo' Mozeliak. They have had two owners in the last 60 years – Gussie Busch and the Anheuser-Busch Corporation, and current owners the DeWitt family, led by chairman and CEO Bill DeWitt Jr. They have had only five managers since 1980 – Whitey Herzog, Joe Torre, Mike Jorgensen, Tony La Russa and current incumbent Mike Matheny. The same longevity and steadiness extends to the front-office operations. Go through the entire organization structure and the leadership positions are held by individuals with decades of tenure at Busch Stadium.

Bill DeWitt Jr explains the underlying philosophy: 'When we bought the franchise from Anheuser-Busch we knew we were buying into an organization that was steeped in history. We did not want to change too much. Our job was to build on the great brand, maintain the standards of performance on and off the field, and continue to make the Cardinals stronger year after

Figure 9.2 National League Championship celebration over the Los Angeles Dodgers at Busch Stadium. Pictured L–R: Bill DeWitt Jr, Manager Mike Matheny, General Manager John Mozeliak

SOURCE: Taka Yanagimoto/St Louis Cardinals

year. The people we inherited had both the experience and the capabilities to help us to achieve that.' In many other franchises a change of ownership would herald wholesale changes of personnel; however, the DeWitt family valued the people assets it had. This continuity of leadership is without doubt a key factor in the success of the franchise under their tenure.

The same level of stable, strong leadership is evident in virtually all of the other case studies included in this book – from Tata in India and Toyota in Japan, to Mayo Clinic in the United States. Each of them share this trait. Each have faced major institutional challenges over time. Their response is not knee-jerk but assured, decisive and calm leadership. A steady hand on the tiller is a major factor in delivering long-term, sustained performance advantage in organizations.

The 'Cardinal Way' – there is no secret sauce

General Manager John 'Mo' Mozeliak heads up the baseball side of the Cardinals' operation. He oversees arguably the most productive player development programme in Major League Baseball. Without the relative financial clout of other teams, Mo and his staff have consistently produced a pipeline of talent that has delivered the franchise's virtually unbroken stretch of winning seasons. Many external observers put this down to the 'Cardinal Way' approach. Mo dismisses this notion as something of a myth: 'There is no secret sauce. The reality is that the Cardinal Way has been overhyped by the media.'

The 'Cardinal Way' refers to a player development handbook that is given to every new player arriving for spring training with the Cardinals. The 86-page booklet (the managers' and coaches' version has 117 pages) covers various elements of their approach. There is a chapter on pitching, another on catching (written by current manager Mike Matheny), guides to infield positioning, bunt plays, team policies and more. The booklet also discusses expectations of player behaviours off the field. The document was first distributed to the players in 2011. It was developed by John Vuch who at the time was responsible for the Cardinals 'farm' system.[4] The material is based on the lessons of former coach George Kissell and many others. It is a living document that is updated regularly.

The idea of the document is to provide a clear guide to players within the system as to how things are done at St Louis. Whether playing in Single-A, Double-AA or Triple-AAA minor league teams the approach is the same. It makes the transition to the Major League team easier for players donning the famous Redbirds uniform. It is no coincidence that a plethora of locally-developed players have successfully made this transition over the years. It makes sense. However, as Mo points out, the Cardinal Way is not the silver bullet: 'Don't get me wrong it is a good thing and provides players with a guide about what it takes to be a Cardinal. However it is no more than that. There is a lot more to what makes us successful than the Cardinal Way.' In reality it is likely that every other team has something similar, although maybe not codified formally in book format. It is hard to imagine that the Cardinals have uncovered some unique insight into baseball coaching that has eluded every other coach in the league. More likely it is a collection of simple, clear, common-sense guidelines for players to follow. And by ensuring everyone is on exactly the same page, literally, it makes it easier to seamlessly integrate into the team when the call comes. It is why the Cardinals are acknowledged by many to have one of the most effective 'farm' systems in Major League Baseball.

The players of the past who helped set the Cardinals' DNA are evident on a daily basis around the clubhouse. No one encapsulates Cardinals DNA more than Red Schoendienst. A 10-time All Star and Hall of Fame inductee, he played for 15 seasons with the Cardinals, out of 19 in total in the Major Leagues. He went on to manage the team, delivering a World Series in 1967, and indeed he stills acts as a special assistant coach. In 2015 he celebrated his seventieth consecutive season in a Major League uniform as a player, coach, or manager! Red and the other former players carry the message of what being a Cardinal is all about. When they talk, the players listen.

The name on the front of the jersey

So if it is not all about the 'Cardinal Way' what else explains the success that St Louis has enjoyed in bringing players through their system? In 2015 St Louis had the best regular season record in baseball (100–62 for a .617 percentage). This in spite of a season of injuries to key players – such as All-Stars Yadier Molina, Adam Wainwright, Matt Holliday and several others – within their line-up. It is telling, however, to review the list of nominees for end-of-season awards. The team with the best record in the league had no nominees in the top 10 in voting for National League Most Valuable Player (MVP).[5] Likewise in polling for the Cy Young Award (for the best pitcher in the league), and Rookie of the Year, the Cardinal roster was virtually invisible. Mike Matheny polled second in the list of National League Managers of the Year. How come the best team in the league was so unrepresented in the individual awards? Because they are the best 'team'. The strength of the team ethos in St Louis is powerful. It harks back to one of the fundamental values of the Cardinals: 'the name on the back of the jersey matters far less than the name on the front'. Mo summarizes this simply by saying: 'the most successful teams tend to do the normal average things well. It is about doing the little things right.' This is a critical cultural anchor point for every Cardinals player.

Fostering a strong team ethic is key to driving performance. A cohesive, tightly bound team will, over the long term, outperform one with individual stars. Nurturing that team-based philosophy is essential for leaders in organizations. It is explicit. It cannot be taken for granted. It needs to be reinforced on a daily basis. The Mayo Clinic example (see Chapter 12) highlights this principle in more detail.

Player character

Another key component in the St Louis scouting approach focuses on the players' characters. The baseball department buys into the same philosophy espoused by the New Zealand All Blacks – 'better people make better All Blacks' (see Chapter 11). The Cardinals have developed a mentor programme (called the 'Cardinal Core') for their minor league players. In part this initiative came following issues with some players in their minor league set-up in Palm Beach in 2009. Three players were suspended for testing positive for banned drugs and another for off-field issues. The programme is also motivated by the 'characters' of the past. Stan Musial is a name that Bill DeWitt Jr namechecks: 'He was the greatest Cardinal of all time. We want our players to emulate his example.' The programme involves many discussions with team leaders and coaches about the character traits of legends such as Musial. These focus on discipline, integrity, the relationship with the community, how they carry themselves off field, and the importance of a strong work ethic. Emerging players are given recommended reading and assigned mentors to work with to develop their character. Personality profiling is included in the scouting process. 'We don't just focus on the baseball. We look for players who fit with the character traits we value and we look to develop them as better men', says Mo.

It is important to remember the combination of the 'what' and the 'how'. In high-performance environments leaders are concerned not just with what you do but also with how you do it. No matter how talented individuals might be, unless they fit into the behavioural norms established within that environment it is unlikely they will prosper. Ignoring this will disrupt the collective. In St Louis, character matters.

The city and its team

The winning record on the field is matched by the performance off the field. St Louis is Cardinal nation. The city and its baseball team are linked inextricably as one. For a start, the Cardinals have been in St Louis since their foundation in 1882.[6] The connection and attachment to the team runs deep for its citizens. Generation after generation of fans have got used to seeing their team win. Cardinal fans of all ages, irrespective of when they were born in the last 90 years, have seen the team win the World Series (11 times) and Championship pennants (19 times).

The great players of the past maintain strong connections not just to the team but the city. Over 100 alumni have chosen to live in the city long after they have finished playing for the ball club. Names such as Lou Brock, Ozzie Smith, Whitey Herzog, Willie McGee and Bob Gibson are very visible and ensure that the link to the Cardinals' fabled history is maintained. This is not an accident of fate. The organization works hard to honour their past greats and keep them involved. They are encouraged to spend time in the clubhouse talking to the current crop of players and interacting with fans as often as possible.

Various community initiatives reinforce the role of the franchise in the city. For example, the Cardinals Care Field Programme supports local teams by building baseball fields in the city – over 21 to date – that are named after the former players. Over US$500,000 in cash grants is allocated to some 200 non-profit, youth organizations each year. These, and other community initiatives, highlight the franchise's civic responsibility.

Cardinal nation

Ballpark Village is one of the most innovative developments associated with baseball. It is a mixed-use development built alongside the new Busch Stadium (Figure 9.3). It houses the Cardinals Hall of Fame and Museum, a range of restaurants, retail units, entertainment venues, residential units and commercial office space. It is designed as an extension of the stadium itself and the result is a vibrant focal point for downtown St Louis. It has reinvigorated local economic activity and complements the energy and excitement of the game-day experience. It ensures that the area around Busch Stadium is vibrant 365 days a year, not just on the 81 regular season home-game days.

The Hall of Fame Museum in Ballpark Village is a treasure trove of Cardinals memorabilia. It houses one of the largest team-specific collections in sport. Bill DeWitt III, President and son of Bill DeWitt Jr, highlights the importance of this: 'We have been buying our own memorabilia for years. Our history is such a strategic advantage that we have invested heavily in it. It is a key part of ensuring we acclaim our heritage and build it as part of the Cardinals brand.'

The stadium layout plays its part too. Bill DeWitt III was the visionary behind the redevelopment of Busch Stadium and Ballpark Village. His background in design is evident in the finished product. From within the stadium spectators enjoy spectacular views of the iconic landmark of the city, the Gateway Arch and the downtown St Louis skyline. From outside the stadium,

Figure 9.3 Aerial view of Busch Stadium and Ballpark Village

SOURCE: Dan Donovan/St Louis Cardinals

its open-ended design draws people in with unobstructed views of the baseball ground, including the playing field itself. It reinforces the symbiotic relationship of the city and the team. In St Louis it is impossible to escape the influence of the Cardinals.

The DeWitt family have placed a big emphasis on cultivating the relationship between the organization and the city. This relationship acts as a tangible source of meaning to staff and fans alike. For further insight into the power of meaning, see Médecins Sans Frontières in Chapter 3.

Filling the baseball ground

We noted earlier that the Cardinals have the second largest home attendance in Major League Baseball. This is in spite of the fact that St Louis is only ranked

22nd of the 30 franchise cities in terms of population size. Every year since 1998, with a single exception in 2003, Busch Stadium has welcomed in excess of 3 million fans per season (in 2003 the figure was just below 3 million). In 2015, total attendance passed the 3.5 million mark. There are several factors that contribute to this phenomenal performance. The rich history and heritage of the franchise helps. So too does the fervent support and connection to the city. As does the fact that it is a consistently winning team. Yet this is only part of the story. The front-office organization deploys a host of mechanisms to fill the stadium game after game.

The Cardinals followed the lead of the San Francisco Giants in introducing a dynamic ticket-pricing model. This allows ticket prices for individual games to vary based on a range of factors, including team performance, pitching matchups, weather and ticket demand. This has proven a real benefit to fans, and the result has been an increase in average attendances. In 2015, 69 per cent of games had tickets available for less than US$10.

The franchise has invested heavily in high-quality promotional offers. Dan Farrell, Senior Vice President (VP) of marketing and sales, explains: 'In the last 5–10 years we have become more strategic with how we use our promotions to build incremental attendance. We invest over US$1 million a year on providing giveaways that are of a really high standard. We spend a lot of time designing the offers and we promote them really well.' An example of this was a Grateful Dead promotional night. Over 4,000 fans came specifically because of the promotion, many of whom had never been to a Cardinals game before! The investment had paid off, the event delivered incremental revenue in multiples of the outlay.

The organization leverages its attraction in really smart ways. For example, in every baseball park the tradition of pre-game national anthems, the singing of 'God Bless America' and the famous seventh-inning stretch song 'Take Me Out to the Ballpark' are staples of the experience. Typically, each night an individual will sing each song. Not at Busch Stadium. The three slots are reserved for groups, typically local schools, where groups of more than 100 kids have the opportunity to take the field and perform each of the rituals. Discounted tickets are offered to the performing groups. It is a marketing masterstroke. The participating school enjoys a build-up to the occasion that generates a buzz for weeks in advance. The kids involved enjoy the unique experience and typically become fans for life – if they weren't already. They are joined by their proud families looking on from the stands. Hundreds of additional tickets are sold to connections of those involved. Everyone benefits. The Cardinals Pom-Cheer-Dance Programme works in a similar way. It offers opportunities to Pom, Dance and Cheer squads to perform before games. Again this creates lifelong connections to the Cardinals and adds to the numbers at each game. Community groups are given the opportunity to participate in first-pitch ceremonies on the field. There are several other group initiatives targeted at community groups, non-profits and businesses, which on any given night help add thousands of ticket sales whilst providing 'wow moments' for their people. Every game night there is a hive of activity around each of these groups.

The sales and marketing department adopt a relationship marketing approach. Rob Fasoldt, Director Of Ticket Sales and Services, explains how this works in practice: 'Our outbound sales agents know that building a relationship is paramount. For example, typically the opening question in a call will be to ask about your favourite Cardinal player or moment.' This leads to fewer calls per agent – they make at least half as many calls as other outbound sales offices – but the quality of the conversations is far higher.

As we learn more about how they operate, the high attendance figures start to make more sense. The results are driven by a smart strategy, executed outstandingly well – the hallmark of a high-performing organization.

Working in partnership

Running Busch Stadium is complex. The 250 full-time staff employed in the front office are supported by a range of third-party service providers to manage all the activities, including security, merchandising, catering, logistics and everything else. However, the Cardinals' organization does not see these providers as separate from the business, rather they regard and treat them as valued partners. This is illustrated by their relationship with Delaware North Companies (DNC) Sportservice, who provide a range of game-day experiences to patrons at Busch Stadium. Vicki Bryant is VP of event services and merchandising at the Cardinals. She is responsible for managing this relationship on behalf of the organization: 'It is critically important for us to really make this an effective partnership. We spend a lot of time making it our business to understand their business model really well. This allows us to make it work for both parties.' Rory Schroeder is general manager at DNC Sportservice in St Louis. He is in his thirtieth season working with the Cardinals and is Vicki's counterpart in the relationship between the two organizations. Rory confirms how they work together: 'I feel as much a part of the Cardinals as I do DNC. In order to deliver the high standards that we both aspire to it has to be that way.' When Rory talks about the Cardinals he uses 'we' not 'they', for example he speaks of the 'fantastic fan base we have'.

Their talk of partnership is not just rhetoric. There are numerous instances of how it actually manifests itself. Once a year a large group of staff from both companies go to the 'lake' – a meeting venue offsite – to review how to deliver on their joint commitment to providing the best possible fan experience in the stadium. The meeting acts as a comprehensive review of how they are doing and results in a plethora of ideas as to how to continually improve.

Secondly, staff from both organizations came together to develop a tailored, detailed training programme covering every aspect of the services provided at Busch Stadium. The 'Team's Team Programme' is rolled out to every employee. Cardinal employees cross train with DNC Sportservice and vice versa.

When Cardinals staff notice issues or receive complaints the conversations they have with Sportservice are not adversarial. As Vicki observes: 'When that happens I can focus on discussing solutions because I know their business so well. Sportservice can do the same.'

The contract between the Cardinals and DNC Sportservice stipulates that the Cardinals have the right to force termination of a DNC Sportservice employee should they feel it necessary. They don't have to use this often but the fact that this clause exists indicates the level of trust and mutual respect between the two entities.

When the Cardinals won the World Series in 2011 Rory and his fellow DNC directors were included in the staff ring ceremony along with their counterparts in the Cardinals front office.

The Cardinals commission 'secret shoppers' to assure the quality of services being provided. The results at Busch Stadium are consistently high compared to other Sportservice venues. Vicki proudly says: 'We are as proud of that as the Sportservice people are.' The Cardinals example is highlighted as best practice when Rory Schroeder meets his counterparts at DNC general manager conferences.

There are many more examples of how the partnership is real. The same ethos applies to other service providers to the Cardinals. For example, the Cardinals nurture relationships with their broadcast partners – KMOX, the local radio affiliate; and Fox Sports MidWest, the TV network. Dan Farrell notes: 'We give our broadcasters samples of our promotional items and encourage them to talk about them. We let them know how ticket sales are going. They play a role in helping us to fill the stadium and they take pride in playing their part.'

Partnership is a deep-rooted part of the culture at St Louis. It permeates every aspect of the organization. By integrating their partners into the business in this seamless way the Cardinals ensure the standards that they cherish are upheld and delivered.

High-performing organizations have a different view of the boundaries of their businesses. They see suppliers as a fundamental part of their business model, not outside it. They integrate them fully through process, governance and behaviour alignment. They invest in the relationships beyond the transactional. They see their partners as colleagues. They celebrate their joint successes. They credit each other for their achievements. And it works.

Everyone owns the performance

Tom Schlaker is Food and Beverage Director at DNC Sportservice. We shadow him on a game night. The stadium is full with over 45,000 fans yet again, and the contest is in the middle of the fifth inning. The condiment carts dispensing ketchup and mustard have been in use by fans for over two hours already as we tour the concourse. It is striking how clean they are. Each cart is as spotless now as it was when the gates were opened. We watch as several fans dollop generous portions of ketchup and mustard on their hot dogs. They spill some on the floor beside the cart. As soon as they leave, a cleaner detailed to look after that area wipes away the evidence. Tom explains: 'These carts are monitored by employees working for us. They take great pride in keeping them pristine and spotless.' He goes on to explain that this area of the stadium is manned by employees sourced through one of their charity partners. In this case it is the Judevine Centre for Autism. The partnership works really well: 'We hire, train and pay the staff and also make a contribution to the Centre. They are brilliant at what they do, super diligent and great employees, as you have just seen. It is a classic win-win-win scenario. We win as we get great staff, the Judevine recruits win as they get huge satisfaction from working for the Cardinals, and the centre wins as it benefits from our contribution whilst showcasing the ability of its people to contribute to society.'

The standards witnessed at the condiment carts are replicated everywhere in the Cardinals' set-up. Bill DeWitt Jr sums it up as follows: 'Everyone in the organization knows that we have high expectations. Our aim is to do everything in a first-class way. They all know that they are responsible for doing all they can to achieve that in every aspect of our operations.' Simple mechanisms reinforce this principle. For example, if an area scores 100 per cent on a secret shop the staff manning that area get a US$100 reward, including the supervisors. As a result they are happy to jump to work on a concession stand if they see the line is too long. Simple but effective. Everyone in the business owns the performance of the business. The alignment between the baseball and business side of the franchise is absolute. What we observe in the stadium is a mirror of the approach Mo describes when he speaks of the team doing the little things right.

Both on and off the field the focus is on continually improving to maintain the Cardinals' competitive advantage – whether within the scouting system, investing in the minor league set-ups, improving facilities in the stadium, or delivering the best possible experience for fans. Bill DeWitt Jr talks of 'never getting complacent and always pushing the envelope to improve'. He concludes our conversation by saying that the DeWitt family is lucky to own a franchise that operates like this. But it is nothing to do with luck and everything to do with hard work. Vicki Bryant summed it up best when she said: 'Success is not owned, it is leased and the rent is due every day.'

We are in the memory business

Engagement is a recurring theme from our visit to the Cardinals: the way the franchise engages with fans, how the organization engages with its partners, the manner in which the leadership engages with staff, and the methods that the baseball operations use to foster engagement between alumni and current players.

Twice yearly, Bill DeWitt III and Mo spend time with a core group of approximately 70 staff. The sessions cover every aspect of the operation, including questions about team affairs. No areas are off limits. So when the season-ticket sales staff are discussing renewals with fans, they can say: 'I had a meeting with Bill and Mo last week and let me share some insights from our discussion.' How many call agents in other franchises can talk about their meetings with the president and the general manager? It makes fans feel like they have an inside track to the thinking of the franchise. The idea for this came from Joe Strohm, VP of ticket sales: 'It is a key advantage that our General Manager cares a lot about the business side of the organization. He knows how ticket sales are going. He interacts with our people. Both Bill and Mo want to know from our front-line staff what fans are thinking and saying.'

Joe emphasizes to his team the importance of building the fans' relationships with the Cardinals: 'Our job is to create memories for our fans. We are in the memory business. No one has to buy a ticket or be a Cardinal fan.'

The best of the best in making connections to fans

Rich Luker is an expert in sports-fan engagement. He is the founder of Luker on Trends and the ESPN Sports Poll. He has carried out extensive research into the relationships between US sports franchises and their fan bases. Whilst we were in St Louis, he visited to present his latest findings from a study piloted by Major League Baseball on fan engagement: 'The Cardinals are the best of the best in making connections to fans'.

Pre-game there is a meeting of all event staff in a briefing room in the bowels of the stadium. The meeting lasts for approximately 15 minutes. Jack Stretch, the event manager, is in charge and the tone is light and fun. Jack is a natural raconteur and holds the room with ease. He cracks jokes, acknowledges birthdays, shares positive feedback from last night's game and generally sets an upbeat mood that everyone feeds off. A newsletter is distributed with some facts on tonight's game (who are the opponents, starting pitchers, league standings etc). It is not what we had expected. We assumed the briefing would be more staid and focused on health and safety issues as opposed to previewing the game. Jack explains what is going on: 'We recognize the importance of fan engagement and these guys are our front-line troops. We want to send them out into the stadium in an upbeat, happy mood. We want them to engage with the fans about the game. We want them to set the tone for the fan experience in the ball park.' After the meeting we arrange to shadow one of the ushers as she greets the fans. The usher's role is to guide fans to their allocated seats. In reality this role is very different each time. On this occasion the usher uses the brief time it takes to show the fans to their seats to engage with them about the game: 'Hey, see who our starting pitcher is tonight? How do you think he will go? We are five games ahead in the NL Central Division, can we make it six tonight?' That is what the best of the best in fan connection looks like! It helps explain why the Cardinal nation comes in such numbers to Busch Stadium.

Powerhouse Principle 8: engagement

There are any number of research studies that highlight the link between engagement and corporate performance. Companies with engaged employees outperform those that don't by over 200 per cent.[7] In research published by the *Harvard Business Review* over 71 per cent of respondents agreed

that engagement was very important to the overall success of the organization.[8] So how do we develop high-performance engagement?

Engagement is a 'contact sport'

Mahatma Gandhi famously said: 'You must be the change you wish to see
in the world.' Building an engaged organization starts at the top. Leaders
must set the example and demonstrate their willingness to engage. If leaders
want things to change, then as leaders they must lead that change. To engage
properly – be it with customers, staff or suppliers – they need to get down
and dirty. It is a 'contact sport'. It is about getting close and personal. The
more face-to-face contact they have the better. At every level within the
Cardinals' organization we see this played out. The leadership group is
actively engaged and visible to staff. The various functional departments
invest time getting to know their suppliers as partners. The franchise
places a huge emphasis on how it engages with fans. It is not lip service, it
is at the core of how things are done.

Link engagement to performance, not satisfaction

The focus of engagement efforts should be to enable performance – allowing people to do their jobs better – and not on satisfaction, happiness or
maintaining harmony. Concentrating on the performance imperative ties
engagement efforts to the overall vision and business strategy. Engaged
employees are those who drive the results, the ones who bring passion to
their jobs, the ones who are willing to go the extra mile, and the ones who
get frustrated if things are not done right. Leaders' engagement efforts
should be focused on providing employees with the tools to do their jobs
well. Performance helps drive engagement, whereas using engagement
to merely focus on 'happy' employees may or may not lead to improved
performance. Engagement is the happy by-product of performance.

Go beyond the 'strictly professional'

The more formal leaders make engagement efforts the more likely they are
to fall flat. Real conversations drive real engagement. To win the hearts
and minds of people, leaders need to be authentic. They should be willing
to have frank conversations. They should not try to hide mistakes or failings.
They should not be afraid to show their personalities. They should allow
themselves to be 'real' and unafraid of showing their emotions. They
should connect with their people.

▶

Don't overengineer it

Many organizations develop sophisticated corporate-wide, branded engagement programmes, typically led by HR and, in many cases, taking months if not years to design. However these programmes seem to deliver little or no tangible impact by the time annual staff engagement surveys are completed. Overengineered engagement initiatives can become impersonal and feel false. Engagement works better with less hype and more substance. Keep it simple. Try stuff, learn from it and improve. If it works, do more; if it doesn't then change it or stop doing it.

Notes

1 The Major League Baseball (MLB) post-season is an elimination tournament held after the conclusion of the MLB regular season. The top-ranked teams during the regular season qualify for these play-off games.

2 http://deadspin.com/2015-payrolls-and-salaries-for-every-mlb-team-1695040045.

3 http://www.forbes.com/mlb-valuations/list/.

4 The term 'farm' system refers to the development programme of teams in the minor leagues with an affiliation to the Major League Baseball organization. The farm system as it is recognized in baseball today was the brainchild of Branch Rickey in 1916. Rickey is the former St Louis Cardinals' field manager, general manager and club president.

5 The 30 teams in Major League Baseball are split into two leagues of 15 teams each, the American League and the National League.

6 The Cardinals were founded in 1882 as an American Association Team called the St Louis Brown Stockings. The team changed its name to the St Louis Browns in 1883. In 1892, the team moved to the National League. In 1899, the name was changed to the Perfectos, and in 1900, the team become known as the St Louis Cardinals.

7 Dale Carnegie [accessed 20 June 2016] The Importance of Employee Engagement [Online] www.dalecarnegie.com/employee-engagement/engaged-employees-infographic/.

8 *Harvard Business Review* (2016) [accessed 15 June 2016] The Impact of Employee Engagement on Performance [Online] https://Hbr.org/resources/pdfs/comm/achievers/hbr_achievers_report_sep13.pdf.

Inside the Mariinsky – the Kirov

10

What makes the Mariinsky Theatre a performance powerhouse?

For more than two centuries the city of St Petersburg has produced some of the world's finest performers in the arts. The city is home to the Mariinsky Theatre (housing the Kirov ballet and opera companies), the Vaganova Ballet Academy and the St Petersburg Conservatory. These three great institutions form a nexus of excellence that defines the city's place at the centre of the modern-day classical arts world.

The greatest artistes of their day have all graced the rehearsal studios and stages of the Mariinsky and Vaganova. The outstanding operatic voices of Ivan Yershov, Fyodor Chaliapin and Sofia Preobrazhenskaya honed their skills here. The roll of honour at the Vaganova is a checklist of some of the greatest ballet dancers of all time. Anna Pavlova, Vaslav Nijinsky, Rudolf Nureyev and Mikhail Baryshnikov are included in the famous names who learned their trade there. The orchestra of the Mariinsky is recognized as one of the finest in Europe and has trained generations of outstanding conductors, developing what came to be known as the 'Russian school of conducting'. The Mariinsky Theatre was the birthplace of numerous operas and ballets regarded as masterpieces of the 19th and 20th centuries. *Swan Lake*, *The Nutcracker*, *The Snow Maiden*, *The Maid of Pskov* and *Sleeping Beauty* are just some of the classics that had their world premiere here.

The Mariinsky is a unique cultural force in the world of arts. The ambassadorial role it has, and continues to play, on behalf of Russian culture is unrivalled and acknowledged the world over. When it comes to the arts, the Mariinsky (Kirov), Vaganova and St Petersburg Conservatory combine to be a performance powerhouse.

Figure 10.1 The Mariinsky (Kirov) Powerhouse Performance model

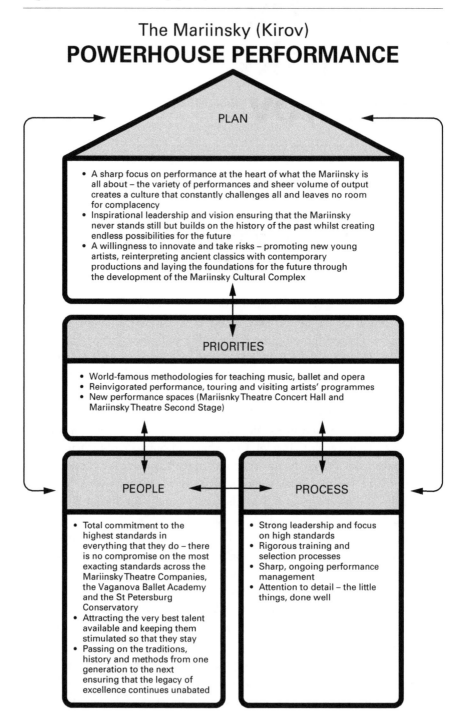

The Mariinsky (Kirov)
POWERHOUSE PERFORMANCE

PLAN

- A sharp focus on performance at the heart of what the Mariinsky is all about – the variety of performances and sheer volume of output creates a culture that constantly challenges all and leaves no room for complacency
- Inspirational leadership and vision ensuring that the Mariinsky never stands still but builds on the history of the past whilst creating endless possibilities for the future
- A willingness to innovate and take risks – promoting new young artists, reinterpreting ancient classics with contemporary productions and laying the foundations for the future through the development of the Mariinsky Cultural Complex

PRIORITIES

- World-famous methodologies for teaching music, ballet and opera
- Reinvigorated performance, touring and visiting artists' programmes
- New performance spaces (Mariisnky Theatre Concert Hall and Mariinsky Theatre Second Stage)

PEOPLE

- Total commitment to the highest standards in everything that they do – there is no compromise on the most exacting standards across the Mariinsky Theatre Companies, the Vaganova Ballet Academy and the St Petersburg Conservatory
- Attracting the very best talent available and keeping them stimulated so that they stay
- Passing on the traditions, history and methods from one generation to the next ensuring that the legacy of excellence continues unabated

PROCESS

- Strong leadership and focus on high standards
- Rigorous training and selection processes
- Sharp, ongoing performance management
- Attention to detail – the little things, done well

The Mariinsky (Kirov) powerhouse

Jewel in the crown of the arts world

St Petersburg is a stunning place. A stroll along the boulevards of the city is like walking through an open-air museum. It is impossible not to be taken in by the magnificent beauty of the place. The architecture is spectacular and the splendour of the city ranks it as one of the most beautiful in the world along with Paris and Rome. It is a fitting home for the jewel in the crown of the arts world that is the Mariinsky Theatre.

Figure 10.2 Facade of the Mariinsky Theatre, St Petersburg, Russia

SOURCE: Keith Levit

In 1738 a decree from Catherine the Great established the Imperial Theatre School at the city's Winter Palace. The decree called for the establishment of a theatre to 'manage performances and music', stating that 'the Russian theatre needs not just comedies and tragedies, but opera too'. The school opened with 24 students – 12 boys and 12 girls. The founding director, French ballet master Jean-Baptiste Landé was tasked with training the students to form the first Russian ballet company. The Imperial Russian Ballet was formed with these students graduating into it and since then the two have been inextricably linked. The school and ballet company quickly developed a strong reputation. Both have gone through name changes since their original founding. To this day, the Kirov ballet and opera companies are world-famous names inextricably linked to excellence in these classical art forms. However, whilst they are most commonly referred to as the Kirov, the companies are officially known as the Mariinsky ballet and opera companies. Both are run by and located at the world-famous Mariinsky Theatre located at the heart of St Petersburg.

Teaching the world to dance

The ballet school also continues to be linked to the Mariinsky. It is now called the Vaganova Ballet Academy, named after the influential Agrippina Vaganova. In the 1920s she consolidated the Italian, French and Russian styles of ballet into a methodical training approach. She published *Basic Principles of Classical Ballet* in 1934, outlining her training system for dancers. This has become known worldwide as the Vaganova method and has served as the basis for training ever since. The Vaganova method emphasizes beauty and expressiveness of the *port de bras* – literally, the 'carriage of the arms' – placing a strong emphasis on preserving the artistry and soulfulness of the performer. She believed that great ballet dancers are artists, not athletes. The method is distinctive for its focus on the total involvement of every part of the person in every movement. Vaganova's philosophy is that there is a connection between the arms, hands, upper body, eyes and facial expressions that are central to the grace of movement of a great ballet dancer. Whilst other ballet schools focus on the legs and feet, the full body focus of the Vaganova Academy is a trademark that sets their dancers apart – that, and an unrelenting focus on striving for excellence. The walls of the stairwells in the building are a shrine to the graduates who have passed through these famous corridors, with plaques hanging on every floor honouring their time at the academy.

The long journey that takes 40 steps

The Rimsky-Korsakov St Petersburg State Conservatory is located directly opposite the Mariinsky on the far side of the road in Theatre Square. It was founded in 1862 by the famous pianist and composer Anton Rubinstein. The conservatory was founded to train and educate the most talented Russian musicians to perfect their art. An influential member of the faculty in its early years was the great Nikolay Rimsky-Korsakov, who established a school of composition that produced some of the world's greatest composers including Pyotr Tchaikovsky, Sergei Prokofiev and Dmitri Shostakovich. In 1944, the conservatory was named in homage to the genius and contribution of Rimsky-Korsakov in establishing its reputation for excellence. The conservatory currently has six faculties – composition and conducting, piano, orchestral instruments, voice and stage directing, musicology and folk instruments. It employs approximately 400 teachers, providing an education for 1,300 students. Graduates of the school are sought after around the world. The best students graduate into the Mariinsky Opera Company and complete the journey across the road. It is a mere 40 metres from the entrance of the conservatory to the doors of the Mariinsky, but for the aspiring graduates they know that only the very best will take the famous 40 steps. It is a tough journey to take and one paved with dedication and hard work.

These three institutions – the Mariinsky Theatre (comprising ballet and opera), the Vaganova Academy and the St Petersburg Conservatory – form a nexus of excellence that defines the city's place at the centre of the modern-day classical arts world.

The Mariinsky can never become like a museum

The Mariinsky Theatre has been led since 1988 by general and artistic director Valery Gergiev. His leadership has seen a renaissance in the reputation of the Mariinsky over this time. The ballet company has always maintained its world-class reputation as the foremost ballet company in the world – and he has sought to ensure that the opera and its associated orchestra matched this high quality. Through balancing respect for the tradition of the theatre with willingness to innovate he has presided over a period that has seen both match the unrivalled quality of the Kirov Ballet. His philosophy is simple: 'The Mariinsky can never become like a museum: frozen in time but lifeless.'[1] He has challenged the status quo and in doing so he has masterminded a period that has seen the production output of the companies increase; presented classical Russian operas in a vibrant, fresh manner; introduced the annual international 'Stars of the White Night Festival'; established international links with many of the world's great opera houses; developed an international touring programme and residencies totalling more than 200 performances a year; and built two modern new performance spaces – the Mariinsky Theatre Concert Hall and the Mariinsky Theatre Second Stage (Mariinsky II).

Figure 10.3 Second (New) Mariinsky Theatre, St Petersburg, Russia

SOURCE: Victor Karasev

The old theatre, which has been a landmark feature of the St Petersburg landscape since 1859, is the golden jewel at the centre of this cultural utopia. The distinctive pastel-green exterior makes it stand out amongst the beautiful architecture of the city. Inside, the crystal chandeliers, classical columns and gold stucco interior make it a must-see for anyone who visits St Petersburg. This classical building is now connected via a footbridge to the modern, glass-based exterior of the Second Stage, the first Russian opera house to be built since the Czars. Mariinsky II, as it is colloquially referred to, is one of the largest theatre and concert venues in the world. Covering almost 80,000 square metres and holding an audience of 2,000, the auditorium is equipped with the latest technology and features perfect acoustics. With its modern glass facade it is a mix of old and new. The third venue, the Mariinsky Concert Hall, opened in 2007; it caters for 1,100 patrons and is across the street from the old Mariinsky Theatre and Mariinsky II. It is built on the site of the old set workshops that were badly damaged in a fire in 2003. The three performance spaces combine to form a unique cultural complex in which Gergiev has successfully married the old and the new. He has created a platform for the Mariinsky Theatre companies to showcase their work: 'The new theatres open up new and incredible possibilities for us all. I truly believe that.'

Pavel Smelkov is one of the Mariinsky opera and symphony conductors and composers. Like virtually all of the members of the opera and orchestra company he is a graduate of the St Petersburg Rimsky-Korsakov Conservatory across the road. He discusses how the Mariinsky has become so great: 'There is a culture of excellence that permeates everything that is done here.' He pays homage to Gergiev – it is noticeable how much he is revered by the staff within the company and is consistently referred to as 'Maestro Gergiev' – for the leadership he has brought to the company during his tenure: 'It is important to have a great leader at the heart of the company. He has set the vision for what we want to be and fostered an environment that adheres to the highest standards possible.' The leadership of Gergiev is an example of the importance of renewal for sustained success. History is littered with institutions and businesses that once led their field but did not last.

> The enduring high performers are those who build on their record and continually strive to improve. They are not afraid to challenge the status quo, whilst respecting the factors that made them succeed in the first place. This demands brave leadership.

Feeding off the environment

Smelkov goes on to explain how the orchestra operates. The orchestra company comprises approximately 300 musicians. There is a rigorous entry test to gain one of the much-coveted places within the company. Each new member of the orchestra begins with a one-year probation period. On average, 80 per cent of those who are accepted survive past the probation period: 'It is not a foregone conclusion. You must demonstrate in that first year that you have the requisite performance standards to uphold the quality of the orchestra.' The main intake for the orchestra comes, as Smelkov did, from the St Petersburg Conservatory: 'The 250-year-old history of the institution means that it is rooted in the tradition and culture of the greatest musicians of the past. The professors of music who teach there are at the highest possible standards. It is a substantial education and those who graduate follow in the footsteps of the likes of Tchaikovsky.'

Smelkov highlights the different criteria they are looking for in a potential recruit for the orchestra. There are five primary components:

- Style: how they play their instrument.

- How they perform: Smelkov says you can tell as soon as they start playing if they have 'it'.

- Team player: someone who can fit into the structure of the team within the orchestra.

- Communicative and creative: a musician who displays the capability to express themselves and an openness to new ideas.

- Attentive to direction: someone who displays all of the above criteria but who will also be comfortable within the structures of the orchestra and under the leadership of the conductor.

Similarly, there is a tough audition process for budding opera singers to join the company. The initial selection group for audition is drawn from a wide list – many will be graduates from the conservatory, many others from further afield. Scouting exercises are done all the time for potential recruits – and modern technology assists in the process. For example, potential candidates can be viewed online via YouTube before being invited to audition. The same criteria are applied to opera singers as to orchestra musicians and ballet dancers. 'We are looking for strong characters and personality that shines through in how they perform', says Smelkov. 'We obviously only look at those who are technically outstanding too but the "*X factor*" comes in the form of their performance.'

New entrants to the orchestra and opera companies quickly pick up on what is required to succeed. As Smelkov noted, 'Once they join the company they are immersed in the environment surrounding them and naturally feed off that.'

The principle of maintaining a narrow performance gap was highlighted in the Curtis Institute of Music (Chapter 6) and is evident in so many of the powerhouses we have studied. This tough selection process is how the Mariinsky maintain a tight performance gap.

It is all about performance

Dr Leonid Gakkel is a professor of music at the St Petersburg Conservatory and a world-renowned musical critic. He is well placed to provide an assessment as to why the Mariinsky is held in such high regard internationally. He is unequivocal that 'the Mariinsky/Kirov sets itself apart based on the uncompromising quality of its productions and the massive repertoire it undertakes. The company has created a prodigious 87 productions in the

Figure 10.4 Mariinsky Theatre, Tchaikovsky Opera – Pikovaya drama – artists bow at the end of the play. Among the artists, Maestro Gergiev

SOURCE: Oleg Proskurin

decade from 2002 to 2012. The output of the Mariinsky is simply on a level higher than that of anywhere else. And yet the quality of these productions is never compromised. They are of the highest possible standards.'

This is an important part of the philosophy of the Mariinsky Theatre. Pavel Smelkov explained further: 'Our core focus is on the production. It is all about the performance. That is the most important thing and it is what this institution is all about.' He further explains that the work output is a key driver in maintaining the high standards: 'Every year we put on six or seven operas (premieres) and two to three ballets. This provides a constant challenge for everyone in the company to maintain standards and not allow complacency to set in. Everything is done to the best professional standards at all times. It means we are always busy, always working and always focused on our work.' As other companies are embroiled in internal difficulties – for example the recent scandal at the Bolshoi Ballet where the artistic director Sergei Filin was the victim of an acid attack that almost blinded him, orchestrated by members of the troupe – Smelkov notes: 'At the Mariinsky we are too busy working to have time to get involved in scandals or egos!' The clarity of focus provided by this philosophy is a cornerstone of high performance. At the Kirov they are clear about what matters most – putting on productions. In other powerhouses the same level of clarity is evident. For example, at Southwest Airlines it is driving on-time performance, customer satisfaction and return on invested capital; at Grameen Bank it is providing financial support to villagers to eradicate poverty; at Médecins Sans Frontières it is serving the medical needs of the communities they support, wherever they are; while in Finland it is providing an equal, high quality education to all.

Each builds a strategy for winning, centred around the sharp focus on what they believe matters most in driving their performance. They define this clearly and explicitly, ensure everyone understands it and then challenge people to continually push the boundaries of what great looks like.

> One of the core principles of high performing is to focus ruthlessly on the things that matter most and set out a clear game plan for driving excellence in whatever that is.

The sheer scale of output from the Mariinsky also explains how it has retained its talent over the years. Any performer at the Kirov is in demand across the best ballet and opera companies in the world. In many cases, they could follow more lucrative careers, financially, if they took up positions elsewhere.

However, the variety of performance options available at the Mariinsky acts as a significant factor in the decision of these artists to stay where they are. It is a much more stimulating and challenging environment to be continuously taking up new roles, compared with many international companies where they would be required to perform a single role for a considerable period of time. The Mariinsky is a culture that fosters continual artistic growth.

The core of what the artists at the Mariinsky are about is performing. The environment is set up to ensure that they are always focused on this. Keeping people focused on what matters most, and repeatedly holding them to account to deliver the highest possible standards is a recurring theme in performance powerhouses from which managers in business can learn. It drives consistent outperformance versus the competition, and is also key to retaining top talent.

High performers thrive in an environment where they are challenged to stay at the top. They enjoy being surrounded by other high performers. They flourish in environments that place this as a priority. It is no coincidence that in every powerhouse example referenced in this book, the best people stay. They recognize the draw of a culture that demands constant growth and learning. They don't want to go anywhere else because they know they will not be challenged as much elsewhere.

Keeping the flame lit

The high standards of performance are maintained through a combination of the large repertoire and continued internal competition for places within the company. For example, there are three orchestras active at all times at the Mariinsky. The top group works with artistic director Gergiev. They tour internationally – indeed the touring programme has increased considerably under Gergiev's leadership with some 30 countries visited since 2005 – and make official Mariinsky recordings. The second and third orchestra groups work on operas, ballets and other performances. Options exist to shift people between the three orchestra groups depending on their performance levels. If a musician's standards drop or if they become tired then they will be shifted from the top group to one of the other groups. The musicians typically are on one-year rolling contracts. In exceptional circumstances longer-term contracts are offered. This ensures that there is a constant performance pressure within the company. In the same way that the New Zealand All Blacks rugby players are under pressure to keep their place on the team, the performers within the Mariinsky understand that there simply is no room for complacency.

Pavel Smelkov summarizes the key to the success of the Mariinsky with four simple principles:

1 Find the best of the best. The company is made up of the very best dancers, musicians, singers and performers: 'We only recruit the highest calibre into the company.' This is consistent with our principle of keeping a narrow performance gap.

2 Ensure people work hard and deliver the best: 'If they are not delivering we replace them with people who do. This is driven by the massive performance workload and combined with an unrelenting focus on the highest possible standards in all we do.' The Powerhouse Principle of clarity of focus is evident in this philosophy.

3 Keep the traditions of the theatre alive whilst staying open to modern influences: 'We are all acutely aware of the people who have gone before us. It is our duty to ensure we honour them through our performances, yet seek new ways of producing these works to make them relevant to modern-day society. Traditions – like a tree – grow from the ground.' This links directly to our Powerhouse Performance model. Always looking to improve, never standing still and continually improving is at the heart of this.

4 Strong leadership, driven by Maestro Gergiev: 'He sets the tone in terms of a phenomenal work rate, stamina and inspiration, which galvanizes all of us at the Mariinsky.' The culture set by the leaders influences how people perform. The Mariinsky Way is defined by this (and is replicated in all the performance powerhouses).

Attention to detail

The Vaganova Academy is housed a few kilometres from the Mariinsky Theatre on Rossi Street in a building designed by the Italian architect Carlo Rossi. Viewed from the outside it is impossible to distinguish it from the other neoclassical structures enclosed by delicate parks. There is no hint from the exterior of what lies within. Once we step inside the modest entrance door, however, the world of classical ballet training opens up. The building is home to some 20 dance studios, where the 300 or more aspiring students ranging from 10–19 years of age are put through their paces by a faculty of over 100 teaching staff (dance, piano and academic). Competition for places within the Vaganova is intense. Thousands of 10-year-old hopefuls attend auditions on an annual basis under the watchful eyes of Altynai Asylmuratova, the artistic director. A former prima ballerina of the Kirov herself, she retired at the age of 39 to concentrate on teaching. She graduated through the Vaganova and was an exceptional artist with perfect technical schooling. It is her job now to guide these young dancers to follow in her footsteps. Of the approximately 3,000 auditionees, a mere 70 or so are chosen. Once the dream begins, however, they face a tough, long road ahead. Less than half of them will go on to graduate and fewer still to secure coveted positions in the Mariinsky (Kirov) Ballet company itself. Only the very best of them will make it as soloists. Those who graduate but are not selected for the Mariinsky will seek work elsewhere, such as with the Bolshoi or the Royal Ballet. A Vaganova education is valued by the best of the rest of the ballet companies in the world.

The dance teachers are all trained to the highest standards and are steeped in the Vaganova technique and traditions. In the same way that students must meet exacting criteria for entry, so too must the teachers. They are not allowed into the dance studios or classrooms otherwise. Typically, they were trained at the Vaganova themselves, performed to the highest levels as professional ballet dancers in their own right and are highly skilled tutors. They pull no punches with their students. As Asylmuratova notes: 'It is tough but it is the best ballet training available anywhere in the world.' Even for the very best dancers the learning never stops.

Mo Mozeliak, general manager of the St Louis Cardinals, talks of the small things done well. The same mantra is repeated at the Vaganova.

Passing on the torch

There is a tradition of the best ballerinas becoming coaches to the younger dancers as they approach the end of their own illustrious careers. Asylmuratova is a case in point. She started to work as a teacher towards the end of her own dancing career and dedicated herself fully to this new role at a relatively young age, 39. The philosophy is that dancers devote themselves to the art form and therefore they have a responsibility to pass on their knowledge to the future stars of ballet dancing. It is in this way that the Vaganova maintains the traditions and standards over the years. There is an endless supply of knowledge passing from one generation to the next. The magic of the Vaganova – its methods and commitment to the very highest standards – is kept alive through the continuity of keeping involved those who have been through the system. As one of these teachers observed: 'Our knowledge and skill are like ripe fruit waiting to be picked.' The depth of the coaching system of the Vaganova School and the Mariinsky Theatre are unrivalled elsewhere in the world.

The relationship that develops between student and teacher is a very close one. They spend many hours alone together in the dance studios of the school, honing and perfecting their technique. There is a lot of one-to-one interaction. The teachers see their role as that of an artist moulding a beautiful statue out of each of their students. In many cases they develop close bonds – almost like that of a parent. The responsibility of the teachers is enshrined in the culture of the school and theatre. When a dancer gives a bad performance it reflects on the person who trained that dancer. It is this tight relationship between teacher and student, along with the sense of duty and responsibility to shape raw diamonds into beautiful gemstones, that is the cornerstone of the Kirov world.

In New Zealand the All Blacks speak of the requirement to leave the jersey in a better place for the next man. This mentality is evident in how the ballerinas pass on the torch to the next generation.

Poetry in motion

The training method established by Agrippina Vaganova is the foundation upon which the fortress that the school has become is built. The training is careful and slow. The dancers learn to perform the movements at a leisurely pace, over and over again, until they understand it completely. The body acts like a memory bank storing the movements until they become second nature, programmed into their muscles. As this effect takes hold, the pace of the movement is sped up. The end result is a dancer in total command of her body. There is nothing mechanical about these dancers. Their bodies are in perfect harmony with their expressions, their souls. It is literally poetry in motion. This is what sets the Kirov dancer apart from others around the world. A Kirov dancer in full flow is an amazing sight. There is a magic of fire that fills the stage.

Ultimately, Altynai Asylmuratova judges her budding ballerinas on how they perform under the spotlight of the stage: 'The performance reveals a lot about the dancers – a talented dancer can appear pale and nervous on stage and a shy child can become a shining star. The best way to gauge how well the intense training is working is by seeing them perform. This will give us a true barometer of their real progress as dancers.'

Music is our one and true monarch

For all involved in the Mariinsky Theatre, there is a special pull to the insti-tution. Gergiev is equally clear that the Mariinsky's aura is a critical factor in attracting the very best talent to the company. 'Why are the greats of the world attracted to play here?' he asks. He sees that part of his responsibility as artistic director is to ensure that this sense of enchantment is maintained: 'We must continue to capture the magic of the Mariinsky to inspire the greatest performers to continue to work here.' At the heart of this lies a deep connection to a calling, a sense of purpose for what the Mariinsky is all about. 'Music is our one and true monarch. Its eternal rebirth, the fact that it continues to resound in people's souls and hearts, filling the air of auditoriums in theatres and concert halls – all this is the meaning and task of our work', says Maestro Gergiev. Pavel Smelkov succinctly sums this up: 'Meaning for us is a matter of fact; the Mariinsky is the Mariinsky.'

Resilience

The citizens of St Petersburg are equally inspired by the notion of meaning associated with the Mariinsky. The theatre might have died immediately after the Russian Revolution in 1918 – it seemed inevitable that the Mariinsky, so closely linked to the Tzar and the ruling elite, would be destroyed and disappear into history in the post-revolution fallout. Yet somehow the Mariinsky was not only saved, but flourished under the new regime. Lenin was persuaded by Anatoly Lunacharsky, his first Commissar for Education and a former champion dancer in his own right, that the arts should belong to the people rather than the ruling elite, as they had done before. The city embraced the Mariinsky. It became a place for Russians to escape to and find expression in their pent-up feelings, and where they could allow their emotions to explode. They protected it; they couldn't let it die – or they might die too. The resilience of the people of St Petersburg was evident too in the Second World War. The city was surrounded by German troops and almost starved over a 900-day period. Many citizens lost their lives. However, St Petersburg survived and the cultural footprint that characterizes this wonderful city, and is really precious to its people, was at the heart of the recovery process. This strength of its meaning to its citizens ensured that after the collapse of the Soviet empire in the 1990s the Mariinsky would continue to survive and thrive. A more open outlook post-perestroika has been embraced by Valery Gergiev and has led to more international visitors, exchange programmes, touring and a spirit of innovation evidenced by the championing of young, talented artists and the revival of classical works.

The resilience displayed by the Mariinsky and the people of St Petersburg is relevant to our discussion on performance powerhouses. They display a level of organizational resilience that helps set them apart from their peers and has allowed them to sustain their position as leaders in their field over several decades. We explore further the principle of organizational resilience at the end of this chapter.

Stronger than ever

It is 2 May 2014, opening night for the new Mariinsky Theatre. A stunning gala performance marks a new dawn in the history of this famous institution. The new centrepiece of the Mariinsky Cultural Complex, Mariinsky II is crammed full with a star-studded audience resplendent in black ties and evening gowns. Vladimir Putin, the Russian President, opens the proceedings, which are being broadcast live on state television. The gala performance features dozens of spectacular pieces, showcasing the full range of talent across the Mariinsky's companies – opera, ballet, orchestra, chorus and youth ensembles. Young and old, current and future stars – it is a stunning evening.

Over the following three days the stages of the old Mariinsky Theatre, Mariinsky II and the Mariinsky Theatre Concert Hall play host to a celebration of the great traditions of the old institution, whilst acknowledging the dawning of a new era that confirms St Petersburg and the Mariinsky amongst the leading centres of culture in the world. Nowhere else combines ballet, opera and orchestra – as well as schools for the arts at this elite level – to this standard. The line of tradition that brought the world Tchaikovsky, Shostakovich, Nureyev, Baryshnikov and the world premiere of classics such as *The Nutcracker* is as strong as it ever was. The Mariinsky (or Kirov) truly is home to some of the world's great performing artists.

Powerhouse Principle 9: resilience

Resilience is a topic that is gaining more focus as the pace of change and levels of stress in the modern world increase. Programmes are being introduced in companies to help individual employees to develop and strengthen their skills to cope with these strains and to become more resilient. In the last year or so we have seen several clients introduce employee welfare programmes designed to address this issue explicitly. However, few if any programmes focus on developing resilience at an organizational level. Yet our research shows that the capability of high-performance organizations to be resilient is a critical defining characteristic.

Understanding what is meant by organizational resilience is a good starting point. It is often thought of as the organization's ability to 'bounce back' when things do not go as planned. We prefer to work with a broader definition – one that includes organizational capabilities to: 1) anticipate (and prevent, if possible) negative events; 2) to adapt to circumstances as they develop; and 3) to emerge stronger from whatever events unfold.

Anticipating events – the importance of getting ahead of the curve

Corporate history is full of stories of once-great companies that were blindsided by events that led to their downfalls. Jim Collins, the author of business bestsellers *Good to Great* (2001) and *Built to Last* (1994), gave us many examples of businesses that were at the tops of their games at the time of writing, but which have subsequently failed. For example, Circuit City, the electronics retailer, went bankrupt; and Fannie Mae, the mortgage lender, collapsed and almost brought the global financial system down with it. The subsequent decline of these institutions led him to write a follow-up book, *How the Mighty Fall* (2009). He pointed to hubris born of success, lack of discipline, and denial of risk and peril as root causes of the failure of these once great enterprises. Our finding is that high performance organizations proactively guard against these dangers. They develop the capability to reinvent themselves as circumstances demand: to flex their strategies or core business models before they become obsolete; to ride the waves of change continually rather than react to them when they are already under water and to ask themselves testing questions about how to stay ahead of the competition. In this way they do not need to develop the skill to 'bounce back' as they are always busy driving forward.

Developing this idea further, we often hear leaders speak with pride about how their organizations are at their best in times of crisis, when heroes emerge from the shadows, everyone goes the extra mile, and remedial and/or coping actions are taken quickly to keep the show on the road. As a matter of fact we have never heard a single leader argue the opposite of his or her team and, human nature being what it is, we are sure that

▶

crisis usually *does* bring out the best in organizations. However, we would argue that judging resilience based on crisis performance is an example of not seeing the wood for the trees. High-performance organizations, while they also perform well in times of crisis, tend to have much fewer crises in the first place.

Effective risk management is at the core of minimizing the incidence of crisis. In practice, however, we find too often that risk management is a peripheral, bureaucratic activity focused on cataloguing the list of things that might go wrong, and then reducing the length of the list by addressing first those that are easiest. Furthermore, identification and evaluation of risks tends to be in the context of what the organization is doing today rather than what it aspires to do tomorrow – avoiding obstacles rather than enabling growth.

High-performance risk management is fundamentally different. Its focus is much more strategic and it is managed in the context of what the organization aspires to achieve. The job of high-performance risk managers is about identifying the biggest obstacles to winning and facilitating leadership teams in proactively addressing these ahead of time. It is also about identifying and tracking leading indicators – both internal and external to the organization – that give early warning as to potential setbacks that might arise in the business's journey. Finally, it is about designing and practising strategies for avoiding (in the first instance) or coping (in the second) with these setbacks in order to minimize their impact.

The best organizations in the world tend also to be the most resilient. However, their capability is often understated and hard for outsiders to discern. Building high-performance risk management as a strategic capability is vital to building resilience and is a must-do for leaders who want their organizations to win.

Adapting to circumstances – things go wrong, cope with it!

No matter how well any business plans ahead or anticipates negative events, they will still occur. What defines a resilient organization is how it deals with these events. A world-class sports coach once told us how he interpreted this message: 'We might lose a game now and then, but as long as we never lose our collective spirit we will come back.' It is the same within organizations. The ability to recover rapidly from setbacks is critical.

This is achieved by keeping a clear focus on the bigger picture and, where required, adapting plans to reflect changed circumstances. In a previous

Powerhouse Principle (see Chapter 2) we discussed the importance of ambition as a starting point for high performance. Resilient organizations do not allow ambition to be diminished in the wake of setbacks. Quite the opposite, they use setbacks as prompts to recommit. At the same time, however, they are not afraid to alter their pathways to getting there. Accordingly, they maintain both the commitment and the capacity to innovate or flex their approaches (new ideas, behaviours, paradigms) for realizing their overall ambitions. Therefore, when things inevitably do not go to plan, the consequences are neither cataclysmic nor fatal. These organizations are already conditioned to challenge the best paths towards their ultimate goals, and setbacks act merely to reinforce this discipline.

Emerging stronger – what doesn't kill me...

Martin Seligman is a founding father of the principle of positive psychology.[2] His belief is that those who thrive in personal (and business) dimensions are people who possess an optimistic outlook on life and the events that befall them. In some this is innate, in others it is a learnt skill. The critical distinction in his view is centred on one's beliefs about adversity. By quickly and decisively dealing with the emotional consequences of adversity and dispelling unrealistic beliefs, one is capable of responding to the setback in a positive manner.

The same is true of organizations. By acknowledging negative events – ie not being stubbornly in denial – but then quickly moving to a positive mindset, organizations recover rapidly and emerge as stronger entities on the other side. The Mariinsky is an example of this, especially under the leadership of Valery Gergiev. We will also see this very tangibly in our study of the Toyota Motor Corporation in Chapter 13.

We highlighted the importance of 'power of purpose' at the end of the Médecins Sans Frontières story (Chapter 3). This is also critical when it comes to organizational resilience. The ability to stay on track and withstand anything thrown at us is greatly enhanced when we are working in an environment with a visceral powerful purpose at its core. This is clearly demonstrated by the people at MSF. Without revisiting the principle again, we highlight it as the final element in developing organizational resilience.

Focusing on developing resilience as a core organizational strength should be on the agenda for any aspiring high-performance operation.

Notes

1 Lisa Kirk Colburn (producer) and Joshua Waltezky (director) (2005) *Sacred Stage: The Mariinsky Theatre* (Documentary), Red Fire Films, United States.

2 Martin Seligman (2002) *Authentic Happiness: Using the new positive psychology to realize your potential for lasting fulfilment*, Simon and Schuster, New York.

11

New Zealand rugby

Better people make better All Blacks

What makes the New Zealand All Blacks a performance powerhouse?

That the New Zealand All Blacks are the best team in world rugby is not in doubt. The statistics speak for themselves. Since 2003 they have played 157 tests. They have won 137, drawn 2 and lost a mere 18. That is a success rate of 87.26 per cent. The next best team in international rugby is South Africa at approximately 61 per cent. Of the other test-playing countries, only Australia and France stand with winning records above 50 per cent. Moreover, New Zealand dominate all formats of the game, not just the men's game. The women's team 'The Black Ferns' has an 87.31 per cent winning record with only England and the United States ever beating them in a test match. The New Zealand Under 20 team has an 86.6 per cent winning record in the Under 20 World Championship, having won all of their first 21 games in this event which was established in 2008. The All Blacks Sevens team is by some distance the most successful international team in the short format of the game. How has a small nation with a population of less than 5 million people come to dominate the sport of rugby union to such an extent? How have the All Blacks become a performance powerhouse?

Figure 11.1 New Zealand All Blacks Powerhouse Performance model

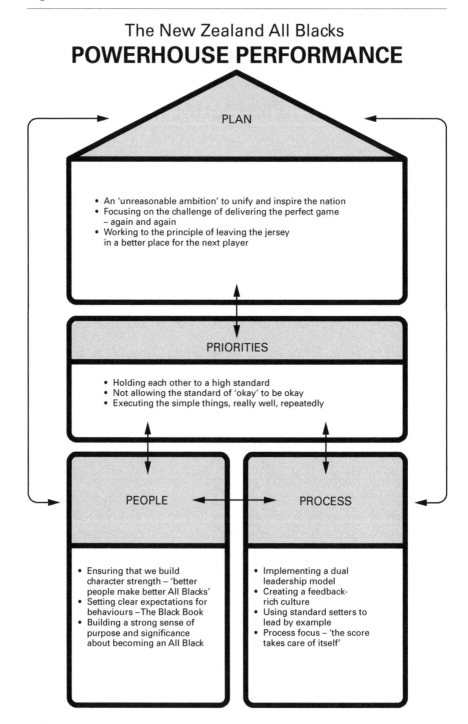

The New Zealand All Blacks
POWERHOUSE PERFORMANCE

PLAN

- An 'unreasonable ambition' to unify and inspire the nation
- Focusing on the challenge of delivering the perfect game – again and again
- Working to the principle of leaving the jersey in a better place for the next player

PRIORITIES

- Holding each other to a high standard
- Not allowing the standard of 'okay' to be okay
- Executing the simple things, really well, repeatedly

PEOPLE

- Ensuring that we build character strength – 'better people make better All Blacks'
- Setting clear expectations for behaviours –The Black Book
- Building a strong sense of purpose and significance about becoming an All Black

PROCESS

- Implementing a dual leadership model
- Creating a feedback-rich culture
- Using standard setters to lead by example
- Process focus – 'the score takes care of itself'

BELONG

TEAM ALL BLACKS

SOURCE: Rafael Ben-Ari

The New Zealand All Blacks powerhouse

'Unify and inspire New Zealanders'

Rugby Union in New Zealand is like a religion. It dominates the national psyche. Young people have a rugby ball in their hands from the moment they learn to walk. New Zealand Rugby is responsible for supporting, growing and promoting the game as well as managing the All Blacks teams. Steve Tew has been working with New Zealand Rugby for over 15 years and has been CEO since 2008. He sees the role of the organization and the All Blacks teams in simple terms: 'Our vision is to unify and inspire New Zealanders.' He sees rugby union as more than just a sport in New Zealand: 'The game is a vehicle for bringing the country together and this must always be at the core of what we are about.'

This provides a powerful purpose for everyone associated with the All Blacks. It is why, when the country was struck by two national tragedies in the space of three months, rugby union played its part. In 2010, a methane explosion at Pike River Mine in New Zealand's South Island resulted in 29 miners being killed. Soon after, in February 2011, a massive earthquake struck in Christchurch. The quake caused widespread devastation to the country's second-biggest city; 185 died and the economic impact was estimated at NZ$40 billion. The players and staff at New Zealand Rugby provided support to various fundraising and community services campaigns. They visited families affected by the disasters, personally thanked the emergency service personnel and were highly visible in many other ways in the aftermath of both tragedies.

Later that year, in September 2011 New Zealand hosted the Rugby World Cup. The event is held every four years and brings the best rugby union nations of the world together to compete for the William Webb Ellis Trophy. The New Zealand Rugby players and coaches saw this as an opportunity to restore a sense of pride in New Zealand and to catalyse recovery from a dark period in the country's history. They were determined to make this World Cup a truly memorable national experience in two ways: first by organizing and running the event so that it was the most enjoyable sporting event the country had ever witnessed; second by winning the tournament on home soil. They delivered on both counts. The nation united behind the 2011 Rugby World Cup, creating a festival atmosphere that brought everyone together and showcasing the best of New Zealand to the world. 'We were able to show that our mantra of unifying and inspiring the nation was more than just words', Steve Tew noted. 'This was a demonstrable example of what the core of New Zealand rugby is all about and what it means to be an

All Black. Rugby to us is more than just a sport. It is part of the DNA of our country and what brings us all together. This is a belief that is central to all we stand for.'

Leave the jersey in a better place

For any New Zealander, becoming an All Black represents the pinnacle of achievement. When a player is awarded his All Black jersey for the first time, it is a proud moment in his life. Every player we spoke to alluded to the same sentiment and sense of responsibility: 'We must leave the jersey in a better place.' This is something that acts as a personal driver to all of them. Position by position, the players in the current squad namecheck those who have worn their jerseys before them. For example, recently retired captain and talismanic leader, Richie McCaw, widely considered to be one of the best openside flankers of all time, wore the number seven on his back. He inherited this jersey from some of the greatest names in New Zealand rugby history, including players such as Dave Gallaher, Ian Kirkpatrick and Michael Jones. In the same way they did for him, McCaw's job was to pass his jersey on to the next man, in a better state than when he got it.

Figure 11.3 The New Zealand All Blacks players perform the haka – a traditional war cry, dance or challenge from the Maori people of New Zealand. It has been performed by the New Zealand All Blacks before every international test match since 1905

SOURCE: JeanFrancois Beausejour/CC BY

Each player is able to produce a similar list of great men who have worn his jersey before him. All understand the privilege and honour that comes with being an All Black and they are determined, to a man, to ensure that they leave the legacy enhanced for their successors. This is a powerful motivating factor that drives their unquenchable thirst for the highest standards of performance.

The notions of '*unify and inspire the nation*' and '*leave the jersey in a better place*' are examples of how the All Blacks develop a deep-rooted sense of purpose. Purpose is a powerful concept when it comes to performance. As we explained in more detail in the Médecins Sans Frontières example (Chapter 3), a precondition for getting people to perform consistently at their best and give discretionary effort comes from having a powerful purpose. It cannot be taken for granted.

> Developing a strong sense of purpose is critical for any organization aspiring for high performance. It needs to be clear, it needs to connect for people, and it needs to be reinforced in practical ways all the time.

The standard of 'okay' is not okay!

The Maori language is native to New Zealand and is an important part of the heritage of the nation. There is an ancient Maori proverb that reads, *Whāia te iti kuhurangi; ki te tuoku koe, me he maunga teitei* – 'Aim for the highest cloud, so that if you miss it, you will hit a lofty mountain.'

The All Blacks' way is to hold themselves accountable to the highest possible standards – both on and off the field. For example, on an annual basis New Zealand Rugby publishes, for all to see, an organizational scorecard that rates how well they achieved the goals and targets for the year, along with the targets for the next year. A weighting is given to each of the core strategic goals, and performance in the past year is assessed. In 2013, the organization rated itself at 82 per cent. This was in spite of achieving record-breaking milestones for on-field performance (the first test nation to record a 100 per cent win record over a calendar year) and financial performance (a second successive annual profit, totalling NZ\$2.9 million, versus a target of NZ\$790,000).[1] The report highlighted the fact that they missed targets for player retention and fan engagement. In a country where every move made by the organization is scrutinized, ad nauseam, this level of transparency and honest self-reflection around organizational performance is unusual. Few, if any, international governing bodies in other sports are brave enough to publish their performance ratings in this manner. It is a major factor in ensuring that the organization never ceases to strive for excellence in everything it does.

The same principle is adopted by the players and coaches in the national team. In spite of completing a historic 100 per cent record in 2013 on the back of winning the Rugby World Cup in 2011, they always see room for improvement. The leadership structure within the squad – made up of coaches, players and support staff – speak of operating to a standard of world class, not just good. Darren Shand is the All Blacks team manager, a role he has served in since 2004. 'What really drives us is the constant challenge to play the perfect game and then do it again the following week', Shand says. In other words, the All Blacks look to deliver consistent perfection. This is the Holy Grail they are chasing. As a result, they analyse every performance with a critical eye on what could have been better. Throughout that 14-game, 100 per cent winning season of 2013, the post-game review processes identified areas where improvements could be made.

The standards against which the team holds itself are set from within. 'We look to ourselves to set the standards we aspire to', Shand observes. 'We set our own agenda and don't benchmark ourselves against our competitors.' As the undisputed number one team in the world, this is another core principle that contributes to the All Blacks' pre-eminence. Complacency is the enemy of improvement when you are at the top and so it is crucial that standards are constantly challenged in the pursuit of perfection. No matter how good they get, you sense that the All Blacks will always look to raise the bar further. For the All Blacks, the standard of 'okay' is not okay! The same zealous pursuit of continual improvement is evident in every example listed in this book.

High-performance organizations never settle for good enough. It can always be better. They never stop thinking about ways to improve. They never assume their performance advantage will last unless they focus on how they keep raising standards. It is a constant narrative. It becomes part of the organizational DNA.

There is always someone else to take your place

Selection policy is important in guarding against complacency. The goal is to have a deep well of talent so that there is intense competition for places. This drives standards higher. If any player feels that his place is secure he may lose his edge. However, if he knows that there are two or three players in his position waiting in the wings for the chance to take the coveted jersey then this ensures he is constantly on his game, looking to improve and never feeling safe in the role. It is this edge that helps drive standards across the entire group.

For the All Blacks, in the same way as we saw at the Curtis Institute of Music (see Chapter 6), the performance gap is narrow. When there is a narrow performance gap everyone feels the pressure to continually improve performance. If, as a player, I fear that my place could be taken by someone else if I allow my performance level to drop off, then I am motivated to ensure I do everything to keep my standards as high as possible. It is a deliberate design feature of the high-performance system.

> The same principle of the performance gap applies in business teams. If you manage the team to ensure that there is a tight range of performance level across the team this will drive continued performance improvement. Allow the performance gap to widen across the team and, over time, complacency sets in and performance drops.

The role of standard-setters

The presence of standard-setters among the squad – especially from those perceived leaders who command respect within the group – is a second crucial factor in avoiding complacency. Brad Thorn was such a player. He is one of very few players to have played international rugby in both codes of the game – union and league. Before playing 60 times for the New Zealand All Blacks he played rugby league for Australia, having moved to the country from his native New Zealand at the age of eight. His collection of titles is unique in world rugby and includes the Rugby Union World Cup, Super Rugby, European Cup, New Zealand National Championship, Rugby League World Club, Super League and Australian National League. Thorn was a leader by example and deed. He had a ferocious appetite for training and a sterling work ethic. This was not always the case, however. Brad had to work hard at working hard.

In a revealing video created by James 'Red' McLeod from Whero Films,[2] Thorn was clear about where his drive came from: 'As a kid I was lazy', Thorn revealed. 'In fact, one of my underage coaches told me when I was 14 years of age that in his 15 years as a coach I was the laziest player he had ever coached!' In his mid-teens, his father, who saw his potential, took him aside one day and told him he was sick of driving him to games when he wasn't working hard enough to maximize his potential. 'He said, "Son you're not fit enough. There is a run in the forest I like to do and I want you to do it too. If you don't, I'm not giving you a lift. You can make your own way to places."' This was the wake-up call that changed Thorn's outlook on life. He adopted his father's phrase, 'Champions do extra', and never looked back. 'From that day I never failed to make a representative squad', he recalls.

Brad Thorn was not a hugely vocal leader, but a quiet, indefatigable role model for others. New Zealand rugby has many such leaders within its ranks. The 'lead by example' ethos of the senior players in the team ensures that from the outset new joiners understand what it takes to reach the highest level. Thorn and others understand the role they play in setting standards.

> How many businesses have an explicit conversation with key influencers within the organization about their role as standard-setters? Very few, if any in our experience. Yet it is one of the strongest factors in helping establish the norms that will result in sustained high performance. Make it an explicit 'ask' of those with influence in the organization. Be clear about what the role is of a standard-setter. Agree on what are the standards to be focused on. Ensure the standard-setters lead by example and deed.

Better people make better All Blacks

The All Blacks philosophy places major emphasis on the importance of character as well as talent. They invest time in focusing on the development of the individual as a person, in addition to the technical aspects of their rugby skills. One of the key personal traits they concentrate on is humility. A practical example of this is the practice adopted by the squad at the end of every training session or match. The players take responsibility for making sure that the dressing room (locker room) is cleaned before they leave. No player is too important to perform this menial task. It is as likely that Kieran Read or Sam Whitelock will do this as it is the newest recruit into the squad. It is a visible reminder of the humility that characterizes what an All Black stands for.

The All Blacks legend Brian Lochore was the originator of this ethos. He represented New Zealand 25 times, as player and as captain, before leading the nation as head coach to its first World Cup victory in the inaugural tournament in 1997. He coined the phrase 'better people make better All Blacks'. 'This is another fundamental belief within our system', Steve Tew says. 'The character of the individual is as important as his rugby-playing skills. You can't have one without the other if you want to be regarded as a great All Black.'

In practical terms, this is reflected in the day-to-day manner in which the New Zealand squad goes about its business. In November 2013, on the eve of the match when New Zealand defeated Ireland in the last seconds to achieve the historic landmark of a perfect year, we were in the All Blacks' hotel meeting some of the management team. The players walked around freely in the hotel lobby, chatting casually with visitors and guests. The atmosphere was relaxed. It would not be unreasonable to expect, less than 24 hours before a crucial game, that players would be protected from the prying eyes of eager fans wishing to catch a glimpse of their heroes. In reality, however, they were happy to interact freely with the public, without the need for any security. Darren Shand explains: 'This is an important part of the Brian Lochore mantra. We make a conscious effort everywhere we go to leave a positive impression. We don't want to be locked away in a cocoon in our hotel. We want to mix and stay grounded.'

In the lead-up to every test match, a key part of the week incorporates fostering links between the squad and the local community. Whether the match is on home soil in New Zealand or abroad in the many countries they visit, a community event is organized to facilitate this. It may involve visiting a local charity, or inviting schoolchildren to meet the squad, but whatever the format, it is a genuine engagement with those around them, and something that reminds the players of their responsibilities as human beings over and above those of professional sportsmen. Shand notes: 'The players totally understand the importance of this and participate fully.'

The 14-year-old with a World Cup medal

After winning the 2015 World Cup Final, the players embarked on a well-deserved lap of honour acknowledging the applause of the crowd. A young 14-year-old boy – Charlie Line – caught up in the jubilation of the moment, jumped the advertising hoardings and, with a sidestep that his heroes would have been proud of, evaded the security guards and ran towards the celebrating players. Before he reached the squad he was intercepted with a thumping tackle from an alert steward. The boy crashed to the ground close to New

Zealand's Sonny Bill Williams. Quickly realizing what was happening Sonny Bill intervened and rescued the young boy. He put his arm around the fan and invited him to join the team on the remainder of the lap of honour. Then he returned him to his mother and, in a gesture that left the boy speechless, took off his winners' medal and placed it around the lad's neck. Charlie Line's face lit up with excitement. Sonny Bill Williams headed down the tunnel to continue the celebrations with his team, without the medal he had spent his sporting life working hard to win. Later, when the boy attempted to reunite the medal with its rightful owner, Sonny Bill simply shrugged his shoulders and said, 'It's not mine now, it's yours.' When asked by the press later why he did it Sonny Bill was typically matter of fact: 'I was walking around doing a lap of honour with the boys and a young fella came running out and he got smoked by the security guard, like full-on tackled him. I felt sorry for the little fella. I just picked up the kid and took him back to his old lady and tried to make the night more memorable for him. Better for the medal to be hanging around his neck than mine.' Even in the midst of celebrating the greatest achievement of their lives, All Blacks players displayed extraordinary humility. Better people make better All Blacks!

Increasingly organizations have come to the realization that behaviours matter. A real insight from our research for this book is the extent to which the institutions we have studied consider values and behaviours to be at the heart of their performance and competitive advantage.

> Making values lived through how people behave means explaining them, modelling them, recruiting to them, allocating resources to them, performance managing against them and recognizing and rewarding them – with zero compromises.

Reed Hastings and Patty McCord of Netflix summarized the challenge of making values matter when they said that 'the *real* company values, as opposed to the nice-sounding values, are shown by who gets rewarded, promoted, or let go'.[3] Achieving and maintaining this standard requires a level of commitment, bravery and discipline. The All Blacks understand this and have made it a core element of their performance system. They now select on character as well as playing ability. It is not enough to have one without the other.

Dual leadership model

The All Blacks squad operates a dual leadership model across management and players. This model dates back to 2004 and the initiative of World Cup-winning head coach, Graham Henry. Their approach to the week leading up to a test match is a good example of how dual leadership works in practice. At the start of the week the management team has a strong input in setting the agenda and schedule. As the week progresses and game time approaches, responsibility transitions to the player leadership group. The dual leadership model, while successful, was one of the areas for improvement identified following the 2007 World Cup campaign when New Zealand suffered a shock quarter-final defeat to France. A strong focus had been placed on leadership in advance of that event; however, in the post-tournament review, as Darren Shand observed: 'The management team felt that they had taken too much of a theoretical approach to leadership rather than a more practical one.'

The decision was taken to focus more on the leadership capability of the players in order to complement the strong capabilities of the core management team. In the four years from 2007 to the 2011 World Cup, this was an area in which they invested heavily. The player leadership group involved key players such as captain Richie McCaw, Brad Thorn, Dan Carter, Mils Muliaina, Conrad Smith, Keven Mealamu and Andrew Hore. They assumed increased levels of responsibility and decision-making authority across a range of areas on and off the field. In the opinion of the management team this was critical to winning the 2011 World Cup and continues to be at the heart of how the team is managed. 'Leadership is key to our success', says Steve Tew: 'The increased role of the player leadership group working in partnership with the management team has really paid dividends.' The result is a strong team focus. 'We operate to a "we over me" philosophy.' Shand puts it succinctly: 'We are a whole team, not a collection of talented individuals.' Essentially it means that egos are left at the door and the best interests of the All Blacks always come first.

Beyond the leadership group, every player in the squad is part of a decision-making group. These groups cover attack, defence, kick-offs, scrums, line-outs, mauls and other elements of the game. Each group is tasked with reviewing performance, analysing opposition, and developing tactics for its area. This means that every player carries some level of leadership role. It is not just the coaching staff's responsibility to lead the team. Leadership within the All Blacks comes from anywhere and everywhere within the set-up.

When new players are selected into the All Blacks squad there is an expectation of personal accountability from the start. During their inductions they are reminded of the players that have gone before them – the legendary figures that have worn the same jerseys that they will. They are also provided with details of the principles, values and ethos of the team. 'We encourage our players to think about what they can do today to improve and make themselves better', says Darren Shand. 'We don't tell them what to do. It is up to each individual to own this for himself.'

All Blacks players are not spoon-fed by management. For example, it is each player's responsibility to manage his own week in the lead-up to a game. This creates self-reliance, and encourages the players to learn the skills of decision making and coping under pressure. This pays off in the key moments of international test matches when they have to make smart decisions under pressure.

The dual leadership model is at the heart of the All Blacks culture. It ensures that responsibility and accountability rest with everyone – players and management alike – to drive that culture to achieve the team's goals. It has led to the development of a capability throughout the group for making good decisions in every aspect of what it takes to win, on and off the field. The Finnish School system (Chapter 7) highlights this principle in more detail.

Process, process, process

A fundamental to success has been a relentless concentration on mastering the basic skills of the game. The All Blacks place huge emphasis on ensuring that every player – regardless of his position on the field – can execute the simple skills of catching, passing, tackling and footwork. It catches some people by surprise when they see the team train. Every training session involves work in these core skills. The players work on simple skill drills over and over again, the sort of basic skills that 8- and 10-year-old kids would do.

The endless hours and constant focus on the core skills pays off in key moments in games. Execution of these skills under intense pressure, at high speed and tempo, has become the hallmark of New Zealand rugby. We could pick countless examples but two will suffice. As we discussed earlier, in November 2013, New Zealand headed into their final test of the year against Ireland in Dublin. They went in with a perfect 13-win, zero-losses record for the year up to that point. No team in the professional era had ever gone through a perfect year. History beckoned. The Ireland players were inspired on the day and with 27 seconds left led 22–17. New Zealand had one final chance. From 60 metres out, they went through

10 phases of play, involving 24 passes and 13 of the 15 players before Ryan Crotty scored in the corner. It was a masterclass in staying calm under intense pressure. If any one of the 24 passes had been missed the game would have been over. Simple skills, executed perfectly. The touchline conversion by Aaron Cruden secured the win, 24–22. History was made.

In the 2015 World Cup Final, the All Blacks jumped out to an early 18-point lead. Australia rallied in the third quarter of the game and reduced the gap to four points. Dan Carter, the New Zealand outside half and World Player of the Year, remained the coolest player on the field. He slotted a 40-metre drop goal and long-range penalty to take his side 10 points clear. A further score then saw them win comfortably. In the clutch moment he relied on the core skills he had worked on in training session after training session. His comment to the media post-game was revealing: 'I've been fighting those thoughts all week – those thoughts about the outcome and whether we were going to win or whether we were going to lose. I just kept pulling myself back to the process to concentrate on the task at hand for the 80 minutes.' Simple skills, executed perfectly.

When the clouds lift, the sun comes out

Bill Walsh, legendary former head coach of the San Francisco 49ers, was one of the great American Football coaches of all time. Shortly after taking over the team in 1979, he oversaw a transformation in their fortunes that led to the 49ers winning four Super Bowls in the next decade. Central to Walsh's philosophy was that the team should not focus on winning but rather on delivering certain standards of performance. When this happened, as Walsh put it, 'the score took care of itself'.

The All Blacks adopt a strikingly similar approach. Speaking with Darren Shand the day before that historic Ireland–New Zealand game, he was very clear about the focus of the team: 'We have not spoken about the possibility of making history by going through a full year with a 100 per cent record. The record would create a distracted mindset. Our focus is on the process of achieving our outcome. If we hit our process goals tomorrow, everything else will follow.'

The All Blacks management team believes in a credo of less is more. When it comes to working with the players, they strive to focus on a small number of things – what matters most. The simple rule of thumb is two things at any one time, not 10 things. This 'specificity' avoids the possibility of cluttering the minds of the players and allows them to be clear on what is important. In the country known as the 'land of the long white cloud' this philosophy is best summed up in the saying: '*When the clouds lift, the sun comes out!*'

> There is a powerful lesson here for business. Focus on the basics. Do the simple things right (*simple skills, executed perfectly*). Develop the 'core' skills so that employees repeatedly perform them well under pressure. Don't overcomplicate. Concentrate on the small number of key things that matter most in determining your success (*less is more*). Ensure everyone knows what they are. Build simple, repeatable processes around the key things so that you know the business is always doing the right thing. Trust the process (*the score takes care of itself*).

Feedback-rich culture

The All Blacks management has created a feedback-rich culture that helps drive consistent performance improvement. They are responsible for putting in place a total support system for the players to allow them to be as effective as possible. The player is at the top of this system and underneath are the coaches, strength and conditioning experts, nutritionists, sports scientists, sports psychologists and video analysts. The cast of support staff is comprehensive; and the model adopts a case management approach. Each player is different – the programme of support they receive is customized to suit their specific requirements. The approach is not a one-size-fits-all. At all times the question is 'How do we get the best out of each individual athlete?'

Detailed data is captured in every training session and match using video analysis and other techniques to provide a rich stream of performance information. For example, after every game each player has access to a personalized review of his performance in that game. The review explores the minutiae of each element of his play – every tackle made, ruck hit, pass and kick executed, line speed in defence, ruck speed at the breakdown. Other international teams carry out similar data mining on performance. However, what sets apart the All Blacks is how they use this data. Steve Cliffe works for Opta, a global sports data company that partners with New Zealand as well as many other national teams. 'New Zealand in general has access to the same information that other teams get from Opta but in my view there is a difference in how they use this data', Cliffe says. 'They ask questions that others don't.'[4]

The All Blacks management team constantly asks searching questions and looks for the data to deliver the answers. The data is relatively easy to gather; the real skill is in having the expertise to analyse it and use it to influence the team's strategy and decision making. In preparation for every game, the video analysis is used to study the opposition and to assist in setting 'process' targets that combat the strengths or exploit the weaknesses of the opponents.

With regard to how feedback is delivered, the All Blacks operate to a simple mantra, namely: 'give feedback in the stomach, not the back'. This captures the essence of the feedback-rich culture that is at the heart of the All Blacks – and the other powerhouses we have studied.

> A high-performance culture demands that everyone within the organization is willing to hold each other to account to a high standard. It demands that they share honest feedback, very frequently, and use this to drive the never-ending push for improved performance.

In comparison to most businesses, the All Blacks are light years ahead in how they use feedback to drive performance. We expand on how organizations can create a feedback-rich culture in the Powerhouse Principle at the end of this chapter.

'The Invincibles'

The New Zealand All Blacks' dominance of world rugby dates back to the start of the 20th century. On their first tour of the United Kingdom in 1905–06 the team won an astonishing 34 of their 35 games. The only defeat was a narrow 3–0 loss to Wales at the end of the trip. The next touring party did not hit the UK shores for another 19 years. However, they came determined to improve on the record of the previous team (nicknamed 'The Originals'). The tour of 1924–25 achieved the perfect record – played 32, won 32. That touring party is immortalized with the nickname 'The Invincibles' in recognition of its achievement. The Originals and the Invincibles set the tone for all future generations of All Blacks. The winning culture epitomized by the modern-day organization comes from them.

No team in any sport has the divine right or ability to win every game it plays. The All Blacks will never stop trying to achieve this goal. They will continue to demand the highest standards, push the boundaries of performance and build on the legacy that has earned them the right to call themselves the most successful sports team of all time.

Powerhouse Principle 10: feedback

Performance powerhouses are driven by what we call a 'feedback-rich culture'. This is one of the defining features of the New Zealand All Blacks' success and is evident in each of the other organizations we studied for this book. The respected author and leadership expert Ken Blanchard is typically credited with the much-quoted phrase *'feedback is the breakfast of champions'*. He says that he first came across the phrase from a colleague, Rick Tate.[5] Ken has taken the mantra further. He says: 'feedback is the breakfast – and the lunch, dinner and midnight snack – of champions!' This is an important distinction.

The first defining feature of a feedback-rich culture is that the volume of conversations about performance is far greater than the norm. There is, in effect, a running commentary on performance as it occurs. High-performing organizations invest energy in learning from today to help them become better tomorrow. The All Blacks learn from every game – win, lose or draw. To develop this culture in businesses, leaders must commit to the practice of high-frequency performance conversations. Feedback should become the norm. To borrow Ken Blanchard's phrase, feedback is not just for breakfast!

Second, to facilitate the volume of performance conversations it is essential to keep these conversations as simple as possible. Short, sharp and to the point. Do not overengineer feedback processes as this will get in the way of enabling more frequent conversations. Work to the principle of 'just enough process' to sustain the practice of consistent, regular, timely review of performance. Eliminate any element of bureaucracy within the process, as bureaucracy becomes simply a barrier to having conversations taking place. The goal should be to make it as easy as possible for people to talk about how they are doing and have regular conversations throughout the organization. The All Blacks have worked hard to ensure their feedback processes are manageable and sustainable as drivers of continued performance improvement.

There is a clear distinction between a 'running commentary'-style feedback conversation and a formal performance review style of discussion. Each is

▶

designed for a completely different purpose. Annual reviews should be used for forward-looking, big-picture discussions about career progression, capability development and future opportunity/prospects – not to discuss specific elements of performance over the last 3, 6 or 12 months. If used for the latter purpose it is inevitable this will lead to frustration and be counter-productive. This happens far too often, and is one reason why companies like Deloitte, Accenture, Adobe and even GE are dispensing with the annual review process in favour of more frequent conversations on performance.

In feedback-rich cultures, performance becomes transparent. Everyone can see how they are doing, all the time. This has two effects. The first is that ownership and responsibility for performance are enabled throughout the organization. The second is that there is no hiding place for poor performers. For some reason, many businesses feel that information on performance – be it at business unit, team or individual levels – should be restricted and in many cases kept private. Our experience is that the more visible and transparent leaders make performance, the more likely it is that everyone will own performance and help improve it. The other effect of greater transparency is that it facilitates self-analysis. People with the capability to assess their own performance accurately are better able to sharpen it in the future. The All Blacks players can do this. They are not 'spoon fed' their reviews. Armed with video analysis of each game and training session they are able to self-diagnose and identify how they can improve, well before they sit down with the coaching staff. Likewise, the All Blacks environment is one where the players are likely to hold each other to account just as much as the coaches do. It is not unusual for players to challenge each other and, more importantly, no one takes offence because everyone knows and trusts it is being done for the good of the team. Businesses need to enable this level of self-analysis and ensure that individuals and teams develop their own capabilities to continually learn, challenge and improve.

The word 'feedback' has negative connotations. Tell someone you are about to give them some feedback and they are likely to interpret it as a signal that 'they are in trouble or have done something wrong'. As noted above, effective feedback should be a running commentary on performance. If performance is good that should be reflected in the tone of the conversation. If it is poor, likewise. More often than not people perform well. Therefore, the balance of feedback discussions should reflect this. The number of positive conversations should outweigh the negative ones – if that is reflective of the performance being delivered. Feedback-rich cultures reflect this balance. There is still room for reflecting on how things can be even better – and more than likely a high-performance culture will focus on this just as much in the good times as when things are tough. If feedback is reserved exclusively for when there is a problem, then that in itself is a problem.

Finally, high-performance organizations recognize that there is a skill in delivering effective feedback. It does not come naturally to many, rather it is something that needs to be developed and cultivated. High-performance organizations invest time in ensuring that their people managers are practised in the art of using feedback to drive performance improvement. They design supporting processes to enable this to happen in the right way, with the right frequency and linked to one goal – ensuring the organization reaches ever high standards of performance.

Our research has taught us that it is virtually impossible to become a performance powerhouse without a feedback-rich culture.

Notes

1 WorldNews.com [accessed 15 June 2015] Steve Tew Very Pleased With NZRU's Profits [Online] http://article.wn.com/view/2014/03/24/Steve_Tew_very_pleased_with_NZRUs_profits/.

2 *Building Blocks: Brad Thorn*, Part 1 and 2, Red McLeod/Whero Films.

3 *Harvard Business Review* (2014) How Netflix reinvented HR, January–February.

4 Extract from newspaper article 'Black Power', *The Irish Times*, 6 November 2013.

5 Ken Blanchard (2015) [accessed 15 June 2016] Feedback Is The Breakfast Of Champions, *How We Lead* [Online] http://howwelead.org/2015/01/07/feedback-is-the-breakfast-of-champions-2/.

Mayo Clinic 12

The three shields of health

What makes Mayo Clinic a performance powerhouse?

Rochester, Minnesota is a small Midwestern US city with a population of approximately 110,000 people, yet it has an annual transient population several times that. It has been described as 'the little town on the edge of nowhere'.[1] Yet people come from far and wide to receive treatment and instruction in one of the world's greatest medical centres. Rochester is famous as the home of Mayo Clinic, the first and largest integrated, not-for-profit medical group practice in the world. In 2015, Mayo cared for over 1.3 million people across its three campuses (Rochester, Minnesota; Scottsdale and Phoenix, Arizona; and Jacksonville, Florida) and within the Mayo Clinic Health System.[2] The 61,000 staff at the Clinic treated patients from all 50 US states and 143 countries. In total Mayo provided 612,000 days of patient care. It generated US$9.8 billion in enterprise revenue – all of which is reinvested into giving patients high-quality care, finding answers to the toughest medical cases and training the next generation of health-care professionals and researchers.

The Mayo Clinic logo is comprised of three shields which represent the three main activities at Mayo – patient care, research and education. The larger centre shield represents the main focus, patient care, while the shields to either side represent the supporting activities of research and education that help keep patient care at the forefront of excellence. In 2015, the research budget for Mayo was US$662.8 million, and Clinic staff produced 6,392 research publications and review articles in peer-reviewed journals. There are currently 9,832 active human research studies under way. Its medical research programme and centres of innovation operate at the leading edge of scientific discovery and innovation in patient care. Mayo is also renowned for the quality of its education programme. The Clinic trains doctors in 271 residency and fellowship programmes, and these are amongst the most sought after in the world, covering virtually all

▶

medical specialisms. Across five schools of education Mayo trains physicians, researchers, and health scientists, continuously raising the standard of health care.

In 2014, Mayo Clinic celebrated its sesquicentennial (150th year). To mark the occasion the organization produced a list of 150 significant accomplishments over its history.[3] The list highlighted the major contribution Mayo has made to the advancement of medical care. From the concept of integrated, multispecialty group practice of medicine, to the creation of integrated medical records, to the discovery of cortisone, to the revolutionizing of open-heart surgery with the Mayo-Gibbon heart–lung bypass machine and the performing of the first heart–lung–liver transplant in the United States, the list is crammed with landmark developments in medical practice that have had a major influence on the development of health care globally.

The reach of Mayo extends well beyond the boundaries of its facilities. Mayo Clinic Care Network ensures more people than ever before benefit from Mayo's expertise. Since launching in 2011, the Mayo Clinic Care Network has grown to include more than 35 health-care organizations across the United States and Puerto Rico, Mexico and Singapore. Organizations continue to join the network, allowing Mayo to reach patients in new ways – many of them never walk through Mayo's doors. The alumni of Mayo's educational programmes practise throughout the United States and the world, propagating Mayo Clinic expertise and upholding Mayo Clinic values. Mayo staff and leaders are continually active participants in national and international journals, boards and societies. Mayo has filed over 5,500 patent applications, has over 2,000 technologies available for licensing, and over 65 start-up companies have been formed around Mayo Clinic inventions.

External bodies recognize Mayo as best in class. Mayo Clinic has ranked at or near the top of the 'Honour Roll' of hospitals through the history of US News and World Report's best-hospital rankings. Mayo has more number one rankings than any other hospital in the nation. In 2016, Mayo was listed for the thirteenth consecutive year on *Fortune Magazine*'s 100 Best Companies to Work For. It has some of the lowest physician (2.2 per cent) and nurse attrition (4.5 per cent) rates in the United States. Mayo Clinic has the highest brand preference among academic medical centres. Ask any medical professional, anywhere in the world, to namecheck the best medical-care organizations and Mayo Clinic will feature on that list every time. This is what makes Mayo a performance powerhouse.

Figure 12.1 The Mayo Clinic Powerhouse Performance model

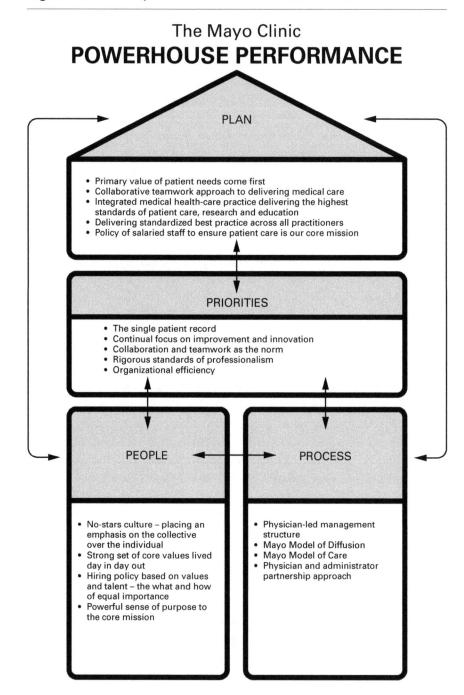

The Mayo Clinic powerhouse

The union of the doctor and the sister

Dr William Worrall Mayo established a medical practice in Rochester, New York in 1864. From the outset he was solely concerned with providing the best possible medical care to his patients. On 21 August 1883 a devastating tornado hit the city, causing 37 deaths and leaving a trail of destruction in its wake. With no hospital in the city, Dr Mayo along with his two sons, Will (who had just completed medical school) and Charlie (a student at home), tended to the injured. The sisters of St Francis, an order of nuns located in the city, also helped treat the victims. In the aftermath of the tornado and the emergency care provided to the citizens of Rochester, Dr Mayo and Mother Mary Alfred Moes, the head of the order, discussed the need for a hospital in the city. Mother Alfred proposed that the Franciscan sisters would raise the money required to build the hospital if Dr Mayo would oversee its clinical services. W W Mayo was sceptical at first, partly because he was not certain that the city was big enough to support a hospital and also because hospitals, at that time, were seen as places where patients went to die. Rather than providing palliative care to people in their final days, he was far more interested in providing high-quality care to make people well. However, Mother Alfred was persistent and persuasive. She was also very adept at raising the necessary finance to fund the construction of the hospital. In 1889 St Mary's Hospital opened its doors for the first time.

The union of the Franciscan order and the Mayo family was to prove a powerful one. Each shared the same commitment to the service of patients. Dr John Noseworthy, the current president and CEO of Mayo Clinic, highlights the characteristics they brought to the partnership, which he credits as the foundation block that has helped make Mayo Clinic so respected globally: 'The interaction of the two universes of the Franciscan sisters and Dr Mayo and his sons was fundamental to establishing the institution we have today. The sisters brought selflessness and devotional attributes, which combined with the science, process rigour and commitment to hard work of the physicians to create a formidable combination. These form the roots of values that are just as strong today as they were when St Mary's Hospital first opened.'

Very quickly the reputation of St Mary's grew. The sisters proved to be highly capable nurses and the Mayo brothers assembled a well-qualified team of physicians to treat patients. They were determined to build an integrated practice in which experts shared information, pooled expertise

Figure 12.2 Following a devastating tornado in 1883, Dr William Worrall Mayo and Mother Alfred Moes formed a dynamic collaboration that laid the foundation of Mayo Clinic

SOURCE: Mayo Clinic

and worked together to deliver care to patients. This concept of integration was novel in medical practice. With the benefit of hindsight it proved to be one of several ground-breaking innovations that set Mayo Clinic on its course to be a standard-bearer for medical care in the world. As demand grew, the hospital expanded. In particular, the skills of the Mayo brothers as surgeons ensured that the 'hospital in the cornfield' came to be acknowledged as a centre of excellence for medical care.

The needs of the patient come first

From the very outset, Dr Mayo was unequivocal about his primary purpose, namely *the needs of the patient come first*. Without question this is the defining focal point for everyone and everything that happens at Mayo. Mayo Clinic Model of Care (see Figure 12.4) provides the practical framework for the delivery of this primary purpose. Everything is rooted in 'patient needs come first'. Every decision, process, system, procedure, structure and even physical layout within Mayo is designed on the basis of how it upholds the primary purpose. It is explicit, internalized by staff, reinforced daily and fundamental to why Mayo exists at all.

Figure 12.3 Modern team providing care to patient. This photograph shows a Mayo physician consulting with a patient

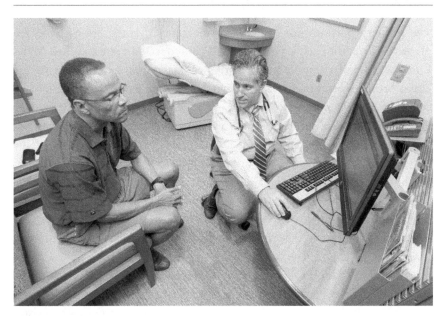

SOURCE: Mayo Clinic

Dr Leonard Berry and Dr Kent Seltman's excellent book on Mayo Clinic, *Management Lessons from Mayo Clinic*, provides many anecdotes and stories as to how the 'patient comes first' ethos is upheld.[4] These stories relate how, time and again, staff at the Clinic have gone above and beyond the call of duty to provide care to their patients. One touching example tells of a truck driver who fell ill as she passed through Rochester. Having parked her rig in front of St Mary's Hospital, the driver rejected the emergency doctor's recommendation that she should be admitted. The reason eventually became clear: the driver was worried about her truck which was parked at the door of the hospital, and also about her dog which was sitting alone in the cab. One nurse on duty happened to have a commercial driver's licence and volunteered to move the truck to a safe parking area while another nurse volunteered to mind the dog. The patient was reunited with both truck and dog several days later after she had recovered.

In any organization, when the core purpose of why it exists is unambiguous and reinforced through daily practice, it becomes deeply ingrained as part of the DNA of that organization. Performance powerhouses do this better than others.

The Mayo Clinic Model of Care

The primary purpose (and value) – patient needs come first – has been preserved from the early days of Dr W W Mayo to the present. When Mayo Clinic was smaller than it is today, the leadership and example set by the Mayo brothers set the standard to which everyone worked. As the institution grew and the number of its staff expanded into the thousands, the way in which its purpose was delivered evolved. In 1998, the Board of Governors decided to codify how its purpose should be delivered in the form of the Mayo Clinic Model of Care (Figure 12.4).

The Model of Care sets out a list of attributes that define Mayo Clinic patient care and the environment within which it is delivered. It is in effect the blueprint for how Mayo delivers the highest-quality patient care and service for which it is renowned, and its existence ensures the Clinic will continue to do so for generations to come.

In addition to the Model of Care, Mayo places a strong emphasis on its core values. Mayo has a Values Council to help infuse its values into Mayo's ongoing work. The council is led jointly by a physician, a Franciscan sister and an administrator. As we toured Mayo during our visit, its values were evident in daily practice everywhere we went. Examples include its distinctive standards of professional dress and decorum which demonstrate respect to patients and colleagues; its embracing of the unique healing environment of art, architecture and landscaping as components of the healing process and the embodiment of Mayo's global vision; and its commitment to 'care for the care givers' through a range of initiatives, including professional development/ mentoring of staff, promotion of interest groups, volunteerism, burnout avoidance, work–life balance and advocacy of healthy living.

Performance is as much about the *how* as it is the *what*. By focusing on both simultaneously, powerhouse organizations establish a coherent strategy for winning and, in tandem, an explicit 'way of working' that helps sustain their superior performance over time.

Figure 12.4 The Mayo Clinic Model of Care

Mayo Clinic Model of Care
Purpose and Vision

The Mayo Clinic Model of Care is defined by high quality, compassionate medical care delivered in a multispecialty, integrated academic institution. The primary focus, meeting the needs of the patient, is accomplished by embracing the following core elements (attributes) as the practice continues to evolve.

Patient Care

- Collegial, cooperative, staff teamwork with true multispecialty integration
- An unhurried examination with time to listen to the patient
- Physicians taking personal responsibility for directing patient care over time in a partnership with the local physician
- Highest quality patient care provided with compassion and trust
- Respect for the patient, family and the patient's local physician
- Comprehensive evaluation with timely, efficient assessment and treatment
- Availability of the most advanced, innovative diagnostic and therapeutic technology and techniques

Environment

- Highest quality staff mentored in the culture of Mayo and valued for their contributions
- Valued professional allied health staff with a strong work ethic, special expertise and devotion to Mayo
- A scholarly environment of research and education
- Physician leadership
- Integrated medical record with common support services for all outpatients and inpatients
- Professional compensation that allows a focus on quality, not quantity
- Unique professional dress, decorum and facilities

SOURCE: Mayo Clinic

The Surgeons Club

One of the cornerstones of patient care at Mayo is collegial, multi-specialism teamwork. Dr W W Mayo preached a simple mantra that *'no man is big enough to be independent of others'*. He was adamant that collaborative approaches were required to enable the practice to best serve the needs of its patients. His two sons were inspired by this. They were relentless in their quest to share knowledge with other physicians. This ran very much against the conventions within the medical profession at that time. Many surgeons closely guarded their skills as they saw them as a source of prestige and a way to ensure they were in demand with patients. The Mayo brothers, by contrast, maintained an open-door policy. They read extensively. They travelled to meet other surgeons, and they established St Mary's Hospital as a destination for visiting physicians to learn and share knowledge.

When Will and Charlie visited other surgeons they found the experience, at times, frustrating. The surgeons would offer little or no explanation during their operations as to what they were doing, nor would they make it easy for the visitors to see for themselves. The brothers vowed to do things differently. They set up their operating theatres in such a way as to make it easy for visiting surgeons to observe without disturbing their work. They installed raised viewing galleries and slanted mirrors. They provided running commentaries during their operations, and asked questions as they worked. They operated with one main assistant to reduce crowding in the operating room. By the early 1900s a flood of physicians travelled to Rochester on a weekly basis to observe the Mayo brothers performing surgeries. In the evenings the visitors would sit and discuss the day's proceedings. These gatherings became known as the Surgeons Club. Word spread fast that aspiring surgeons looking to enhance their skills should go to Rochester to see the brothers in action. This gave rise to a learning environment unrivalled elsewhere. One Canadian writing about the Mayo brothers for the *Canada Lancet* described the set-up as 'the greatest postgraduate centre of the century, with possibilities practically illimitable'.[5]

Will Mayo summed up the purpose of these observational visits perfectly in an address to Rush Medical School graduates in 1910. He said: 'The sum total of medical knowledge is now so great and widespread that it would be futile for one man to attempt to acquire, or for one man to assume that he has, even a good working knowledge of any large part of the whole. The very necessities of the case are driving practitioners into cooperation.'[6]

Matt Dacy is the Director of Mayo Clinic's museum and one of the most authoritative sources on the history and heritage of Mayo. He explained that the very name – Mayo Clinic – was derived directly from this practice: 'At the time visiting doctors used to refer to "the Mayos' clinic" at St Mary's Hospital in Rochester. They were referring to the practice of observing the brothers perform surgery and to these clinics as great sources of learning for surgeons.' Over time, the term 'Mayos' clinic' stuck and in 1914 it became the official title of a new building constructed for the practice. Now it is an iconic brand associated with excellence and admired globally.

Rapid diffusion of best practice

One challenge facing every major health-care organization is the slow speed at which new evidence-based best practices become the standard of care for particular conditions. Dr Stephen Swensen, Medical Director of the Office of Leadership and Organizational Development at Mayo, highlights this as another critical factor in Mayo Clinic's performance culture: 'Typically across health care it takes up to seven years for new methods and practices to be adopted consistently. At Mayo we have accelerated this process so that it takes six months.' The Mayo Clinic Model of Diffusion (see Figure 12.5) is a structured methodology for diffusion of best practices in a rapid timescale. At its core are three key enablers – systems engineering, infrastructure and culture.

Disciplined approach to work practices

Systems engineering has been an organizational capability at Mayo since the early 1900s and the days of Dr Henry Plummer. A brilliant physician, scientist and engineer, Plummer helped establish systems, principles and organizational structures that define Mayo today. He brought a disciplined approach to organizing work practices, regarding this as a worthy management activity central to meeting patient need. Mayo hired industrial engineers to further develop organizational competence in this area. This was another example of how the Clinic broke the mould of traditional health-care institutions and built competitive advantage into its approach. Rapid diffusion of best practice is enabled by this engineering focus. The approach leverages experts (medical and systems engineers), facility and workflow analysis, flowcharts and control charts, accountability matrices, human factors and usability studies, process re-engineering and workload modelling to design optimum solutions for disciplined implementation of care process models and new practices across all Mayo facilities. We expand further on the systems engineering capability at Mayo later in this chapter.

Figure 12.5 The Mayo Clinic Model of Diffusion: spreading and standardizing excellence

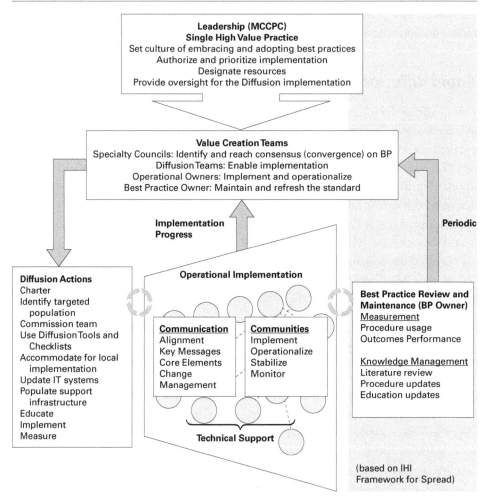

SOURCE: Dr Stephen J Swensen, Dr James A Dilling, Dr C Michael Harper Jr and Dr John H Noseworthy (2012) The Mayo Clinic Value Creation System, *American Journal of Medical Quality*, **27** (1), pp 58–65

Making the right thing to do the easy thing to do

The diffusion model is also supported through a focus on infrastructure support. In essence the aim is to create an environment where the *right* thing to do is the *easy* thing to do. To meet a six-month diffusion target – that is industry leading – Mayo concentrates on five main infrastructure supports (leadership, information technology, education, measurement and The Centre for the Science of Health-Care Delivery). It all starts with leadership and an organizational structure that makes it easy to standardize best practice rapidly. Mayo organizes itself around a single Clinical Practice Committee and a range of Speciality Councils with physicians and administrators working together to set best practice across the sites. Information technology plays a key role too, with the electronic patient record project being just one example of this. Real-time education and decision support is facilitated by systems such as 'Ask Mayo Expert' which are available to all staff via the corporate intranet. This particular application provides quick 'at the touch of a button' access to Mayo-vetted best practices, national clinical guidelines and Mayo's foremost experts in every discipline. Mayo measures its success using a range of relevant metrics including the percentage of staff educated on best practice, compliance with process and quality of patient outcomes. Finally, a specialized research group analyses and defines best care and publishes it within and beyond the Mayo network. Together, the components of this approach ensure that rapid diffusion endures as an organizational strength.

> Performance powerhouses demonstrate the capability to improve at an accelerated rate compared to their competitors. They design institutional supports to enable rapid adoption of best practice in a consistent fashion across the organization. It happens through design, not by accident of fate.

Standardized adoption of best practice

The third enabling factor in rapid diffusion of best practice is cultural. The world of health care is full of highly qualified physicians 'who know best'. In many cases it is very difficult to tell these physicians that the method they have used for several years may no longer be necessarily the best way. If the prevailing culture is such that these physicians are allowed to adopt a 'know all' mentality where their judgement or methods are never questioned or challenged, then it becomes virtually impossible to ensure new practices that serve the best needs of the patient become the norm. Doctors at Mayo buy into the philosophy that standardized adoption of best practice is the most patient-centred approach. They subscribe to adopting new practices in consistent ways, when they prove to be better. They are open to learning all the time and believe fundamentally in the power of the collective over the individual. As Will Mayo said: 'One of the conditions essential to the future success of Mayo Clinic is continuing interest by every member of the staff in the professional progress of every other member.'[7] This defines the supporting culture that has allowed Mayo to thrive.

> Performance powerhouses build and create environments where the *'right thing to do'* is the *'easy thing to do'*. By setting up the organization in this way through a combination of planning, process design, governance, leadership and culture they build an organizational capability that sustains their competitive advantage in the long term.

The collective expertise of Mayo

The primary value of 'patient needs come first' is followed closely by the second foundational value – that of integrated, multispecialty group working, whereby teams of specialists combine their skills to serve patients

Figure 12.6 Teamwork in service to patients is the hallmark of Mayo Clinic. This photograph shows Dr Charles H Mayo and a nurse caring for an infant, circa 1920s to 1930s

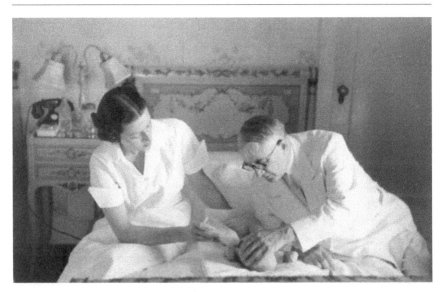

SOURCE: Mayo Clinic

and advance medical science in a collaborative manner. It is a critical enabler of the primary value. The collaborative approach harks back to the days of the Mayo brothers. Will Mayo in his speech to graduates in 1910 said: 'The best interest of the patient is the only interest to be considered, and in order that the sick may have the benefit of advancing knowledge, union of forces is necessary.'[8] For staff at Mayo and those who admire it from afar, this is highlighted as a source of 'organizational advantage' and another factor that makes the Clinic unique in the health-care sector. Jeff Bolton, Chief Administrative Officer and Vice-President of Mayo Clinic, says: 'When patients visit Mayo they don't just get a doctor, they get the collective expertise of the Clinic. Everyone works together to provide what is needed.' The collaborative approach manifests itself in several ways:

- no place for egos;
- a salary policy that fosters teamwork;
- everyone owns the patient;
- collaborative culture.

No place for egos

First, there is a filtering process when it comes to the recruitment of staff at Mayo Clinic. Mayo is not a place for big egos. It attracts, and indeed seeks out, astonishingly well-qualified professionals who share a passion for practising integrated medical service provision for patients. The hiring process places huge emphasis on the value of teamworking. Those for whom this is not part of their make-up simply do not survive at Mayo. Dr Noseworthy reaffirms this: 'If you want to be a star this is not the place for you. We emphasize collaboration and teamwork over individuals seeking the limelight. That is at the core of our value set.'

Salary policy that fosters teamwork

Mayo's remuneration policy reinforces this philosophy. Everyone is recompensed on a salaried basis. There are no incentive payments or rewards based on either the number of patients or the number of procedures performed. As a result there is no economic motive for a Mayo doctor to mine patients or hold on to them in ways we might see in other medical practices. Most doctors in OECD countries work on a productivity model. In other words they are paid more for doing more. At Mayo it is different. Its salary policy ensures that there is no inherent misalignment of interest between a physician and a patient.

Physicians have no financial interest, for example, in ordering a CT scan, or removing a gall bladder. This means that patients can be sure that a Mayo doctor will only perform procedures or order tests if it is in their best interests. Mayo also promotes collegiality. If a particular physician is best suited to serving the needs of a patient then there is no question but that the patient will be referred to the best qualified person, irrespective of who has seen that patient first. Equally, there are no impediments to physicians providing support to fellow physicians when patients are referred in this way. A Mayo doctor does not lose income by seeking the support of others or by taking time to assist colleagues. The result of this pay structure is that it incentivizes physicians to work together and to focus solely on the needs of the patient.

Everyone owns the patient

Third, the integrated patient record – an innovation way ahead of its time when introduced first by Dr Henry Plummer in the early 1900s – ensures that the process of collaborative medicine is facilitated seamlessly. The patient record is owned by Mayo and not by any individual doctor. In reality, Mayo has had a 100-year jump on the rest of the medical profession in working in this way, which has been adopted now as a standard by many health-care organizations. All information pertaining to the diagnosis, treatment and care of a patient is available in one location. This enables any health professional within the system to rapidly and effectively participate in the treatment of that patient. Indeed, Mayo Clinic is currently investing in its biggest project yet – a US\$1.3 billion spend – to develop a new electronic health record across the institution. The 'Plummer Project' – aptly named after Henry Plummer – is taking the single patient record to the next level, reaffirming the strategic importance of the collaborative medicine philosophy that has helped make Mayo so unique.

The introduction of the single patient record by Dr Plummer in 1907 is one of the seminal moments in the history of Mayo. Resulting from this innovation, Mayo creates a unified medical record for each patient. Each new patient is assigned a unique number and every piece of data pertaining to that patient is stored in a single location (now electronically). This includes everything from outpatient diagnostic tests to in-hospital nursing notes. Every interaction with the patient is added to the record in a standardized format, which ensures that any physician – inside or outside the hospital – has the full history of that patient at his or her fingertips. From the outset Plummer wanted patient records to be permanent and lasting. He went so far as to examine various options for inks and papers that would be guaranteed to survive, and even tested them by putting notes on the roof of the Clinic building during the winter months – if the ink stayed legible on the paper he knew he had a patient record that would still be readable decades later. Plummer's innovation has had many positive impacts. His intent was to use it to improve the diagnoses and treatment of patients by having better information available all the time. It unquestionably achieved this; however, it has acted also as a driver of quality at Mayo. Any doctor working at the Clinic knows that patient records are there for all to see, all the time. This creates positive peer performance pressure. Likewise, records serve as an effective teaching tool. The ability to cross-reference records enables physicians to address problems they haven't seen before, by interrogating the archives and reviewing how others have handled similar cases. It encourages them to reach out to experts in these cases and ask for their assistance. It enables the teamwork philosophy to be applied practically. As such, the single patient record enables and incentivizes learning, teamwork and quality at Mayo.

Collaborative culture

Fourth, the culture of seeking help is deeply ingrained in all staff to the extent that it has become second nature. Highly qualified surgeons are never afraid to seek advice from others, particularly on complex cases. It is not regarded as a sign of weakness but rather affirmation of the underlying philosophy of 'patient needs come first'.

This practice of working together is further reinforced by the communication processes and protocols surrounding the care of patients. For example, before each day's surgery there is a pre-operative briefing involving every member of the surgical team. Team members discuss their respective roles and raise any concerns relating to the specifics of the cases in front of them. The briefing does not take the form of a mechanical checklist review, rather it is a discussion to ensure the team is ready for what lies ahead. The introduction of this briefing has increased significantly the communication flows between members of the surgical team, reducing errors and waste in the operating theatres, and reinforcing the teamwork ethos across Mayo. Physical work-spaces are also designed to foster collaboration. Each examination room is configured in the same way so that any doctor can work in any room.

Dr Bradly Narr is the Chair of Anaesthesiology and a 20-year veteran at Mayo. He takes us on a tour of the 87 operating rooms (ORs) in St Mary's Hospital so that we can see a typical working day for the surgeons in the

Clinic. He points out the detailed patient information on display in the OR during a complex open-heart-surgery operation. The OR has a bank of screens displaying real-time patient diagnostic data throughout the procedure: 'The transparency of this data ensures the full team knows precisely the condition of the patient throughout. We have some of the most advanced diagnostic equipment and we have designed our ORs to ensure that we get the full benefit. It enables anyone in the team to intervene as required and increases the effectiveness of the full surgical team.'

We are better because we are here

The collaborative approach not only provides a platform for serving the needs of the patients, but it also creates an environment that enhances quality continually. The Mayo brothers created the best postgraduate learning environment in medicine and this remains the case today. Because doctors work together, they always learn from each other. This drives quality on a daily basis. Doctors improve while at Mayo *because they are there*. The peer learning culture ensures that this is the case. Dr Noseworthy is unequivocal about this: 'The transparency of how we work drives quality and is one of the unique characteristics that has helped define Mayo.'

A defining characteristic of a performance powerhouse is the impact it has on people who spend time there. Powerhouses are places that stimulate improvement in people simply by immersing themselves in the performance environment around them.

Commitment to research and education

The scale of investment in research at Mayo is massive – over 3,000 people are dedicated to research activity, working in 29 different research laboratories with an annual research budget in 2015 of US$662.8 million. On Mayo Clinic's logo, the patient care, research and education shields deliberately overlap. Dr Noseworthy explains: 'We invest heavily in our research capability. The purpose of all our research is to enable us to meet the needs of our patients. It is not research for the sake of science.'

When we visited the Neurology Department on the eighth floor of the building we found a large wall chart in the corridor. It laid out a timeline of research activity across the 16 disciplines within the department, including for example neuromuscular, neuroimmunology and cerebrovascular. Under each discipline the chart highlighted the research activities carried out over the last decade and the future goals of the research programme in that discipline. Staff walk past the wall chart every day. It is a tangible reminder not just of the achievements of the recent past but of Mayo's continued commitment to conducting groundbreaking research that will form the basis of medical breakthroughs in years to come. As doctors treat patients and see opportunities for advancing patient care, they work together with Mayo scientists and research teams to develop new and improved diagnostic tools, medications, devices, treatment protocols and more. At Mayo, physicians deal with some of the most complex, difficult cases that other clinics are simply not capable of addressing. The end result – new solutions, fresh answers, improved patient care, better health.

In addition to research, Mayo's commitment to education is just as strong. In 1915 Mayo Graduate School of Medicine was established, with a focus on training medical specialists. It was the first education programme of its kind. Today this programme extends across five schools, and the medical school, residency and fellowship programmes are amongst the most sought after by the most promising physicians of the future. The learning only starts with formal training. Throughout their careers, physicians at Mayo are committed to continued education. Built into the contracts of Mayo doctors is an allocation of 18 days' professional improvement. This harks back to the days of the Mayo brothers who placed such a strong emphasis on learning from others. The education programme also serves as a powerful recruiting tool for talent. More importantly, time spent in its residency and fellowship programmes provides Mayo with the opportunity to assess the fit of potential recruits. Having studied under their watchful eyes, Mayo's leadership knows whether or not an applicant has the values required to thrive within the unique culture that is Mayo Clinic.

Physician-led leadership

Mayo Clinic is a physician-led organization. Aside from the president and CEO, all other leadership positions are part-time and held by physicians or scientists. They typically devote between 10 and 40 per cent of their time to their leadership roles and the remainder to continued clinical practice across the three shields of patient care, research and education. Leadership positions rotate regularly and all physician leaders are partnered with administrator leaders to provide support – also on a rotating basis. This rotation policy serves two purposes. First, it ensures that the transition from practice to leadership and back again is a natural one. The physicians or scientists never leave clinical practice. Second, it fosters an environment that encourages leadership development and fresh ideas. Mayo produces many of its own leaders rather than relying solely on external recruitment for its succession planning. This helps maintain the culture and ethos that is deeply ingrained in Mayo staff DNA. It also prevents fiefdoms from developing. At Mayo the mission is all important, not the individual. This structure – which is unusual in medicine where typically less than 5 per cent of CEOs are physicians – impedes development of the type of 'us versus them' cultures that can be common elsewhere. It also ensures that the primary focus of patient need is always at the heart of decision-making processes at leadership levels. As few as 10 per cent of the 232 physician leadership positions (called 'Chairs' in Mayo lexicon) are held by people with Masters' degrees in management, business or health-care administration. All of the administrative partners assigned to support the physician leaders are qualified to this level. The net effect is that Mayo Clinic is run by a teamwork model of physicians as leaders, supported by administrators who bring diverse skills, to achieve shared goals that reflect the primary mission. Unlike other health-care organizations, Mayo is not led by business people with a core focus on profit maximization.

Mayo leaders are performance managed on their leadership capabilities. Their clinical expertise is proven by the time they are appointed to leadership roles. However, the organization realizes the importance of their roles as leaders. To that end, they assess regularly the perceptions of staff. A leadership heat map is produced with an emphasis on staff perceptions of Chairs' leadership capabilities. Perceptions are based on responses to three key questions: 1) Does your Chair take an active interest in your career? 2) Does your Chair value your ideas, seek them out and act on them? 3) Does your Chair communicate transparently with you? If the answers are positive they know the Chair is performing the leadership role effectively. If not, then the Chair is supported through coaching to achieve improved leadership effectiveness. It is a simple yet elegant process for assessing leadership capability.

In performance powerhouses leadership can come from anywhere and everywhere in the institution. Everyone has a leadership responsibility. Everyone feels accountable for the performance of the organization. Distributed leadership creates a total commitment by all to driving performance.

My best day's work

On top of the highest quality of care, Mayo has also earned a reputation for efficiency that sets it apart from other health-care providers. Dr Plummer brought medical and engineering capabilities together and implemented innovative systems, processes and structures. It is this blend of disciplines that has proven to be a significant factor in the Mayo success story. William Mayo describes his decision to convince Henry Plummer to join him at Mayo as his 'best day's work'. The efficiency focus provides institutional advantage across two dimensions. First, and most importantly, the patient experience benefits from operational efficiency. Second, the organization enjoys a cost advantage in terms of productivity of physicians, scientists and nursing staff and the optimization of procedures and processes.

The patient experience

Mayo has continually invested in improving the patient experience in practical ways through disciplined approaches to delivering care. In 1947, they set up an internal business consulting group to examine their systems and procedures and identify improvements in record management and information flow. One of their first initiatives was to visit the Metropolitan Insurance Company in New York to learn how they could improve efficiency with regard to patient record management. Ever since, the group has searched out best practice and how it might be applied to the benefit of patients. For example, when it comes to patient queuing processes they have benchmarked against the best, such as Disney or the very efficient airlines, to learn how they can improve queuing times and experience. This has led to innovative ideas being implemented and a maximum patient waiting time of 15 minutes. They have adopted process improvement tools including the 'lean' approach developed by Toyota to eliminate waste and 'Six Sigma' initiated by Motorola to identify and eliminate defects in processes. They run simulation models to test new processes, and carefully design facilities to maximize patient experience through efficient flow of people, data and materials. Janine Kamath, Chair of Internal Business Consulting and Management Engineering at Mayo, says: 'We now have a staff of 200 working in this area with a singular mission. We use engineering principles to identify how we can deliver the patient-centred philosophy. We benchmark against best practice elsewhere, identify ways in which we can do things better and then work in an integrated way with the front-line medical staff to manage the change process.' The end results speak for themselves. Mayo patients rave about the experience of attending the Clinic.

Destination medicine

This focus on continual improvement and innovation also brings direct business benefit. The combination of systems engineering discipline, adoption of best practice from within and outside health care, and rigorous change management processes, including the Model of Diffusion, ensure that the Clinic not only delivers outstanding patient care and satisfaction but does so without compromising patient safety while simultaneously keeping costs under control. Since 2008, the strains of the financial downturn compounded by the changing structures of the US health-care system have resulted in increasing pressure on cost for every health-care facility in the country. Mayo is not immune to this; however, through having such a strong focus on efficiency they have weathered the financial storm better than most other institutions.

Mayo Clinic's focus on speedy and efficient clinical health care is akin to a well-oiled machine in which all of the working parts combine to provide effective results. It allows Mayo to deliver '*destination medicine*' – the practice of bringing people to an integrated health-care facility where all their requirements are met by experts under a highly efficient model. It is one of the reasons that patients travel there in their thousands every week to be treated.

One visitor from the West Coast summed it up perfectly: 'I have travelled with my mother who is receiving treatment at St Mary's. She was diagnosed yesterday after a battery of tests by a team of docs, she underwent her surgery this morning, and they have told us she should be good to go tomorrow. I am amazed at how much they do so quickly. I figured we would be here for at least a week or 10 days. These guys just get on with it.'

Innovation by design

Aside from the efficiency focus brought by Janine Kamath and her department, Mayo also invests heavily in innovation. The Centre for Innovation (CFI) is led by Dr Douglas Wood. He explains their remit: 'We apply a creative, problem-solving approach to revolutionize the experience and delivery of health care by going beyond process analysis and quality improvement. Our design-thinking philosophy fuses with traditional science to help us transform the way people experience health and health care.'

The centre is over eight years old now and is home to a team of 14 designers. While Kamath's group focuses on quality and efficiency improvement, the CFI acts as an incubator for new ideas, nurturing them to grow and mature until they are ready for patients. The staff at CFI are agitators constantly challenging for improvements in patient care and experience. To date they have brought over 300 projects to fruition, helping to keep the Clinic at the forefront of innovative clinical care. Lorna Ross, a design strategist at the CFI, is passionate about her role: 'We will always poke and challenge to be better. It is a key element of Mayo culture. The organization really values the role we play in helping to foster that culture.' The establishment of the CFI has brought a structured approach to innovation at Mayo. As with so much else, this does not happen by chance. The Clinic has always had a strong reputation for innovation, dating back to the Plummer single patient record, the Mayo brothers' clinics and countless other examples of leading-edge thinking in its 150-year history. The workspace at the CFI is dominated by a sign on the wall: *'start small – think big – move fast'*. It sums up the philosophy of the unit. No one at Mayo thinks that they are as good as they could be. They can always do better. They will never stop asking how.

The three shields of health

Mayo Clinic is the epitome of what we define as a performance powerhouse:

- It is founded on an ambitious vision for an integrated health-care practice that breaks the mould.
- It is rooted in a core purpose and value of 'patient needs come first', which has prevailed through its 150-year history and been delivered consistently and outstandingly well.
- It is a magnet for incredible talent who are loyal to that powerful core purpose.
- It is a demonstration of the principle and impact of collaborative teamwork, ensuring that the sum of the parts equates to far more than the individual elements within.
- It exemplifies carefully designed processes, structures and governance that enable the organization to remain true to its principles and efficiently deliver a service experience that is second to none.
- It embraces new ideas and change for the better in controlled and carefully managed ways.

- It is an institution with a distinct and almost unique set of behaviours and culture that has made it an iconic brand the world over.
- It is an organization that has stood the test of time and one that will endure for many decades to come.

The three shields of health, the symbol of excellence.

Powerhouse Principle 11: teamwork

A key driver of Mayo Clinic success is its total commitment to teamwork and collaborative medicine. Dr Charles Mayo, the younger of the famous brothers, once said: 'The keynote of progress in the 20th century is system and organization. In other words, "teamwork".' It is hardly surprising that in our journey through performance powerhouses we have found that teamwork is universally important in driving performance. Every business leader understands that effective teams deliver outstanding results, but not all understand the key requirements for building high-performing teams. From our interactions with the institutions featured in this book we have developed a list of nine conditions for driving high-performance teamwork. We call it our CHAMPIONS model:

C = common purpose and mission. First, everyone must be on the same page – a common purpose, clearly articulated, understood by all and that acts as the focal point for the organization. In the case of Mayo Clinic that is the primary purpose of *'patient needs come first'*. It is a constant. It does not change. It drives everything and everyone.

H = hard-work ethic. High performance is hard work. It does not come easy. Fundamentally every winning team we encounter understands this. Team members are not afraid to 'roll up their sleeves' and do what it takes. As the New Zealand All Blacks put it: 'the standard of okay is not okay'. This ethic manifests itself in rigorous standards of execution on a daily basis. Doing the simple things really well makes a big difference. To achieve this leaders must demand it.

A = attitude and aptitude. When building a high-performing team it is essential to get the right people into the team. In our view, this comes down to a combination of attitude and aptitude – the blending of the *how* and the *what*. The *how* is the attitude. We always start here. Getting people to buy into the organization's underlying culture, hard-work ethic and values is vital. Without this the fabric of the team culture is lost. The *what* is aptitude. Hiring people with the expertise and capabilities for the job is important but talent alone is not enough. Talent absent of attitude does not work.

M = model for distributed leadership. The most effective teams we encounter work to a distributed leadership model. In effect, responsibility for leadership goes well beyond the formal hierarchy or defined organizational structure. These structures are still important in terms of how teams are organized. However, in tandem with this, we notice that within high-performing teams leadership responsibility extends to every member of the team. Leadership can come from anywhere and everywhere. Members assume ownership for performance, they feel empowered and act accordingly.

P = problem-solving mentality. The road to high performance is never straightforward. Obstacles and issues will always present themselves. However, what sets the best apart from the rest is their ability to tackle these problems with resolve to overcome them constructively. This demands honesty, a feedback-rich culture, a solutions mindset and a can-do attitude. Psychologists talk of the importance of individuals having positive mental attitudes – we think of this requirement as having a positive team attitude.

I = invested in each other. One of the criteria we used to select the institutions we visited was that they were places where people improved by being immersed in the performance environments around them. In institutions that share this attribute, people recognize that they are better *because* of those around them. Therefore, they really care about what everyone else is doing. They know that their success is dependent on others. This means they are heavily invested in each other. They are relying on those around them to uphold high standards and to continually drive each other on to achieve more.

O = one-team philosophy. The best teams are those whose individual members work to collective rather than individual objectives. In effect they live to the mantra '*if one wins we all win, if one loses we all lose*'. There is no place for inflated egos in such teams. Indeed, across all the powerhouse examples we studied for this book, we encountered outstanding individuals in each one, yet little evidence of – and certainly no tolerance for – prima donnas. Powerhouses are

▶

full of stars but none shines brighter than any other. In both St Louis Cardinals and Mayo Clinic the same phrase was used to sum this up: 'The name on the front of the jersey is more important than the name on the back.'

N = never happy. High performers are never satisfied. They always think that there is room for improvement. High-performance teamwork demands that the pursuit of perfection is eternal. These teams challenge each other to find ways to be better all the time. They ask difficult, penetrating questions. They learn from their experiences – good and bad. They embrace peer review. They encourage each other to grow and develop. They benchmark against the very best. They set the current standard as the baseline for the future and think about how they can keep improving on it.

S = structured teamwork. The teams we observed set about developing high-performance teamwork by design rather than default. Effective teamwork is an outcome of carefully planned processes, structures, governance practices, communication protocols and cultural norms driven by values and reinforced through behaviours. How these are designed varies from institution to institution but in each case they are deliberately and carefully constructed to reinforce the end goal: building a high-performance team.

Notes

1 Helen Clapesattle (1969) *The Doctors Mayo*, Mayo Foundation for Medical Education and Research, Rochester.

2 Mayo Clinic Health System is a network of clinics and hospitals serving more than 70 communities in Minnesota, Wisconsin, Iowa and Georgia. The community-based doctors and their patients are supported by the highly specialized expertise and resources of Mayo Clinic. This partnership is dedicated to providing quality health care close to home.

3 Mayo Clinic [accessed 15 June 2016] Contributions to Medicine: 150 for the 150th [Online] http://mayocms.cws.net/content/150years.mayoclinic.org/files/150-Contributions-to-medicine(5).pdf.

4 Leonard L Berry and Kent D Seltman (2008) *Management Lessons from Mayo Clinic: Inside one of the world's most admired service organizations*, McGraw Hill, New York.

5 Helen Clapesattle (1969) *The Doctors Mayo*, Mayo Foundation for Medical Education and Research, Rochester.

6 Willam J Mayo (1910) Rush Medical School Graduation Speech, Mayo Clinic Historical Unit.

7 Charles Mayo [accessed 15 June 2016] Quotations from the Doctors Mayo, *Mayo Clinic History and Heritage* [Online] http://history.mayoclinic.org/toolkit/quotations/the-doctors-mayo.php.

8 Willam J Mayo (1910) Rush Medical School Graduation Speech, Mayo Clinic Historical Unit.

Toyota Motor Corporation

Everybody wins

What makes Toyota a performance powerhouse?

Without question, and as evidenced by most normal business metrics, Toyota is and has been a top dog in the global automotive industry for many years. Toyota's total production for 2014 was 9.2 million units, and global revenues for the year to March 2014 were 25.7 trillion yen – equivalent to US$249.5 billion. In each of these metrics Toyota ranks in the global top three. Net profit in 2014 amounted to 1.8 trillion yen, equating to a healthy return on equity by industry standards of 13.7 per cent, and US$100 invested in Toyota shares in February 2010 would be worth almost US$200 in February 2015 at an annual rate of total return of 14 per cent. Moreover, in Interbrand's 2015 listing of 'Best Global Brands' Toyota ranked number one in automotive and number six overall, with an estimated brand value of US$49 billion.

Toyota is also a leader in its sector in innovation, and commercialization of innovation at large scale. Notable examples over its history include product innovation, for example the hybrid-engined Prius model, and latterly the hydrogen fuel-cell-powered Mirai; brand innovation, such as Lexus; and process innovation, as evidenced by a myriad of examples that continue to be widely leveraged as elements of the Toyota production system.

By these standards, and many others, Toyota is a performance powerhouse.

The Toyota Motor Corporation powerhouse

Making cars Motomachi-style

Making cars can be a serene activity. As we stand overlooking the assembly line of Toyota's Motomachi plant, we watch Crown, Estima and Mark X

Figure 13.1 Toyota Powerhouse Performance model

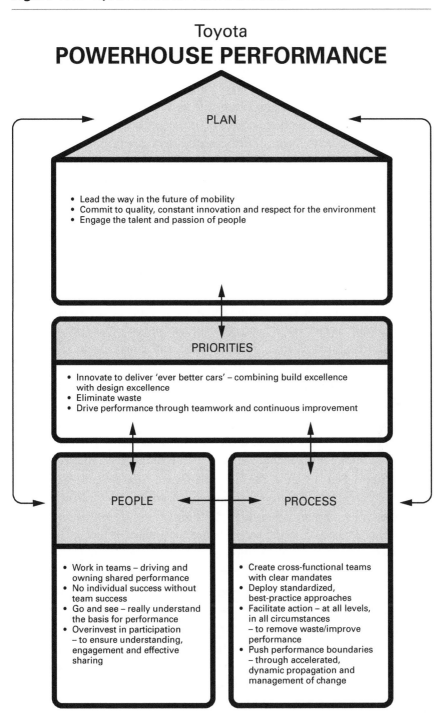

cars progressing in what appears to be a random order of models, colours and fit-outs towards completion at a rate of one car every three minutes – an interval known as the *takt* time.

Motomachi is located in the heart of Toyota City – a mid-sized urban centre (2010 population 461,000) situated 35 kilometres from the city of Nagoya in Japan. The site dates back to 1959 and is the second-oldest in Toyota's manufacturing network. It is one of 10 sites (out of 12 in total in Japan) located within an hour's drive of Toyota's global headquarters, and it was the first facility in Japan dedicated to the manufacture of passenger cars. The sophistication of Motomachi's automation and other technologies is at the lower end of Toyota's scale, and in aspects of its physical appearance the site looks its age. However, key well-known elements of the Toyota production system (TPS) are evident in the steady rhythm by which manufacturing activity progresses throughout the factory.

Operators at Motomachi are organized on the assembly line in cells where, depending on the activity, they work individually or in small teams. They join the cars at the point where they enter their cells, and work on the moving vehicles for the three minutes that it takes for the car to pass to the next one. Work in each cell is busy, concentrated and controlled. It progresses with a choreography that is clearly defined and from which there is no deviation, and it is evident that the operators know exactly what they are doing. The sounds are of hammers, pneumatic screwdrivers, welding torches and other assembly machinery rather than conversation or shouting.

Above the line, in several locations and in plain sight for all to see, are *Andon boards*, simple low-tech displays that show red/green status lights for each cell along the line, together with details of the target number of cars to be produced in the shift, the current running total and the variance – positive or negative – between the running total and that required in order to hit the target output by the end of the shift.

The only disruption to the serene 'dance' unfolding below occurs when an abnormality – most likely quality-related – is detected at one of the cells. As soon as this happens, the operator pulls a cord at their cell – the *Andon* cord – the effect of which is to bring the entire line to a halt. Immediately on the Andon boards, the status light for the cell in question turns from green to red, and the supervisor for that part of the line scrambles to the scene to discuss the problem and support the operators in getting it resolved. Fortunately, on this occasion the issue appears to be manageable such that within a couple of minutes the line is back up and running at the same pace as before, with no loss of product.

We observe the systems used to manage the flow of parts to the assembly line and keep levels of inventory on the floor (and indeed inside the factory) to a minimum. Parts are delivered to the site, typically on trolleys or in trays, and always with minimal external packaging, often directly by the suppliers. They are placed in clearly marked bays – called *kanbans* – on the floor, and nothing comes into the site unless there is an available bay. Toyota operators, working from the predetermined manufacturing schedule, pick the specific parts for each vehicle at each cell, and place them in carefully laid-out kits, which are delivered on conveyors to the cells at the same time as the relevant cars. In this way, Toyota ensures that the right quantity of the right parts are in the right place when they are needed, and waste – or *muda* in Japanese – of both materials and process, is minimized.

Kaizen *in action*

We see several examples of *kaizen,* or continuous improvement, throughout the factory – small changes to the manufacturing process identified and trialled by operators, each one delivering incremental improvements in the productivity of the lines, the comfort and therefore productivity of the workers, or in the levels of *muda* associated with the assembly process. One example of this is their doorless assembly system – whereby the doors of the cars are removed at the beginning of the assembly line, to be processed separately offline before being replaced on the almost finished vehicle at the end of the line. What seems at first glance like the introduction of an unnecessary complication to the assembly process actually delivers concrete benefits in that it eliminates the need for operators to open and close swinging doors to carry out work inside the cars. This brings positive consequences for productivity and also worker safety – while also enabling a narrower, more space-efficient assembly line within the factory.

A smaller example of kaizen is the 'synchronized dolly' – effectively a bench holding the required tools and parts for a particular cell that moves down the assembly line in tandem with the operator and the car being worked on. As a result, as the car progresses, the dolly is always by the operator's side, saving them from having to walk over and back to pick up the materials that they need. When the car moves on to the next cell, the dolly moves back to the start, with the operator, ready for the next vehicle in line.

Toyota as a high-performance case study

As a study in institutional high performance, Toyota is a fascinating and much-researched case. As far back as 2004, the American academic Dr Jeffrey Liker, from the University of Michigan, published *The Toyota Way*, the product of over 20 years' research, including many visits to Japan and interviews with well over 100 Toyota employees at all levels of the business. Liker describes Toyota's model as being built around two elements of DNA – respect for people and continuous improvement – and identifies 14 business principles at the core of Toyota's success. This book has become a bestselling work that remains required reading for students and practitioners of management and lean manufacturing worldwide. It has also given rise to a series of additional works by Dr Liker and colleagues, exploring other aspects of Toyota's model. Separately in 2008, the Japanese Professors Osono, Shimizu and Takeuchi of the Hitotsubashi University Graduate School of International Corporate Strategy, published *Extreme Toyota: Radical contradictions that drive success at the world's best manufacturer*. Once again, this book is the product of in-depth research, this time involving over 200 interviews with employees across the company. They characterize the company as a study in contradictions – for example moving gradually while taking big leaps, cultivating frugality while spending huge sums, and respecting the hierarchy while allowing freedom for dissent.

The insights contained in each of these authoritative works have been tested, and in many respects validated, by Toyota's experiences in the period since their publication. This is because Toyota's business and its high-performance model are emerging from a period that can only be described as challenging. Its reputation was significantly damaged in 2009–10 by a series of highly publicized quality issues relating to, amongst others, floor mats, accelerator pedals, propeller shafts and brake systems. Exacerbated in some respects by poor management of communications, these issues led ultimately to the recall of over 7 million cars in Toyota's key US market and 9 million in total worldwide. Customer perceptions of the Toyota brand in the United States dropped from 83 per cent positive/17 per cent negative in late-2009 down to 59 per cent positive/41 per cent negative in mid-2010. In part as a result of these issues, the effects of which were compounded by the global economic slowdown, Toyota's financial performance crashed, with revenues declining from 26 trillion yen in 2008 to 20 trillion yen in 2009, to 18.9 trillion yen in 2010, while profitability slumped to the point where the business made a net loss of 437 billion yen in 2009, with the Automotive division continuing to lose money into 2010.

The period since 2011 for Toyota has been one of renewal and recovery, leading to the restoration of both business performance and customer perceptions to the levels outlined at the start of this section. Our sense, however, is that this renewal and recovery has been achieved by re-energizing rather than reinventing the high-performance model that had underpinned the company's success in the first place, which we would like to frame around four key themes as follows:

1 vision and challenge – stretched and made real;

2 performance through problem solving;

3 continuous, dynamic, broad-based improvement;

4 teams of people driving and owning performance.

Vision and challenge – stretched and made real

The starting point for Toyota's high-performance model is the same as that which we encounter in every example that we study around the world – namely definition and mobilization around a clear purpose, and a level of ambition that can comfortably be described as unreasonable. Toyota's Japanese term for this, translated into English, is 'challenge'. Throughout its history, and in relation to all aspects of its business, from manufacturing to sales to new product introduction, Toyota's development has been led by the organization's passion to achieve shared objectives associated with really stretching targets. Lean manufacturing was a response to the challenge of delivering global competitiveness through step-change reduction in manufacturing costs and, at the same time, radical reduction in defects. Similarly, Toyota's development and launch of the highly innovative and successful Lexus model came in response to three specific challenges set by company leadership – to build 'the finest cars ever built', 'the finest dealer network in our industry and to treat each customer as we would a guest in our home' and 'to ensure that a Lexus with 50,000 miles on the clock wouldn't feel, sound or perform any differently to one fresh out of the factory'.[1]

For us, however, the best, recent example of this aspect of Toyota's high-performance model in action relates to the business overall in the aftermath of the recall-related crisis described above. In tandem with dealing with the short-term fallout of the recalls, the newly appointed President of Toyota, Mr Akio Toyoda (a great-grandson of the company's original founder, Sakichi Toyoda) took action to refocus and re-energize the company for the longer term. In 2011 he gathered his global executive team to develop a new vision for the business. The output of that exercise was the text shown in Figure 13.2, which remains in force today:

Figure 13.2 Toyota global vision

Toyota will lead the way to the future of mobility, enriching lives around the world with the safest and most responsible ways of moving people.

Through our commitment to quality, constant innovation and respect for the planet, we aim to exceed expectations and be rewarded with a smile.

We will meet our challenging goals by engaging the talent and passion of people, who believe there is always a better way.

As corporate vision statements go, in terms of its depth, scope and ambition Toyota's is different to the norm. In and of itself this is a strident call to action for Toyota's workforce. It captures both ambition – 'will lead the way to the future of mobility', and purpose – 'enriching lives around the world'. Crucially it is unbounded in time – that is to say, its focus can be taken to be long term, yet it also clearly starts now. Finally, throughout its second and third paragraphs it sets down clear markers for the organization as to how these objectives should be achieved.

Vitally, and unlike many corporate vision statements, it is more than just words on a page – being really, viscerally and urgently 'owned' by Mr Toyoda and his workforce. It is prominently on display in company facilities in Japan, and cited routinely by him and members of his leadership team in setting the context for discussions on strategy and performance. (As an aside this vision statement was originally created by Toyota's leadership team in English rather than Japanese – another major departure recognizing the increasingly global nature of the business and its emerging 'lingua franca'.) As such, Toyota's global vision statement indicates *true north* for all of its stakeholders, including its workforce, suppliers and investors.

Performance through problem solving

In the context of Toyota as a high-performance organization, vision and ambition is, however, only the starting point. In Toyota's world, the effect of setting an ambition in excess of current performance is to define a problem that has to be solved. As such, in addition to energizing the workforce, Toyota's ambitions spark both strategic and operational problem solving, the effectiveness of which is enhanced by Toyota's culture and behavioural 'code'. Put another way, if the vision statement indicates where Toyota wants to go and why, what follows is aimed squarely at designing how the business will 'get there from here'. In this respect, problem solving as a capability within Toyota compares with those of strategy development and deployment in other organizations.

Problem solving in Toyota is conducted with a level of rigour that is rarely matched elsewhere. It is carried out in relation to big, structural initiatives that relate directly to Toyota's global vision, as well as for more detailed operational initiatives that might emerge from factory-floor kaizen processes. Toyota's problem-solving approach is built around 'Plan – Do – Check – Act (PDCA)', a framework that was originally introduced to Japanese manufacturers by the US quality pioneer W Edwards Deming in the 1950s. The logical and performance basis for PDCA, as illustrated in Figure 13.3, is 'fail to prepare, prepare to fail'.

Figure 13.3 Plan, do, check, act model

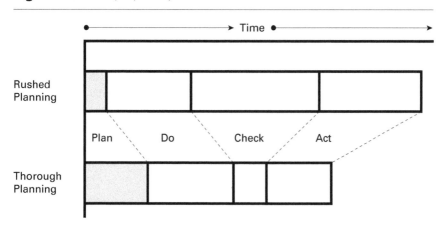

The starting point for problem solving at Toyota is to get under the skin of cause and effect and, from there, to break down an overall problem into tangible, manageable and individually addressable pieces. 'May your future be lit by knowledge of the past' is a quote from Toyota's founder, Sakichi Toyoda, that has prompted the development of a series of root-cause analysis tools, many of which are now established business standards. In Toyota it is impossible for workers to create a plan to get to somewhere if they don't understand why they are where they are.

The most famous of these tools is called 'five whys', where the question 'why?' is asked iteratively and in sequence until the point of clarity of cause and effect is reached.

As an example of this, one element of Toyota's global vision relates specifically to safety and is about 'zero casualties from traffic accidents'. Their initial application of five whys to this problem – asking the question 'Why do we have traffic accidents today?' – has resulted in the overall problem being broken down into five focus areas, as follows:

- parking;
- active safety;
- pre-collision safety;
- passive safety;
- emergency response.

Asking the second-level 'why?' question – for example, 'Why do we have parking-related traffic accidents?' – allows these focus areas to be further sub-divided into individually addressable, project-sized chunks on which individual teams can focus. In this specific, parking-related example, these include driver visibility, awareness of space/clearance, and capabilities with regard to steering and application of pedals. Continuing to ask 'why?' through the third, fourth and fifth levels (and onwards if required) allows Toyota engineers to focus on specific interventions that get to the heart of the problems under consideration and to develop technological and other innovations that result in the overall ambition being achieved.

The effectiveness of these root-cause analysis tools is reinforced by the involvement in them of what might in other organizations feel like too many people. Visitors to Toyota often remark on the large number of people attending meetings; however, in a world where every action is aimed at eliminating waste, or *muda*, this is viewed as an investment that brings two benefits – it allows the addition of insight that might otherwise be missed, and it allows insight to be captured and distributed through the organization such that other discussions, on other topics, might be better informed.

The final steps in Toyota's problem-solving model are design and implementation of actions, or counter-measures. There is a tension here that is well highlighted by Professors Osono, Shimizu and Takeuchi, in that on the one hand the business is risk averse, while on the other hand it is committed to achieving the leap in capability and performance to which it has signed up. Toyota manages the tension between risk aversion and risk taking through the effectiveness and speed of its organizational learning. Toyota has effectively two means of managing innovation risk: offline modelling simulation using advanced, computer-based tools; and deployment of carefully managed, physical experiments using research facilities, test markets or even the manufacturing lines themselves. The first of these allows them to mimic real-world experiments in a virtual environment, the results of which lead quickly on to the second. For example, during its initial development, the aerodynamic design of the Lexus model, having been created using engineering software models, was then tested hundreds of times in a wind tunnel before being finalized. The level and accuracy of Toyota's data capture from these experiments is a key source of their advantage that allows them to focus and de-risk each individual bet that they make.

Continuous dynamic, broad-based, synchronized improvement

The Japanese term kaizen, which is synonymous with Toyota, translates as 'change for the better'. Kaizen is embedded in the culture and practice at Toyota in a way that is both intense and challenging. Taken to the limit, kaizen means continuous improvement every day, for everyone. Kaizen at Toyota is company-wide, being practised at all levels from senior management to the shop floor. Moreover, kaizen processes themselves are subject to continuous improvement – in effect Toyota applies kaizen to kaizen.

Applying kaizen to deliver sustained high performance in a business like Toyota's requires addressing another tension at the heart of its model. On the one hand it is a business that thrives on standardization – Toyota wants cars to be made in the same way in multiple sites and locations across the world in order to ensure consistent high quality and also low cost. On the other hand they want to improve – all the time – the way they make cars, in order to achieve ever better quality at ever lower cost, and in particular to achieve the performance ambitions that they have set for themselves. The way they square the circle is through discipline, rigour and speed with regard to implementing and improving standard approaches.

At any point in time, the standard approach is simply the best-known way to do something. Standards within Toyota are situational and in context, which is to say that standards for a given process, while incorporating what we might describe as corporate best practice, may well vary from one location to the next to reflect individual circumstances and needs – Toyota's is explicitly *not* a 'copy exact' manufacturing model. For example, the standards for how the doors of Toyota Crown, Estima and Mark X cars are assembled at Motomachi differ materially from those for assembling the doors of similar models at other Toyota sites. Differences between these standards reflect differences between sites with regard to line configuration, manning, deployment of automation technologies and also operator capabilities. What is important, however, is that standards in each location are internally consistent, thoroughly documented and followed to the letter until and unless they are changed.

Standards at Toyota, however, are dynamic. They change both regularly and quickly – in some instances dozens of times per year – to facilitate implementation of the outputs of the problem-solving initiatives described earlier and to enable achievement of stretching target outcomes through continuous improvement. Processes for changing standards are carefully controlled, with new standards incorporating changes being documented, 'locked-in' and followed to the letter in the same manner as those they replaced.

Sharing of standards, innovations and best practice is vital to driving Toyota's continuous improvement capability, and a key enabler of sharing is the principle and practice of *yokoten*. This is short for *yokoni tenkai suru* and translates as 'unfold or open out sideways'. *Yokoten* is about creating the capacity for as many people as possible to share as much knowledge as possible as quickly as possible. The capture and management of tacit knowledge through physical and web-enabled means is as developed within Toyota as in most other large corporations. However, as we discuss more in the next section, its organization thrives on first-hand, person-to-person sharing of knowledge. Toyota's practice of having more people attending meetings than is strictly necessary is one example of *yokoten* in action.

Complementing *yokoten* is Toyota's age-old principle of *genchi genbutsu*, literally 'go and see'. This was initiated in Toyota's early days by Taiichi Ohno and is enabled by the practice of *gemba* walks, whereby managers routinely visit factory floors (*gemba* means 'the real place, where work is done') to engage with people and activities and really *know* the basis for performance. In part to facilitate *genchi genbutsu*, Toyota manufacturing plants, including Motomachi, are designed with gangways and viewing platforms that allow visiting groups to view what is going on without impeding work on the floor.

When it comes to performance, Toyota achieves what might appear to be high-risk, transformational outcomes by actioning many incremental, relatively low-risk steps. The consequence of Toyota's continuous improvement capability is that the capacity and boundaries of its high-performance model are pushed every day in every location across the network. Primed by their commitment to deliver more – whether in terms of volume, quality or cost – and conditioned by their ownership of their ambitions, individual teams look to leverage successful innovations and practices from elsewhere and to develop their own ideas. In effect they try to keep up and push ahead at the same time. Relative to other organizations where the approach to continuous improvement is more deliberate and static, Toyota's dynamic capability results in real, system-wide performance advantage.

Teams of people, driving and owning performance

'Respect for people' is one of two tenets of Toyota's DNA highlighted by Dr Jeffrey Liker in *The Toyota Way*. Toyota's corporate perspective is that 'there is no limit to how far human wisdom can be developed'. As such, the stated ambition is to 'continually aim to achieve mutual understanding, fulfil mutual responsibilities and combine the power of our individual employees'. As you can see from the above, Toyota is about individuals, however explicitly in the context of the collective. Its organizational structure, culture and operating processes are designed to maximize individual potential and, as a result, collective performance.

Looking first at structure, in contrast to many other large corporates, by-and-large Toyota's is organized vertically rather than in a matrix. Ownership for performance from top to bottom of the organization is delegated clearly to teams, and from there to sub-teams as required. The organization shies away from creating situations of dual accountability. For example, shift managers working at Motomachi are responsible for the overall performance of the line; however, they delegate responsibility for individual sections of the line to supervisors working under their direction who, in turn, delegate responsibility for individual cells to the relevant operators. Performance is measured at all levels, and performance of individual areas is considered explicitly in the context of line performance as a whole. Teams and sub-teams within this environment are empowered to achieve defined outcomes over both the short and medium term – in the context of customer requirements and of other initiatives that are going on around them and also in a manner that is consistent with what they consider to be 'The Toyota Way'.

Having designed the structure to facilitate clear, unambiguous collective focus, Toyota then, by way of its culture and processes, establishes the conditions to allow these teams to be effective. Toyota's culture reflects its origins as a family-owned business and the continued influence, completely disproportionate to its shareholding, of its founding family. One such family member, Kiichiro Toyoda, in the earliest days of the business in the 1940s, espoused as a value that 'everybody should win' and this notion is captured, modelled and reinforced to this day in all aspects of the company's operation. In Toyota culture the collective outcome is most important and there is no individual success without team success. The primary (albeit not exclusive) measures of performance are team-based, and Toyota's reward and recognition systems emphasize team over individual contributions. Toyota prides itself on being a humble organization that avoids, both individually and collectively, many of the obvious trappings of its success.

Toyota's culture is also based on trust. Employees at all levels of the organization, having been made accountable for delivering short- and medium-term performance outcomes, are empowered and trusted to achieve those goals. Equally they are empowered and trusted to take appropriate action to prevent and/or address any negative issues. The presence and use of the *Andon* cord on Motomachi's assembly line, as described at the beginning of this chapter, is an example of Toyota's culture of trust in practice – pulling the cord to stop the entire assembly line is a big call for an operator to make, with potentially significant business consequences in terms of customer service and/or cost. However, either of these outcomes is recognized as being better than one where a quality-related or, worse, a safety-related abnormality makes it through the system, and in this context the operators are trusted to make the call as they see fit.

Enabling a high-trust, empowered environment results from Toyota's focus – in principle and in practice – on building and sharing experience. The organization has a strong learning culture that manifests itself as commitment to individual training – both on the job and academic – and as corporate investment in academic and other institutions – for example Toyota Technical Institutes (TTIs), both in Japan and the United States. In Japan in particular, Toyota has low levels of people attrition, such that employees routinely build 'mastery' of the roles that they have before these are expanded to take in new areas of responsibility.

Finally Toyota processes – ranging from shop-floor kaizens to global dealer meetings – are many, and are designed to bring people together within and across teams. Toyota's organization thrives on a large number of formal and informal networks that are vehicles for sharing information and experience, and processes are designed and facilitated to encourage ideas in the context of achieving shared objectives. Involvement in these processes tends to be, for the reasons we pointed out earlier, greater than we might otherwise expect; however, this reflects Toyota's deliberate policy of over-investing in bringing its people together.

Ever better cars

In summary, then, we can see how Toyota's high-performance model is built around the four themes we have described:

- It is primed by vision and challenge, which is collective and meaningful in nature and cascaded from the very top of the organization to the levels of individual teams across the many divisions around which the company is organized.
- It is enabled by defined, focused and rigorous approaches for solving the 'problems' of bridging the gaps between current and target performance.
- It is further enabled by the principles and practices of kaizen, which embed problem solving and continuous improvement everywhere, every day in the fabric of how the organization operates.
- Finally, the model is held together by glue in the form of Toyota's approach to team working, which insists on collective ownership of shared challenges and measures team and individual performance in that context, and which promotes and enables collaboration as the key vehicle for making sure that, over the long term, ambitions are delivered. Ultimately the name of the game is ensuring – to quote Kiichiro Toyoda once again – that 'everybody wins'.

As Toyota's performance over many years has shown, this is a model that works. Moreover, the extent of Toyota's recovery from the reputational and other challenges experienced through the recall of 2009–10 shows that its high-performance model is also resilient. Its effectiveness can also be judged by the extent to which it – in whole or in part – has been studied and copied by other institutions over the years.

At a corporate level, Toyota's leadership is now mapping out its plans for sustained leadership for the next 10 years and the next 100 years – to deliver its global vision and, in particular, 'ever-better cars' that meet our transport needs in this century and the next. The history and heritage of Toyota is evident throughout Toyota City, and in particular on both the walls and the floors of the Motomachi manufacturing site and also the Kaikan visitor centre. Beside its history, however, is tangible evidence of Toyota's future, in the form of concept vehicles both wacky and traditional, designed to enable effective, sustainable and cost-effective mobility that – to quote the company – 'brings smiles' to the faces of individuals, families and all manner of business owners into the next generation and beyond.

Powerhouse Principle 12: improvement

As we have seen, continuous improvement is at the heart of Toyota's high-performance model. The concept and practice of kaizen has been made available for many years to manufacturing and service companies as a core element of the lean operations philosophy. However, what is notable for us from our research is the effectiveness with which Toyota applies continuous improvement to its continuous improvement approach itself – what we described earlier as applying kaizen to kaizen.

This is because improving the *rate* at which an organization improves is at the heart of enduring high performance. Increasing this rate is the key means by which organizational leaders address competing tensions between delivering on short-term commitments while at the same time enabling more long-term growth.

In a world of constantly increasing workload, many smart, competent leaders choose to deal with these tensions by prioritizing one over the other. Some manage and measure their success in the context of their short-term commitments, adopting a 'mañana' attitude to growth on the basis that they are too busy to worry about it now. Others focus on chasing the growth 'silver bullet' while betting that their teams can heroically keep things going until the promised land appears. Such focus can seem both understandable and rational. However, not only does it fall short of the standards for high performance; when kept up over time it *increases* the risk of failure.

By contrast, leaders in high-performance organizations – of which Toyota is one – recognize the limitations of this approach, and instead look to take on both tensions in parallel (Figure 13.4). They work explicitly and constantly on improving the capability and capacity of their organizations and, beyond this, on *improving the rate at which they improve*. To use an automotive analogy, this means increasing the rate of acceleration – rather than speed – of a car.

Figure 13.4 High-performance competing tensions

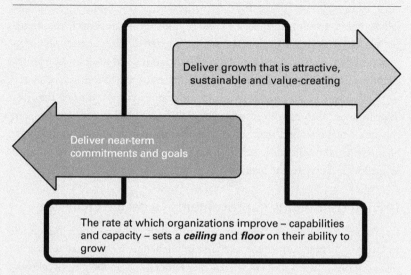

Deliver growth that is attractive, sustainable and value-creating

Deliver near-term commitments and goals

The rate at which organizations improve – capabilities and capacity – sets a *ceiling* and *floor* on their ability to grow

SOURCE: Kotinos Partners

Organizational fitness

The rate at which an organization improves is, in some respects, a measure of organizational fitness. In practice it sets both a ceiling and a floor on the organization's ability to grow. It sets a ceiling in that leaders should not take on new initiatives if, in doing so, they are putting at risk their ability to meet existing commitments. At the same time it sets a floor, in that most organizations, if they have the capacity and capability to hand, have little trouble identifying and acting on exciting opportunities for long-term performance improvement and growth.

Continuous improvement and standardization – it's about managing change...

Key to Toyota's success in improving the rate at which it improves is its approach to standards and standardization. Standards for operating processes across the company are rigorously defined, followed and enforced – *until the point where they are changed*, and they can change often, in some instances dozens of times in a year. Counter-intuitively, the key enabler of standardization as a driver of high performance in Toyota is the dynamism of its approach to *propagating and controlling change*. This allows them to encourage and embrace innovation – and through it to consistently push the

▶

limits of best practice – and to have the whole organization operate at or close to those limits all the time. The alternative is a situation where the (slow) speed and intransigence of the organization's approach to change act as *barriers* to innovation. In such a scenario, while standardization may still be effective in reducing the risk of failure – in itself an important outcome, in particular where the consequences of major failure are severe – its potential as an enabler of *outperformance* is lost. Rather than, as Toyota does, pushing and standardizing to best practice, organizations in this latter scenario find themselves effectively *resisting* innovation, *demoralizing* their thought leaders, and forcing standardization at performance levels much closer to the average.

Driving continuous improvement – a design challenge

Improving the rate at which an organization improves – applying kaizen to kaizen – is first and foremost a *design* challenge. It runs across all four pillars of our powerhouse model, starting with taking on the idea of increasing organizational fitness as an explicit objective, deciding what this means in the context of the organization's vision and strategy, and then designing and implementing a structured, comprehensive and aligned programme of change. In our experience it is best set up (and resourced) as an ongoing area of focus for the leadership team. What it delivers, though, is the ultimate form of proprietary competitive performance advantage – that which is embedded in the fabric of the organization and the way it works. Truly this view is worth the climb.

Note

1 Emi Osono, Norihiko Shimizu and Hirotaka Takeuchi (2008) *Extreme Toyota: Radical contradictions that drive success at the world's best manufacturer*, Wiley, New Jersey.

Conclusion 14

Becoming a performance powerhouse

We set out at the start of this journey to explore the secrets of sustained high performance – to understand the business and organizational models of a group of diverse performance exemplars, our powerhouses, and to see if they shared common attributes that we could highlight and present as guidance for managers. Finally we set out to develop a way of thinking about performance that would enable rapid performance transformation.

Our desire to answer these questions has led us on a quest of discovery that has taken in all five continents of the world. We have visited amazing institutions, met fantastic leaders – at all levels of their organizations – and witnessed great performance models and environments at first hand. We have covered fields ranging from business to academia, from sports to the military, from charities to culture, and from education to medicine.

Our research, while not exhaustive, has been significant in both its scale and scope. As such it has led us to our first conclusion that institutional high performance arises by design rather than by accident – that high-performance institutions are made, not born.

Second, we have concluded that the source of high-performance institutions' advantage is intrinsically organizational in nature. While many of the institutions discussed have been led by charismatic individuals at different points in time, each of these leaders has recognized and embraced the reality that high performance is by definition a collective endeavour. They all have focused on engaging, mobilizing and enabling their organizations to deliver again and again to the highest standards, in the toughest circumstances, against the objective measures that matter to them.

Third, we are clear that high-performance organizations do share common characteristics – the 'what' of performance. We believe that these powerhouse principles are at the core of enduring institutional success, regardless of the definition of that success. Through these pages, we have identified and discussed 12 specific principles that we observed consistently, in different manifestations, in the institutions we researched. We believe that these principles are instructive, and that understanding them provides a powerful basis for managers and leaders of aspiring high-performance institutions to make progress. In summary, the 12 powerhouse principles are:

- ambition;
- purpose;
- measures;
- standards;
- gap;
- decisions;
- code;
- engagement;
- resilience;
- feedback;
- teamwork;
- improvement.

Enduring high performance – from the 'what' to the 'how'

So now that we have a view as to what the outcomes are that leaders of any institution should work towards, let's examine our fourth and final conclusion – that there is a way for managers to approach the job of transforming institutional performance that works to deliver rapid, sustainable results. Notwithstanding that our studies describe journeys to enduring high performance that in most instances have been evolutionary rather than revolutionary, we believe that with increased clarity as to the target outcomes it is possible to effect transformation in performance much more quickly. For us, as set out in the opening chapter, the journey to sustained high performance is about working *within and across* the four pillars of our Kotinos Powerhouse Performance model, as shown in Figure 14.1:

Figure 14.1 Kotinos Powerhouse Performance model

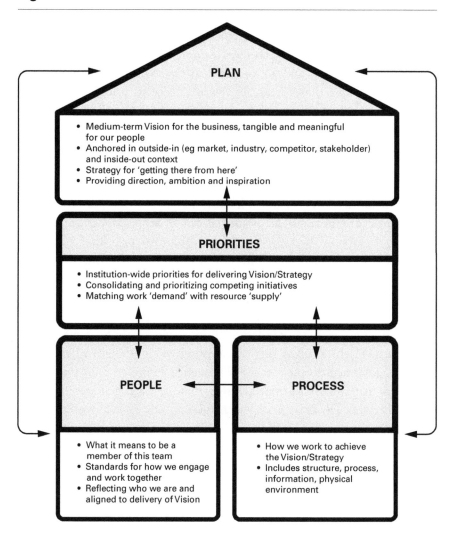

- The *Plan* pillar is about establishing (and maintaining) clarity of direction. We can state unequivocally that every institution we have studied for this book is clear about *what* it is looking to achieve, *why* it is looking to achieve it, and *how* it is going to get there. Moreover, it has encapsulated and articulated this for its people and other stakeholders such as to eliminate ambiguity, and to engage hearts as well as minds. Organizations with clear, powerful direction *all the time* have a sense of where 'true north' lies and, as a result, they have a point towards which they can align the actions and decisions they take. This brings clear performance benefits in the form of energy, coordination and pace.

- The *Priorities* pillar is about establishing clarity of short-term, organization-wide focus. It requires teams to identify the most important areas for attention and to mobilize around concrete milestones for progress against those areas. This work needs to bridge between the reality of where the organization is, and the ambition for where it wants to get to, by when. It needs also to ensure that work is appropriately focused, scoped and resourced to deliver. In short, this pillar is the point where work 'demand' is aligned with resource 'supply'. As with the *Plan* pillar, our research suggests that the more clarity that exists down through an organization with regard to its institutional priorities, the greater the alignment of effort and decisions that can be achieved. Crucially, when we look at how high-performance institutions prioritize and focus their efforts, we see them uniformly working on delivering short-term performance *and* medium-term capacity and capability *in parallel*. Notwithstanding the pressures on leaders – especially in publicly quoted business institutions – to focus all their efforts on delivering in the now, powerhouses do this in tandem with improving the rate at which they improve. In the process they demonstrate both strength of character and commitment to their vision. Through working on *Plan* they define success in terms of sustained, rather than one-off, high performance, and then through *Priorities* they energize and focus their teams' efforts to achieve it.

- The *People* and *Process* pillars together define the way in which leaders and teams across the organization work together – in essence the governance model by which the institution is run. In our view, thinking about governance is, at the same time, the 'stuff' of management and one of the tasks to which leaders look forward to the least. In a high-performance context, however, as evidenced by our research, this is where the rubber hits the road. In designing an institution's governance model, its leaders go much further than even they might think in creating the environment that enables sustained outperformance.

  The *People* pillar is about defining and implementing a behavioural code, or 'way', for the institution. Almost all of the studies we covered have established distinct 'ways' for their organizations, either explicitly or implicitly, which translate their values into standards for how people behave and act. Moreover, in several instances we came across examples of teams at middle or lower levels of an institution taking the overarching corporate codes and interpreting them to relate to their specific jobs. When it comes to behavioural codes, however, the defining characteristic of high-performance organizations is that they are *lived*. People understand what they are and why they are there; they buy in to them and, day in and day out, are happy to be held to their standards. 'Fit', or the assessment of individuals' capacity to adopt and live the code, is a key criterion for both recruitment and progression in each of these cases. Paraphrasing the words of Southwest Airlines it is about 'hiring for attitude and training for aptitude'.

Finally the *Process* pillar is about designing the 'mechanical' model by which the institution is run. The most tangible aspect of this model relates to management process; however, process design in turn reflects and influences organizational structures, definition roles and responsibilities, design of information flows, and even design and layout of physical space. We deliberately address *People*, which relates to behaviour and culture, ahead of *Process*, which concentrates on the more mechanical areas of organizational design. This reflects the interdependencies between these two areas and, above all, the opportunity for building capacity to perform and grow that is presented by institutionalizing great behaviours. High-performance institutions create time to think by operating on the basis of 'just enough process'.

The four pillars proposed in our model in some respects are unsurprising, and it may feel that proposing these as the path to enduring high performance is both obvious and underwhelming. In response, however, we would argue two things. First, there is no silver bullet when it comes to enduring high performance – the term itself makes it clear that we are talking more about marathons than about sprints. Second, the transformational 'magic' comes through working *across* the pillars to make sure the individual outputs are internally consistent, aligned and 'tensioned' to deliver the sustained high-performance outcome that leaders desire. Taken and managed together, the pillars give rise to a systemic and structural advantage that is intrinsic to the organization and hard for competitors to replicate.

The other point to note is that sustained high performance is a vocation not a project. Rather than being short-lived, the pillars remain in place as an enduring performance framework. However, the pillar outputs *must* evolve over time – sometimes both rapidly and significantly – to reflect changes in circumstances both inside and outside the institution. Managing this is, in itself, a defining capability of high-performance organizations.

Our powerhouse approach to performance transformation has emerged from the research process of the last five years, and been further refined and tested through our work with clients, which has proceeded in parallel with our research. Based on these experiences, we believe that this approach works. Focusing attention on the pillars – most notably exploring the cause-and-effect interdependencies that exist between them – provides a really powerful basis for senior leadership teams to unlock rapid performance transformation.

We opened this book at Oslo's City Hall, attending the award of the Nobel Peace Prize to Grameen Bank and its founder Muhammad Yunus. In closing it now, it seems apt to consider once more the words of this great man: 'One cannot but wonder how an environment can make people despair and sit idle and then, by changing the conditions, one can transform the same people into matchless performers.'[1]

Whilst this quote was made in the specific context of poverty we can – with due acknowledgement and respect – lift and apply it to the fundamentally different context of institutional high performance. Our study of performance powerhouses around the world demonstrates that leaders in high-performance organizations work endlessly and tirelessly to create the specific conditions for their people to maximize performance. This requires insight, dedication and energy; however, it is not magic. Rather than being accessible to only a chosen few, our view is that any organization can – with enough of these qualities – achieve sustained high performance over time. By working within and across the pillars of our Powerhouse Performance model, to put in place the powerhouse principles we have described, we believe that any organization can become a powerhouse in its field.

The beauty of the examples we have highlighted is that enduring high performance reflects fundamentally simple, common-sense notions executed outstandingly well. We leave the last word to Muhammad Yunus: 'I learned that things are never as complicated as we imagine them to be. It is only our arrogance that seeks to find complicated answers to simple problems.'

Note

1 Muhammad Yunus (1999) *Banker to the Poor: Micro-lending and the battle against world poverty*, PublicAffairs, New York.

INDEX

Note: *Italics* indicate a Figure or Table in the text.

CPSIA information can be obtained
at www.ICGtesting.com
Printed in the USA
BVHW01s1215180118
505662BV00008B/215/P